Lecture Notes in Computer Science 6220

Commenced Publication in 1973
Founding and Former Series Editors:
Gerhard Goos, Juris Hartmanis, and Jan van Leeuwen

W0192940

Ngoc Thanh Nguyen
Ryszard Kowalczyk (Eds.)

Transactions on Computational Collective Intelligence I

 Springer

Editors-in-Chief

Ngoc Thanh Nguyen
Wroclaw University of Technology
Institute of Informatics
Str. Wyb. Wyspianskiego 27
50-370 Wroclaw, Poland
E-mail: thanh@pwr.wroc.pl

Ryszard Kowalczyk
Swinburne University of Technology
Centre for Complex Software Systems and Services
P.O. Box 218
Hawthorn, Victoria 3122, Australia
E-mail: rkowalczyk@ict.swin.edu.au

Library of Congress Control Number: 2010931853

CR Subject Classification (1998): I.2, C.2.4, I.2.11, H.4, H.3, D.2

ISSN   0302-9743
ISBN-10   3-642-15033-0 Springer Berlin Heidelberg New York
ISBN-13   978-3-642-15033-3 Springer Berlin Heidelberg New York

springer.com

© Springer-Verlag Berlin Heidelberg 2010
Printed in Germany

Typesetting: Camera-ready by author, data conversion by Scientific Publishing Services, Chennai, India
Printed on acid-free paper   06/3180

Preface

We would like to present, with great pleasure, the first volume of a new journal, *Transactions on Computational Collective Intelligence* (TCCI). This journal, part of the new journal subline in the Springer series *Lecture Notes in Computer Science*, is devoted to research in computer-based methods of computational collective intelligence (CCI) and their applications in a wide range of fields such as the Semantic Web, social networks and multi-agent systems. TCCI strives to cover new methodological, theoretical and practical aspects of CCI understood as the form of intelligence that emerges from the collaboration and competition of many individuals (artificial and/or natural). The application of multiple computational intelligence technologies such as fuzzy systems, evolutionary computation, neural systems, consensus theory, etc., aims to support human and other collective intelligence and to create new forms of CCI in natural and/or artificial systems.

TCCI is a double-blind refereed and authoritative reference dealing with the working potential of CCI methodologies and applications as well as emerging issues of interest to professionals and academics.

This inaugural issue contains a collection of articles selected from regular submissions and invited papers of substantially extended contributions based on the best papers presented at the first International Conference on Computational Collective Intelligence: Semantic Web, Social Networks and Multiagent Systems (ICCCI 2009) during October 5-7, 2009 in Wroclaw (Poland). This issue introduces advances in the foundations and applications of CCI and includes 10 papers.

The research area of CCI has been growing significantly in recent years and we are very thankful to everybody within the CCI research community who supported the idea of creating a new LNCS journal subline – the *Transactions on Computational Collective Intelligence*. With this strong support and a large number of submissions already received by TCCI we believe that this very first issue will be followed by many others, reporting new developments in the CCI domain. We would like to thank all the authors for their contributions. This issue would also not have been possible without the great efforts of the Editorial Board and many anonymously acting reviewers. Here, we would like to express our sincere thanks to all of them. Finally, we would also like to express our gratitude to the LNCS editorial staff of Springer, in particular Alfred Hofmann, Ursula Barth and their team, who supported us in the creation of the TCCI journal and in the editorship of this issue in a very professional way.

May 2010   Ngoc Thanh Nguyen
                                                                                             Ryszard Kowalczyk

Transactions on Computational Collective Intelligence

This new journal focuses on research in applications of the computer-based methods of computational collective intelligence (CCI) and their applications in a wide range of fields such as the Semantic Web, social networks and multi-agent systems. It aims to provide a forum for the presentation of scientific research and technological achievements accomplished by the international community.

The topics addressed by this journal include all solutions of real-life problems for which it is necessary to use computational collective intelligence technologies to achieve effective results. The emphasis of the papers published is on novel and original research and technological advancements. Special features on specific topics are welcome.

Table of Contents

HYDRA: A Middleware-Oriented Integrated Architecture for e-Procurement in Supply Chains

Giner Alor-Hernandez[1], Alberto Aguilar-Lasserre[1], Ulises Juarez-Martinez[1],
Ruben Posada-Gomez[1], Guillermo Cortes-Robles[1], Mario Alberto Garcia-Martinez[1],
Juan Miguel Gomez-Berbis[2], and Alejandro Rodriguez-Gonzalez[2]

[1] Division of Research and Postgraduate Studies, Instituto Tecnológico de Orizaba
[2] Computer Science Department, Universidad Carlos III de Madrid
{galor,aaguilar,ujuarez,rposada,
gcortes,magarcia}@itorizaba.edu.mx,
{juanmi-guel.gomez,alejandro.rodriguez}@uc3m.es

Abstract. The Service-Oriented Architecture (SOA) development paradigm has emerged to improve the critical issues of creating, modifying and extending solutions for business processes integration, incorporating process automation and automated exchange of information between organizations. Web services technology follows the SOA's principles for developing and deploying applications. Besides, Web services are considered as the platform for SOA, for both intra- and inter-enterprise communication. However, an SOA does not incorporate information about occurring events into business processes, which are the main features of supply chain management. These events and information delivery are addressed in an Event-Driven Architecture (EDA). Taking this into account, we propose a middleware-oriented integrated architecture that offers a brokering service for the procurement of products in a Supply Chain Management (SCM) scenario. As salient contributions, our system provides a hybrid architecture combining features of both SOA and EDA and a set of mechanisms for business processes pattern management, monitoring based on UML sequence diagrams, Web services-based management, event publish/subscription and reliable messaging service.

Keywords: EDA, SOA, Supply Chain Management, Web services.

1 Introduction

A supply chain is a network that enables the distribution options for procurement of both raw and finished materials, which can be transformed into finished goods and distributed to the end customer through various distribution channels. Commonly, the main goal of a supply chain is satisfy the customer's requests as soon as they appear. However, to satisfy these requests, it is necessary to consider notification services and event management as required mechanisms due to continuously changing data. From this perspective, a supply chain can be considered as a network of services, driven by events. Furthermore, a supply chain is made up of diverse kinds of components, such

N.T. Nguyen and R. Kowalczyk (Eds.): Transactions on CCI I, LNCS 6220, pp. 1–20, 2010.
© Springer-Verlag Berlin Heidelberg 2010

as applications and information sources, which reside in different organizations and trust authorities. These components have been built using different technologies, and run in different execution environments. Service-Oriented Architecture (SOA) is an architectural paradigm for creating and managing "business services" that can access these functions, assets, and pieces of information with a common interface regardless of the location or technical makeup of the function or piece of data [1]. This interface must be agreed upon within the environment of systems that are expected to access or invoke that service. With a SOA infrastructure, we can represent software functionality as discoverable services on the network. SOAs have been around for many years, but the distinctive feature of the SOAs we address is that they are based on Internet and Web standards, in particular, Web services. A Web service is a software component that is accessible by means of messages sent using standard web protocols, notations and naming conventions, including the XML protocol [2]. The notorious success that the application of the Web service technology has achieved in B2B e-Commerce has also lead it to be viewed as a promising technology for designing and building effective business collaboration in supply chains. Deploying Web services reduces the integration costs and brings in the required infrastructure for business automation, obtaining a quality of service that could not be achieved otherwise [3], [4]. In a basic SOA, producers of these services may publish information about them in a service registry, where service consumers can then look up the services they need and retrieve the information about those services to bind them. Then, the primary value of SOA is that it enables the reuse of existing services and information, either standalone or as part of composite applications that perform more complex functions by orchestrating numerous services and pieces of information. For instance, at a shipping company, a tracking number allows a retail customer to check on the status of the shipment. When coupled with other information, the tracking number allows retail customers to check on their shipment over the Internet, by phone, or by walking into a distribution and receiving center. The same tracking number can be used by the shipping company's business partners to offer tracking services to their own customers. Thus, a simple service is reused in different ways and combined with other services to perform a specific business function. However, an SOA infrastructure does not address all the capabilities needed in a typical SCM scenario. It does not have the ability to monitor, filter, analyze, correlate, and respond in real time to events. These limitations are addressed with an Event-Driven Architecture (EDA). An EDA combined with SOA, provides that ability to create a SCM architecture that enables business. An EDA is an architectural paradigm based on using events that initiate the immediate delivery of a message that informs to numerous recipients about the event so they can take appropriate action [5]. In this context, an event is a trigger that typically corresponds to the occurrence of some business activities, for instance, the receipt of an order. An EDA comprises event consumers and event producers. Event consumers subscribe to an intermediary event manager, and event producers publish to this manager. When the event manager receives an event from a producer, the manager forwards the event to the consumer. If the consumer is unavailable, the manager can store the event and try to forward it later. Then, the primary value of EDA is that it allows companies to identify and respond to events coming from SCM collaborations that need to be addressed by one or more systems through event management. The events, collected via an EDA, can be analyzed and correlated to identify relevant patterns, and then aggregated to build up information that is needed to solve the procurement problem. With this process, companies can proactively address and respond to real-world scenarios in real time. Based on this understanding, in this paper we propose a Middleware-oriented Integrated Architecture system that offers a brokering service to facilitate the business processes integration in supply chains. Our brokering service is part of a complex system named BPIMS-WS which provides a virtual marketplace where people, agents and trading partners can collaborate by using current Web services technology in a flexible and automated manner [6]. Our brokering service provides the following contributions: (1) A hybrid architecture that borrows features from service-oriented and event-driven architectures to provide support for B2B and SCM collaborations, (2) A business processes pattern management component for the orchestrations of business processes, (3) A mechanism based on UML sequence diagrams to monitor the interactions involved in business collaborations, (4) A Web services-based management component with capabilities for discovering the availability, performance, and usage, as well as the control and configuration of Web services, (5) An execution event publish/subscription mechanism to incorporate information into business processes and decisions through event publication, (6) A messaging service that provides a guaranteed delivery and processing in a reliable way. This proposal is an extended version presented in [7].

2 Middleware-Oriented Integrated Architecture for e-Procurement

The middleware-oriented integrated architecture has a layered design. Furthermore, our proposal presents a component-based and hybrid architecture, borrowing features from SOA and EDA. In an SOA context, our approach acts as a Business Process Management (BPM) platform based on the SOA paradigm, facilitating the creation and execution of highly transparent and modular process-oriented applications and enterprise workflows. In an EDA context, our approach provides a software infrastructure designed to support a more real-time method of integrating event-driven application processes that occur throughout existing applications, and are largely defined by their meaning to the business and their granularity. Regardless of the event's granularity, our proposal focuses on ensuring that interested parties, usually other applications, are notified immediately when an event happens. These features are performed by our brokering service. Its general architecture is shown in Fig. 1. Each component has a function explained as follows:

SOAP Message Analyzer determines the structure and content of the documents exchanged in business processes involved in SCM collaborations. Since our proposal is based on Web services, this component determines the information involved in the incoming SOAP messages by means of XML parsers and tools. A DOM API is used to generate the tree structure of the SOAP messages, whereas SAX is used to determine the application logic for every node in the SOAP messages. A set of Java classes based on JAXP was developed to build the XML parser.

Service Registry is the mechanism for registering and publishing information about business processes, products and services among supply chain partners, and to update and adapt to SCM scenarios. We used a UDDI node which is an industry initiative to create a platform-independent, open framework for describing services, discovering businesses, and integrating business services. In our UDDI node, commercial enterprises, services and products both are classified and registered. For the classification of business processes, products and services in the registry, we use broadly accepted ontologies/taxonomies like NAICS, UNSPSC and RosettaNet. NAICS is a standard classification system for North American Industry; UNSPSC provides an open, global multi-sector standard for efficient, accurate classification of products and services and; RosettaNet defines the technical and business dictionaries.

Subscription Registry is the mechanism for registering interactions in which systems publish information about an event to the network so that other systems, which have subscribed and authorized to receive such messages, can receive that information and act on it appropriately. According to the cause of an event, knowledge often referred to as event causality in this work, we have considered both vertical and horizontal causality meaning that the event's source and cause reside both on different and on the same conceptual layers in an architectural stack, respectively. From vertical causality, this registry has support for storing execution events that represent runtime occurrences such as service or component invocations under a vertical causality. Life-cycle (such as stopping or starting a business process), management (when thresholds have exceeded defined limits or ranges) events, which are also part of a vertical causality, are considered as future work. From horizontal causality, this registry has support for Platform-layer, Component-layer and Business-layer events. Platform-layer events signify platform-level activities, such as the modification of a data source or the addition of a new service. Component-layer events signify component-level activities, such as the transformation of a view or a state-machine transition. Finally, Business-layer events signify business-level activities, such as the creation of a new user or the removal of an account.

Discovery Service is a component used to discover business processes implementations. Given the dynamic environment in SCM, the power of being able to find business processes on the fly to create new business processes is highly desirable. A key step in achieving this capability is the automated discovery of business processes described as Web services. In this sense, this component discovers Web services like authentication, payments, and shipping at run time from a SCM scenario. These Web services can be obtained from suitable service providers and can be combined into innovative and attractive product offerings to customers. When there is more than one service provider of the same function, it can be used to choose one service based on the client's requirements. Inside the discovery service, there is a query formulator which builds queries based on the domain ontology that will be sent to the registry service. This module retrieves a set of suitable services selected from the previous step and creates feasible/compatible sets of services ready for binding. The discovery service uses sophisticated techniques to dynamically discover web services and to formulate queries to UDDI nodes.

Dynamic Binding Service is a component that binds compatible business processes described as Web services. The binding of a Web Service refers to how strong the degree of coupling with other Web Services is. For instance, the technology of one Web service provider might be incompatible with that of another, even though the capabilities of both of them match with some requirements. In this sense, the module acts as an API wrapper that maps the interface source or target business process to a common interface supported by our proposal.

Dynamic Invoker transforms data from one format to another. This component can be seen as a data transfer object which contains the data (i.e., request or response) flowing between the requester to the provider applications of Web services. We used Web Services Invocation Framework (WSIF) that is a simple Java API for invoking Web services, no matter how or where the services are provided.

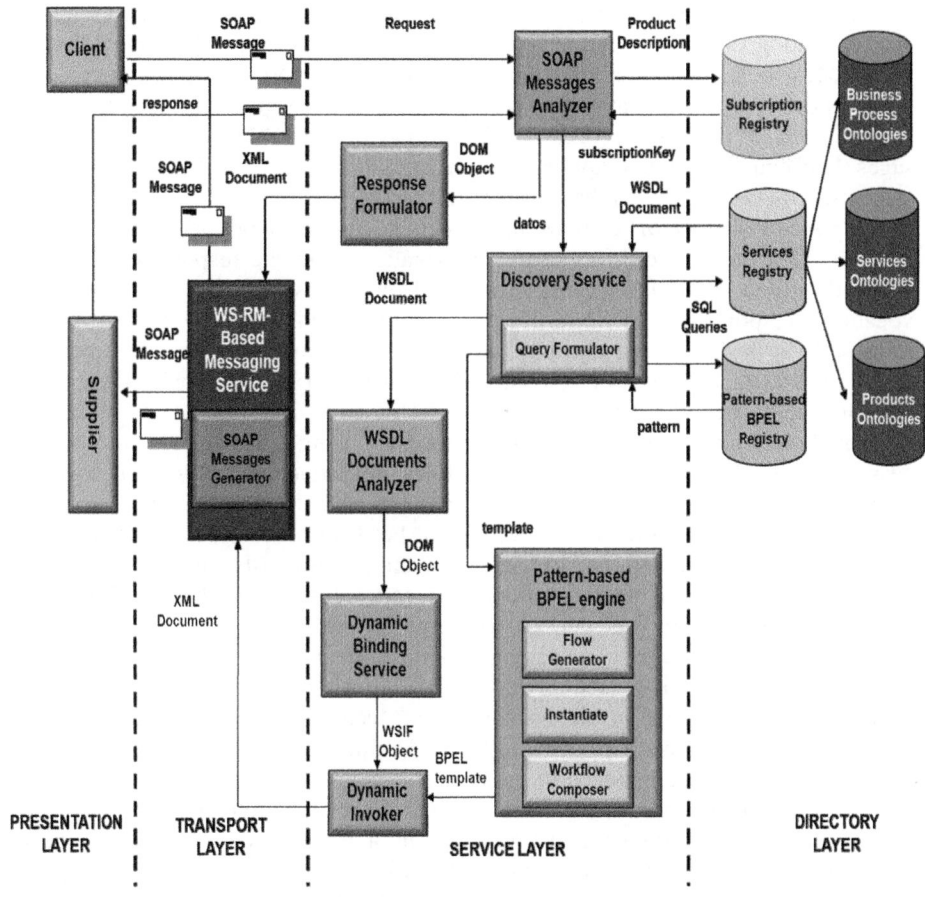

Fig. 1. General architecture of the Web services-based brokering service

WSDL Document Analyzer validates WSDL documents that describe business processes by their interfaces which are provided and used by supply chain partners. WSDL documents employ XML Schema for the specification of information items either product technical information or business processes operations. In this context, this component reports the business processes operations, input and output parameters, and their data types in a XML DOM tree. We used WSDL4J to convert the XML DOM nodes in Java objects.

WS-RM-based Messaging Service is the communication mechanism for the collaboration among the actors involved along the whole chain. One of the most critical aspects in SCM is to maintain its continuous operation as long as possible. In order to bring effective communication mechanisms along the chain, information technologies are considered to be the ideal solution for solving the problems related to reliability. Reliability of Web services is impacted by several factors including but not limited to, the reliability of the Web service end-points; the performance and fault-tolerance characteristics and the extent to which Web services can handle concurrent client access, among others. Our architecture uses the Web Services Reliable Messaging (WS-RM) which is a protocol that provides a standard, interoperable way to guarantee message delivery to applications or Web services. In this sense, our proposal provides a guaranteed delivery and processing that allows in a reliable way, delivery of messages between distributed applications in the presence of software components, systems, or network failures through WS-RM.

Response Formulator receives the responses from the suppliers about a requested product. This module retrieves useful information from the responses and builds a XML document with information coming from the service registry and the invocations' responses. This XML document is presented in HTML format using the Extensible Stylesheet Language (XSL). The answer contains information pertaining to the product (according to the requested product) and the electronic address of the enterprise that offers that product.

Workflow Engine coordinates Web services by using a BPEL-based business process language. It consists of building a fully instantiated workflow description at design time, where business partners are dynamically defined at execution time. In supply chain management, workflows cannot be determined since business partners are not known beforehand, and because they are continuously changing their client-provider roles through collaboration. For this reason, we have designed and implemented a repository of generic BPEL workflow definitions which describe increasingly complex forms of recurring situations abstracted from the various stages from SCM. Its design is presented in [8]. This repository contains workflow patterns of interactions involved in an e-procurement scenario. These workflows patterns describe the types of interactions behind each business process, and the types of messages that are exchanged in each interaction.

According to the emphasis on automation, our architecture can be accessed in two modes of interaction, either as a proxy server or as an Internet portal. In the first mode, the brokering service can interoperate with other systems or software agents. In the second mode, our architecture acts as an Internet portal that provides to the users a range of options among the Web services available through the brokering service. Finally, the HYDRA architecture has a layered design following four principles: (1) Integration, (2) Composition, (3) Monitoring and (4) Management, which are described next.

3   Web Services Discovery in HYDRA

Web services discovery involves locating business processes that provide a particular service which can be used by supply chain partners satisfying their commercial needs.

HYDRA provides basic services for publishing and querying Web services. These services represent the basic operations in HYDRA. The structure and behavior of the Web services discovery in HYDRA can be understood with the following example. Assume that a client has a production line which cannot be stopped. At certain moment, the client detects his stock levels have diminished and therefore she needs to find what providers are available related to her product. By doing this, the client must select the type of the product she wants from a range of options offered through an Internet portal. Then, HYDRA obtains the request and formulates a query to the service registry. The result to the query is a list of all the suppliers that includes the requested product in their stocks. Next HYDRA extracts the required information and builds an XML document. This XML document is presented in HTML using a stylesheet. The answer contains information relating to the provider and product.

By means of basic Web services, a client can know what registered enterprises in the service registry can offer a certain product.

4   Web Services Orchestration in HYDRA

Orchestration is currently presented as a way to coordinate Web services in order to define business processes. The utility of Web services is further enhanced by the introduction of mechanisms for composing them in order to generate new Web services and applications. The composition of Web services is defined as a process that enables the creation of composite services, which can be dynamically discovered, integrated, and executed to meet user requirements. In HYDRA, a composite Web service is obtained by the orchestration of several simple Web services. Composite Web services can be created in both design and execution time. In HYDRA, for the execution of a composite Web service it is firstly necessary to locate a suitable template from the BPEL repository that describes the intended commercial activities. In this schema, the templates are completely determined since commercial partners are known beforehand. For instance, in a purchase order scenario of books, the client might be interested in buying a book in the store that offers either the lowest price or the minimum delivery time. If a client wants to buy several books at the lowest price, HYDRA will retrieve the location of the BPEL workflow template that uses the purchase-criteria selected from a database. Once the template is located, HYDRA uses the WSDL document and the related configuration files in order to instantiate them. HYDRA obtains the templates that can be used to find the suppliers that offer the product required by the client. A query to a database containing the WSDL documents provided by HYDRA can retrieve the appropriate Web services to obtain a number of pieces of commercial information like price, delivery time, quantity, and purchase access point of the product. These services, based on UNSPSC and RosettaNet ontologies, are get_PriceandDeliveryTime, get_ProviderQuantity, and get_ProviderURLBuy, respectively. The related WSDL documents are then analyzed, and all the relevant information is retrieved and used to complete the templates. The first step to complete the templates is to include the namespaces of the services on top of the BPEL document identifying them with a number. A list of partnerLinkTypes is also included and a portType is placed within each partnerLinkType element. The portType name is divided into two parts: the namespace and the portType name of the remote service. The second step is to complete the executable BPEL document by including or modifying some elements. Once Web services namespaces, partnerLinks, input and output variables, and invocations to external services have been included, a namespace and a partnerLink must be added for each Web service along with input and output variables. The instantiated templates are allocated in a BPEL engine for execution. To communicate with the running workflow, HYDRA builds SOAP messages containing the information provided by the client. Following our example, the client sends to the running workflow, the book code and the required quantity in a SOAP message. The workflow verifies also that the sum of all the quantities is at least the quantity requested by the client. If it is not true, an empty list is sent back to the client as response, which means that client's request could not be completely fulfilled by any of the registered stores. Whenever the workflow has been successfully terminated, it sends back to the client the list of suppliers satisfying his requirements. Then, the workflow is de-allocated from the workflow engine. After the client selects the suppliers, a BPWL4WS template for placing a purchase order is now retrieved from the repository, completed and executed as described before. By enacting this workflow the purchase orders are sent to the suppliers and the corresponding answers from each supplier are eventually received.

So far, we have only shown one example that illustrates the use of a composite Web service. However, a wide variety of other composite Web services involving some optimization criteria have also been developed and tested, like minimum delivery time and distributed purchases, to mention a few.

In the next section, we describe how business processes descriptions can be monitored at execution time. This is one of the more relevant aspects of HYDRA in relation to the deployment of business processes.

5 Process Activity Monitoring in HYDRA

The need to conduct business in real-time is among the most daunting yet strategic challenges facing today's enterprise. Enterprises that operate in a SCM scenario can instantly detect significant events to identify problems and opportunities, and manage the appropriate response to reap significant profits and build competitive advantage. For these reasons, enterprises are turning their attention toward implementing solutions for real-time business activity monitoring (BAM) [9]. In this context, HYDRA offers capabilities for business activities monitoring. For the monitoring process, it is necessary to listen to the request/response SOAP messaging of Web service-based business collaboration. The SOAP messaging identifies the participants and their communications during the long-running interactions of the participants in the collaboration. For this end, HYDRA intercepts all SOAP messages to generate a UML sequence diagram from the information about the participants and the order in which the messages are exchanged. For the monitoring of activities, a set of Java classes has been developed to represent a UML diagram in a SVG (Scalable Vector Graphics) representation that can be visualized in an SVG enabled Internet browser. This whole process can be depicted in figure 2. The exchange of SOAP messages during some kinds of business collaboration may be developed very quickly. Therefore, to avoid reducing the performance of the Web services execution, the dynamic generation of UML diagrams uses a buffered mechanism to deal with a fast pacing production of SOAP messages.

In the next section, we describe how business processes described as Web services can be managed in HYDRA.

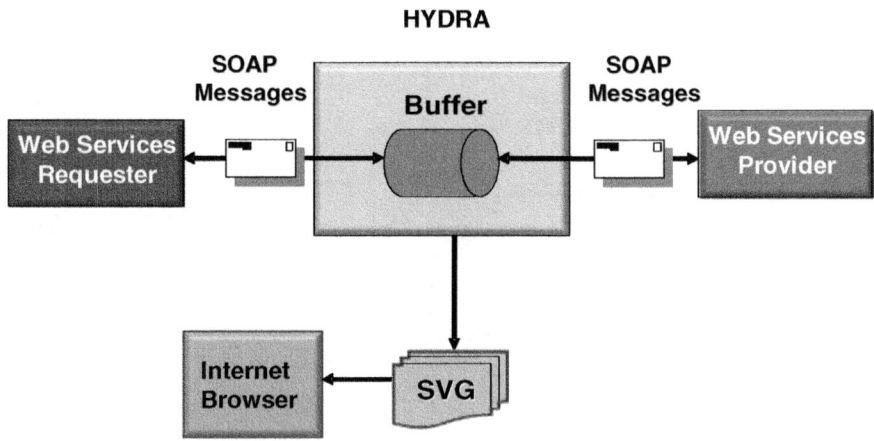

Fig. 2. Process activity monitoring in HYDRA

6   Web Services Management in HYDRA

As Web services become pervasive and critical to business operations, the task of managing Web services and implementations of our brokering service architecture is imperative to the success of business operations involved in SCM. Web services Management refers to the problem of monitoring and controlling the Web services themselves and their execution environment, to ensure they operate with the desired levels of quality [10]. In this sense, we developed a basic web services manager with capabilities for discovering the availability, performance, and usage, as well as the control and configuration of Web services provided by HYDRA. The underlying technology used for the implementation is JMX (Java Management eXtension), but conceptually could be extended to support other management technologies such as CIM (Common Information Model) and SNMP (Simple Network Management Protocol) [11]. The JMX architecture consists of three levels: instrumentation, agent, and distributed services. JMX provides interfaces and services adequate for monitoring and managing systems requirements. This functionality involves abstracting resources by using components called MBeans (Managed Beans) and remote instrumented resources, accessible through JMX connectors. An MBean is a Java object that represents a manageable resource, such as an application, a service or a device. The architecture for Web services management in HYDRA is shown in figure 3.

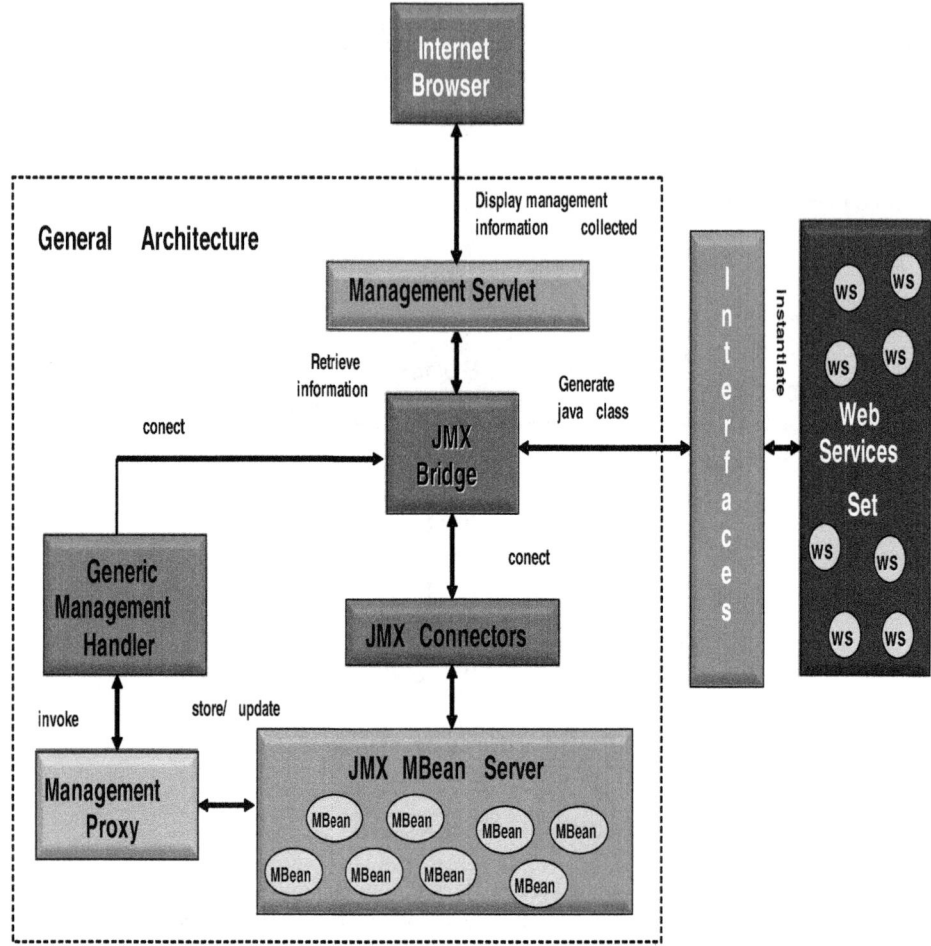

Fig. 3. Architecture for Web services management in HYDRA

The main component for web services management is a JMX Bridge, which acts as a bridge between the collection of resources managed by JMX and Web services. In HYDRA, Web services interfaces to JMX are available. Rather than provide a JMX specific Web service interface, HYDRA provides a Web service interface to a manageable resource. Under our approach, the resources can be implemented on different technologies because it is only necessary to define a Web service interface for a resource. In order to do this, we used MBeans to represent the resource being managed.

The JMX Bridge provides information that identifies or describes the MBean instance that represents a specific managed resource. The general architecture for Web services management is presented in [12]. The most significant aspect of our approach is a JMX-based management Web service that allows the storage of MBeans within a JMX MBean Server that can be accessed and manipulated from an AXIS-enabled remote console. Under this approach is possible to monitor the status of JMX-enabled services and components through an AXIS (SOAP) client interface. The MBean server tracks global information and statistics about Web services. In order to do this, a Web-based interface was developed, which displays this data based on a hostname and port pair specified in a simple form embedded in a servlet. Collectively, this functionality represents the direction towards active management of JMX-enabled data and application resources over a standard AXIS (SOAP) interface. This illustrates an approach to managing Web services by instrumenting AXIS through the use of handlers to provide a JMX-based systems management interface.

In this case, AXIS handlers were developed and added to the handler chains of our various Web services to allow statistics about those services to be gathered. The JMX MBean Server which tracks the service statistics is instantiated globally within the application server's JVM, allowing statistics to be tracked across all instrumented Web applications. A screenshot of this tracking is presented in figure 4.

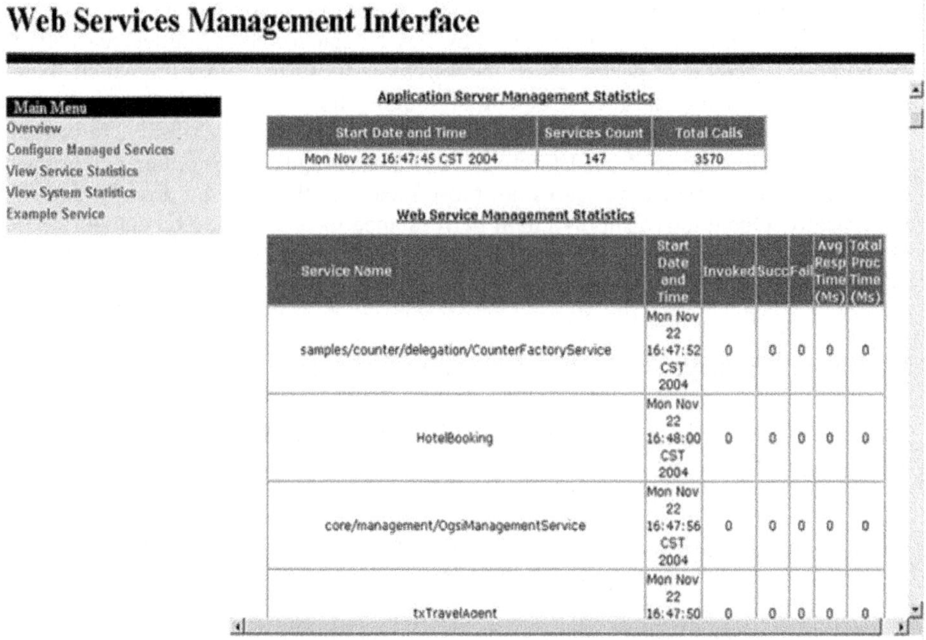

Web Services Management Interface

Application Server Management Statistics

Start Date and Time	Services Count	Total Calls
Mon Nov 22 16:47:45 CST 2004	147	3570

Web Service Management Statistics

Service Name	Start Date and Time	Invoked	Succ	Fail	Avg Resp Time (Ms)	Total Proc Time (Ms)
samples/counter/delegation/CounterFactoryService	Mon Nov 22 16:47:52 CST 2004	0	0	0	0	0
HotelBooking	Mon Nov 22 16:48:00 CST 2004	0	0	0	0	0
core/management/OgsiManagementService	Mon Nov 22 16:47:56 CST 2004	0	0	0	0	0
txTravelAgent	Mon Nov 22 16:47:50	0	0	0	0	0

Main Menu
Overview
Configure Managed Services
View Service Statistics
View System Statistics
Example Service

Fig. 4. Graphic Interface for Web services management in HYDRA

Finally, for each Web service deployed by HYDRA, the following statistics are tracked:

1) Current state
2) Total number of managed SOAP services deployed
3) Total number of RPC calls to all managed services combined
4) Total number of successful invocations

5) Number of failed invocations (requests received by the server but resulted in an exception)
6) Average response/transaction time for successful requests

To illustrate the functionality of HYDRA, we describe next an e-procurement scenario that integrates several products and services among clients, suppliers and providers that has already been implemented.

7 Performance Measures in HYDRA

An important component in supply chain design and analysis is the establishment of appropriate performance measure. A performance measure, or a set of performance measure, is used to determine the efficiency and/or effectiveness of an existing system, or to compare competing alternative systems. Available literature identifies a number of performance measures as important in the evaluation of supply chain effectiveness and efficiency. In HYDRA, these measures may be categorized as either qualitative or quantitative. Qualitative performance measures are those measures for which there is no single direct numerical measurement, although some aspects of them may be quantified. Examples of these measures are Customer satisfaction, Flexibility, Information and material flow integration, Effective risk management and Supplier performance. Quantitative performance measures are those measures that may be directly described numerically. Quantitative supply chain performance measures may be categorized by: (1) objectives that are based directly on cost or profit and (2) objectives that are based on some measures of customer responsiveness.

8 Case of Study: An e-Procurement Scenario

The case of study describes how our brokering service facilitates the discovery of Web services that are offered by different enterprises that sell electronic components. Suppose the following scenario:

1. The enterprises sell on-line electronic components. The enterprises have registered their products and their business processes as Web services in the UDDI node of our brokering service.
2. A potential client (enterprise) starts a supply chain to procure products by requesting a purchase order by means of Web services.
3. In this scenario, we approach the fundamental problem of determining how a client can discover and invoke the Web services available to carry out e-procurement?

On the one hand, we assume that the business processes of the registered enterprises in our architecture are based on the commercial behaviors described in RosettaNet PIPs. On the other hand, we do not assume, however, that all suppliers use the same data fields for product descriptions and follow the same protocol for their interactions with customers. The whole e-procurement business process based on the fourth kind of response (detailed below) is shown in figure 5. In this scenario four types of re-sponses can be observed:

1) The request is not understood, i.e. the architecture cannot process the client's request because it is ill-formed. Some factors, such as lack of parameters or invoking a Web service with a wrong operation name, produce an ill-formed request. In this case, an error message indicating that the request cannot be processed is returned.

2) No provider is found for the requested product, i.e. the architecture re-turns an empty list indicating that no provider can supply the requested product. This situation is derived from two factors: (a) the requested product is not registered in our architecture and therefore providers are not available, and (b) the requested product is registered but is not associated with a supplier.

3) A provider for the requested product is found, i.e. the architecture returns a list of the enterprises that appear as the product providers. This is the better case because the requested product is registered and is associated with a pro-vider. In this case, a list of providers that offer the requested product in their stocks is displayed.

4) A provider is found but the product is not available at that time. In this case, our architecture may engage in obtaining such a product from the registered providers.

In what follows, we address only the fourth case observed, when some providers are found but none of them have enough number of products at the time to fulfill the request. The proposed solution is based on the use of business processes patterns de-scribed as BPEL workflows, after an event-based subscription pattern that occurs in the fourth kind of response has been identified. The event-based subscription pattern is used to obtain a list of suppliers offering the requested product in sufficient quantities. The event-based subscription pattern is explained as follows: Firstly, the architecture creates new instances for both service and subscription registries (Steps 1-4 in Fig. 5). This step is an initialization phase in which our architecture is ready for listening client's requests. The client submits a request by sending a SOAP message containing the product description (Step 5 in Fig. 5). This request corresponds to the RosettaNet PIP 2A5 (Query Technical Information). A screenshot of products selec-tion is shown in Fig. 6a. The SOAP message analyzer extracts the product description to be sent to the discovery service. The query formulator builds a query to determine the qualified suppliers. The query formulator transforms the product description into SQL sentences and builds a query to the service registry. The query is executed and the response is a set of WSDL documents of candidate suppliers (Steps 6-9 in Fig. 5). Each WSDL document represents the RosettaNet PIP 2A5 from available suppliers. For each WSDL document, the access point, operations, messages and parameters are retrieved through the WSDL document analyzer. Then, the binding service identifies the type of communication protocol specified in each WSDL document and invokes the Web service of each candidate supplier (Step 10 and 11 in Fig. 5). The architec-ture receives the supplier's response (Steps 12 and 13 in Fig. 5). Then, the SOAP message analyzer determines which of the four types of responses mentioned before

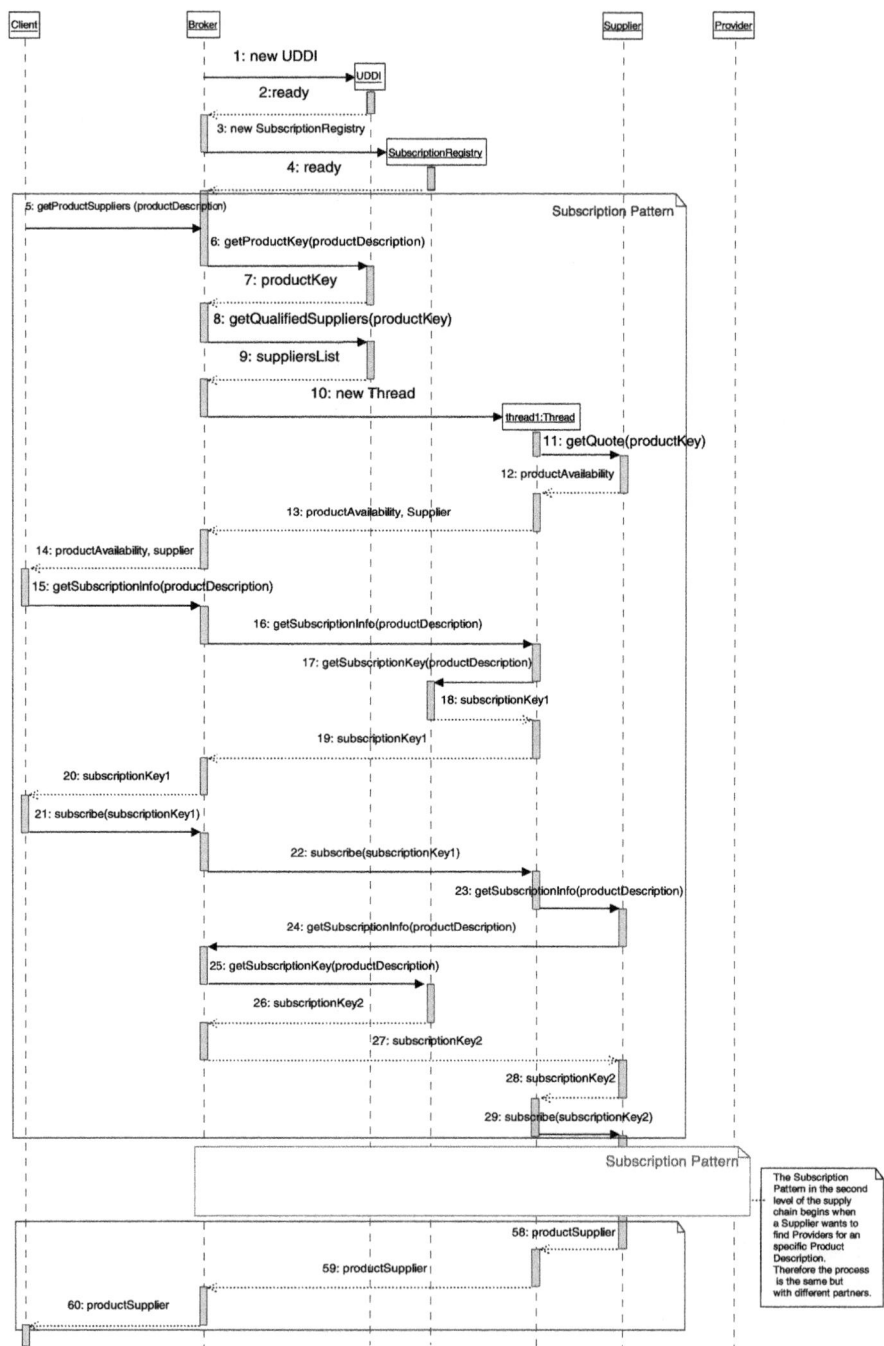

Fig. 5. Interactions involved in e-procurement business process

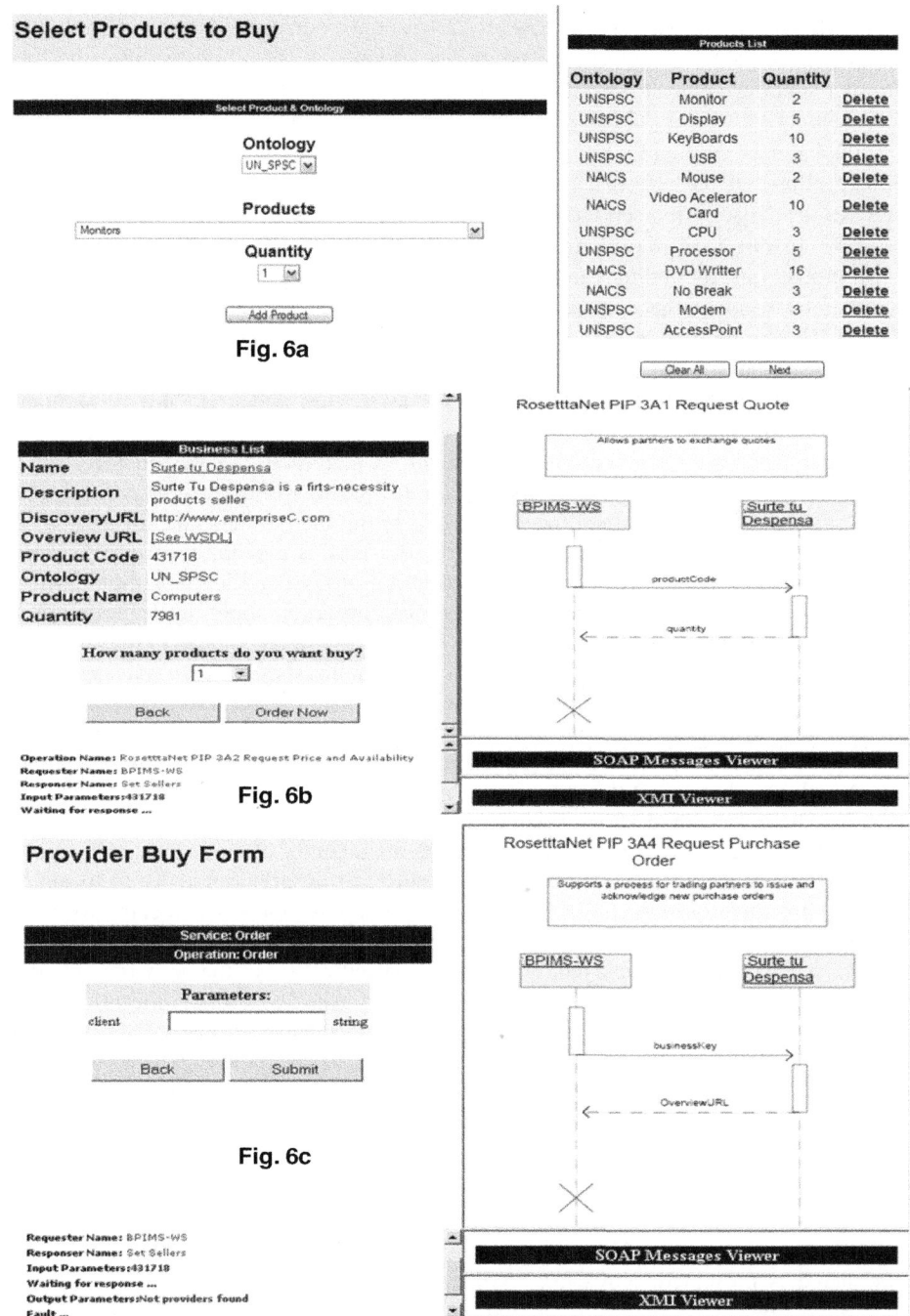

Fig. 6. (a) Products selection in HYDRA, (b) HYDRA displays information about a requested product when the subscription pattern finishes both second and first level of SCM, (c) HYDRA displaying the Web service specification of a purchase order from a supplier

was included in the message. Whenever the response corresponds to the fourth case, an execution event is triggered by asking the client if it is willing to subscribe for a product supplier when it becomes available (Step 14 in Fig. 5). If the client accepts, the architecture uses a publish/subscription mechanism within the subscription registry, publishing the client's requested product description and generating a subscriptionKey that will be returned to the client (Steps 15-20 in Fig. 5). Then the client invokes the subscription service by sending a SOAP message containing the subscriptionKey. In this case, the client will be waiting for an answer (Step 21 in Fig. 5). During this wait, the architecture requests a corresponding subscriptionKey from the supplier by sending the client's requested product description (Steps 22 and 23 in Fig. 5). The supplier stores the product description and generates a subscriptionKey as a response to the request (Steps 24-26 in Fig. 5). Next, another execution event is triggered by invoking the supplier's subscribe service and waits for a supplier's answer (Steps 27-29 in Fig. 5).

During this wait, the event-based subscription pattern in the second level of the supply chain management begins when a supplier wants to find providers for a product description. Therefore, the process is the same but the partners take different roles, i.e., the supplier acts as a client and the provider acts as a supplier of our brokering service. When the provider's response is returned the second level of the SCM, the architecture analyzes it and retrieves the useful information about the requested product. With this information, the architecture is able to send a response to the supplier's subscribe service request. Here the second level of the supply chain management is completed. In a similar way, the supplier will answer to the subscribe service request and his wait will finish (Step 58-59 in Fig. 5). Finally, the architecture is able to answer the client's subscribe service request and as a consequence, the client's wait will finish and the client is getting the information about his requested product (Step 60 in Fig. 5). The information about a requested product by the client is shown in Fig. 6b. At this point, the client is already able to select the quantity of the requested product.

Once selected, the architecture makes a query to the service registry to locate the URL where the RosettaNet PIP 3A4 (Request Purchase Order) is located to obtain and analyze the Web service specification. Next, a graphic user interface of the Web service specification is displayed, enabling the visualization of the activities involved in the purchasing order process. The client is then asked to provide the information required to complete the purchase. This graphic interface is shown in Fig 6c. Upon completion, the Web service corresponding to the RosettaNet PIP 3A5 is invoked (Query Order Status) to verify that the purchase was successful. Finally, the results to the user are displayed.

9 Related Works and Discussion

In [13] a system named eXFlow for business processes integration on EAI and B2B e-commerce is presented. However, eXFlow only provides support for Web services discovery, invocation, orchestration and monitoring. Web services management is not considered and since eXFlow is based on SOA architecture, asynchronous messaging is not provided. In [14] another system named THROWS is proposed, an architecture for highly available distributed execution of Web services compositions. In the

THROWS architecture, the execution control is hierarchically delegated among dynamically dis-covered engines. However, THROWS is in the design phase, thus it is still under development. In [15] an architecture for semi-automatic Web services composition is provided, combining both centralized model and peer-to-peer approaches. This proposal only has support for Web services discovery, invocation, orchestration and monitoring. Web services management is not considered, and the architecture is being developed. In [16] a system which acts as an Integration Broker for Heterogeneous Information Sources (IBHIS) was developed. IBHIS is already implemented but process activity monitoring is not included. In [17], a system named IRIS (Interoperability and Reusability of Internet Services) for Web services composition through a set of graphic interfaces. In IRIS, Web services discovery and orchestration are provided by an ontology-based registry approach. However, IRIS is focused on the simulation of Web services composition; therefore Web services execution is not included. In [18] is proposed a framework named KDSWS (Knowledge-based Dynamic Semantic Web Services) which addresses in an integrated end-to-end manner, the life-cycle of activities involved in brokering and managing of Semantic Web Services. However, agent monitoring is not considered and the architecture is subject to ongoing work. In [19] an architecture for Web services discovery is proposed by using a goal-oriented approach. Web services discovery is carried out by means of services chains satisfying certain constraints. This architecture only provides support for Web services management and monitoring, and it is in the design phase. In [20] is proposed a framework for Dynamic Web Service Invocation. This framework is based on SOA architecture. Publication/subscription and notification mechanisms are used in Web services discovery in UDDI nodes. However, an experimental prototype is provided, which does not consider Web services orchestration, monitoring and management. In [21] was developed a system named METEOR-S (Managing End-To-End OpeRations for Semantic Web services) which is a constraint driven Web Service composition tool. In the METEOR-S architecture, web services management is not considered. Nevertheless, METEOR-S has been implemented and is working well.

More recent works have proposed others approaches for e-procurement in SCM. In [22] is presented an overview and a classification of B2B approaches. Business-and implementation-related specifications are classified in terms of the Open-EDI reference model. Furthermore, the path from a business model down to deployments artifacts for SOA environments is outlined. In [23] an agent-mediated coordination approach is proposed to dynamic supply chain integration. A prototype has been implemented with simulated experiments highlighting the effectiveness of the approach. In [24] is proposed a service oriented knowledge-based architecture to support supply chain application. The proposed architecture has the capability to meet the on-demand requirements of dynamic supply chains. Business requirements and potential benefits associated are discussed. In [25] an approach that improves requirements engineering as part of the UN/CEFACT's Modeling Methodology for specifying B2B systems is presented. This approach helps to avoid inconsistencies between worksheets capturing the business experts' knowledge and the modeling artifacts. This is realized by integrating a worksheet editor into a UMM modeling tool. In [26] is established a two-period replenishment model of (s, S) strategy to analyze the operation cost efficiency of the traditional procurement in strategic partnership, e-procurement and the mixed procurement strategy respectively. The model quantifies the effect of the Internet on procurement management. Finally, in [27] is proposed a new solving scheme for modern e-commerce system frameworks. The solution of sharing function and data for each node of a modern business flow is designed including data reuse, elastic cart, order of automatic collection, trusteeship calculating of logistics cost request and automatic chamberlain based on Web Services.

10   Conclusions

SCM is an important yet difficult problem to be addressed in its full complexity. However, we believe that hybrid architecture, borrowing features from SOA and EDA, may provide the fundamental structure in which the solutions to the diverse problems that SCM conveys can be accommodated. In this paper, we have described an architecture namely HYDRA we have developed so far that provides a comprehensive framework for developing business integration, collaboration and monitoring in SCM scenarios. HYDRA provides a set of Web interfaces where different enterprises can offer its products and services in SCM scenarios. To achieve this, HYDRA offers mechanisms to publish and discover the business process provided by enterprises. Enterprises must register their business processes described as Web services to enable to potential clients to integrate their processes with them through HYDRA.

Among the applications we envisioned for our proposal, the orchestration of long-term supply chains involving operation research methods to minimize costs, reduce delivery times and maximize quality of service along with artificial intelligence methods to provide semantic matching and to define business partners profile management is now under consideration.

Acknowledgements

This work is supported by the General Council of Superior Technological Education of Mexico (DGEST). Additionally, this work is sponsored by the National Council of Science and Technology (CONACYT) and the Public Education Secretary (SEP) through PROMEP. Furthermore, this work is supported by the Spanish Ministry of Industry, Tourism, and Commerce under the EUREKA project SITIO (TSI-020400-2009-148), SONAR2 (TSI-020100-2008-665 and GO2 (TSI-020400-2009-127).

References

1. Papazoglou, M.P.: Service-Oriented Computing: Concepts, Characteristics and Directions. In: Proceedings of the Fourth International Conference on Web Information Systems Engineering. IEEE Press, Los Alamitos (2003)
2. Vinoski, S.: Integration with Web Services. IEEE Internet Computing, 75–77 (November-December 2003)
3. Adams, H., Gisolfi, D., Snell, J., Varadan, R.: Custom Extended Enterprise Exposed Business Services Application Pattern Scenario, (January 1, 2003),
   http://www-106.ibm.com/developerworks/webservices/
   library/ws-best5/

4. Samtani, G., Sadhwani, D.: Enterprise Application Integration and Web Services. In: Fletcher, P., Waterhouse, M. (eds.) Web Services Business Strategies and Architectures, pp. 39–54. Expert Press, Ltd., Birmingham (2002)
5. Sriraman, B., Radhakrishnan, R.: Event-Driven Architecture augmenting Service-Oriented Architecture. Sun Microsystems (January 2005)
6. Alor Hernandez, G., Olmedo Aguirre, J.O.: BPIMS-WS: Service-Oriented Architecture for Business Processes Management. Advances in Artificial Intelligence, Computing Science and Computer Engineering. Journal of Research on Computing Science 10, 255–264 (2005)
7. Alor-Hernández, G., Aguilar-Lasserre, A.A., Juárez-Martínez, U., Posada-Gómez, R., Robles, G.C., Martinez, M.A.G., Gómez, J.M., Mencke, M., González, A.R.: A Hybrid Architecture for E-Procurement. In: Nguyen, N.T., Kowalczyk, R., Chen, S.-M. (eds.) ICCCI 2009. LNCS, vol. 5796, pp. 685–696. Springer, Heidelberg (2009)
8. Sandoval Hernandez, C., Alor-Hernandez, G., Olmedo, J.O.: Dynamic generation of organizational BPEL4WS workflows. In: Proceedings of the 1st International Conference on Electrical and Electronics Engineering and X Conference on Electrical Engineering (ICEEE-CIE 2004), pp. 130–135. IEEE Press, Los Alamitos (2004)
9. Dresner, H.: Business Activity Monitoring: New Age BI? Gartner Research LE-15-8377 (April 2002)
10. Casati, F., Shan, E., Dayal, U., Shan, M.C.: Business-Oriented Management of Web Services. Communications of the ACM 46(10), 55–60 (2003)
11. Sidnie, M.F.: SNMP: A Guide to Network Management. McGraw Hill Series on Computer Communications (September 1, 1994) ISBN: 0070203598
12. Alor Hernandez, G., Olmedo Aguirre, J.O.: Managed Web Services using WS-Manageability. In: Gelbuck, A., Calvo, H. (eds.) Advances in Computing Science in Mexico. Research on Computing Science Series, vol. 13, pp. 255–264 (2005) ISSN: 1665-9899
13. Chung Nin, N.C., Wen-Shih, H., Tse-Ming, Seng-cho, T.: eXFlow:A Web Services-Compliant System to Support B2B Process Integration. In: Proceedings of the 37th Hawaii International Conference on System Sciences (2004)
14. Lakhal, N.B., Kobayashi, T., Yokota, H.: THROWS: An Architecture for Highly Available Distributed Execution of Web Services Compositions. In: Proceedings of the 14th International Workshop on Research Issues on Data Engineering: Web Services for E-Commerce and E-Government Applications. IEEE Press, Los Alamitos
15. Budak, A.I., Aleman-Meza, B., Zhang, R., Maduko, A.: Ontology-Driven Web Services Composition Platform. In: Proceedings of the IEEE International Conference on E-Commerce Technology. IEEE Press, Los Alamitos
16. Turner, M., Zhu, F., Kotsiopoulos, I., Russell, M., Budgen, D., Bennett, K., Brereton, P., Keane, J., Layzell, P., Rigby, M.: Using Web Service Technologies to create an Information Broker: An Experience Report. In: Proceedings of the 26th International Conference on Soft-ware Engineering. IEEE Press, Los Alamitos (2004)
17. Radetzki, U., Cremers, A.B.: IRIS: A Framework for Mediator-Based Composition of Service-Oriented Software. In: Proceedings of the IEEE International Conference on Web Services. IEEE Press, Los Alamitos (2004)
18. Howard, R., Kerschberg, L.: A Knowledge-based Framework for Dynamic Semantic Web Services Brokering and Management. In: Proceedings of the 15th International Workshop on Database and Expert Systems Applications (2004)
19. Srinivasan, A., Sundaram, D.: Web Services for Enterprise Collaboration: A Framework and a Prototype. In: Proceedings of the 30th EUROMICRO Conference (EUROMICRO'04). IEEE Press, Los Alamitos (2004)

20. Jian-Jun, Y., Zhou, G.: Dynamic Web Service Invocation. In: Proceedings of the IEEE International Conference on E-Commerce Technology for Dynamic E-Business (CEC-East'04). IEEE Press, Los Alamitos (2004)
21. Aggarwal, R., Verma, K., Miller, J., Milnor, W.: Constraint Driven Web Service Composition in METEOR-S. In: Proceedings of the 2004 IEEE International Conference on Services Computing (SCC'04). IEEE Press, Los Alamitos (2004)
22. Jurgen, D., Christoph, G., Hannes, W., Marco, Z.: A Survey of B2B Meth-odologies and Technologies: From Business Models towards Deployment Artifacts. In: Proceedings of the 40th Hawaii International Conference on System Sciences 2007. IEEE, Los Alamitos (2007)
23. Minhong, W., Huaiqing, W., Jiming, L.: Dynamic Supply Chain Integration through Intelligent Agents. In: Proceedings of the 40th Hawaii International Conference on System Sciences 2007, pp. 1–10. IEEE Press, Los Alamitos (2007)
24. Wei, D., Paul, M., Juanqiong, G., Ping, Z., Xi, Y., Tiedong, C., Xin, W.: Services Oriented Knowledge-based Supply Chain Application. In: Proceedings of the 2007 IEEE International Conference on Services Computing (SCC 2007). IEEE Press, Los Alamitos (2007)
25. Christian, H., Marco, Z., Philipp, L., Rainer, S.: Worksheet-Driven UMM Modeling of B2B Services. In: Proceedings of the IEEE International Conference on e-Business Engineering, pp. 30–38. IEEE Press, Los Alamitos
26. Guangshu, C.: The Analysis of Supply Chain Procurement Strategy in E-Commerce. In: Proceedings of the International Symposium on Electronic Commerce and Security (2008)
27. Hao, Y., Cheng, L.V.: Research on the Solving Scheme of E-commerce System ase don Web Services. In: Proceedings of the International Conference on Management of e-Commerce and e-Government, pp. 230–233. IEEE Press, Los Alamitos

Tableaux with Global Caching for Checking Satisfiability of a Knowledge Base in the Description Logic $\mathcal{SH}$ [⋆]

Linh Anh Nguyen[1] and Andrzej Szałas[1,2]

[1] Institute of Informatics, University of Warsaw
Banacha 2, 02-097 Warsaw, Poland
[2] Dept. of Computer and Information Science, Linköping University
SE-581 83 Linköping, Sweden
{nguyen,andsz}@mimuw.edu.pl

Abstract. Description logics (DLs) are a family of knowledge representation languages which can be used to represent the terminological knowledge of an application domain in a structured and formally well-understood way. DLs can be used, for example, for conceptual modeling or as ontology languages. In fact, OWL (Web Ontology Language), recommended by W3C, is based on description logics.

In the current paper we give the first direct EXPTIME (optimal) tableau decision procedure, which is not based on transformation or on the pre-completion technique, for checking satisfiability of a knowledge base in the description logic $\mathcal{SH}$. Our procedure uses sound global caching and can be implemented as an extension of the highly optimized tableau prover TGC to obtain an efficient program for the mentioned satisfiability problem.

1 Introduction

Collective intelligence refers to intelligence emerging from cooperation or competition of groups of (intelligent) agents. When such cooperation or competition occurs in distributed and open environments, new agents and services are allowed to join them while other may disappear, e.g., undertaking other activities. This happens, for example, in the Semantic Web. Achieving complex tasks by software agents requires cooperation supported by communication in a common language and conceptual space. Shared understanding of concepts and relationships is usually achieved by terminological knowledge and ontologies. It should be emphasized that one cannot expect a common or global conceptual space in such open environments. Instead, many local ontological structures, some shared by agents and others not, are much more likely. For example, if a new type of product or service appears, some agents can extend their local ontologies while other agents still have to properly situate new concepts.

[⋆] Supported by grants N N206 399134 and N N206 370739 from the Polish Ministry of Science and Higher Education.

N.T. Nguyen and R. Kowalczyk (Eds.): Transactions on CCI I, LNCS 6220, pp. 21–38, 2010.

Description logics (DLs) are a family of knowledge representation languages which can be used to represent the terminological knowledge of an application domain in a structured and formally well-understood way [1]. DLs can be used, for example, for conceptual modeling or as ontology languages. In fact, OWL (Web Ontology Language), recommended by W3C, is based on description logics. DLs provide important techniques for knowledge representation and collective intelligence. They allow users to represent the application domain in terms of concepts, individuals, and roles, and to reason about them. A concept is interpreted as a set of individuals, while a role is interpreted as a binary relation among individuals. A knowledge base in a DL usually contains:

- a TBox consisting of terminological axioms
- an ABox consisting of assertions about individuals
- possibly also of an RBox consisting of role axioms.

The meaning of diverse information content, if specified by means of DLs, is made accessible to software agents for use and reasoning. On the other hand, DL-based reasoning has to be supported by software tools. Therefore, efficient implementations of DL reasoners are substantial for automating knowledge intensive tasks.

One of the basic inference problems in DLs, which we denote by Sat, is to check satisfiability of a knowledge base. Other inference problems in DLs are usually reducible to this problem. For example, the problem of checking consistency of a concept w.r.t. a TBox (and an RBox, if the logic allows), further denoted by $Cons$, is linearly reducible to Sat.

In this paper, we consider the Sat problem in the description logic $\mathcal{SH}$, which extends the basic description logic $\mathcal{ALC}$ with transitive roles and hierarchies of roles. Both the problems Sat and $Cons$ in $\mathcal{SH}$ are ExpTime-complete. The lower bound follows from Schild's result that the $Cons$ problem in $\mathcal{ALC}$ is ExpTime-complete [21], while the upper bound follows from Tobies's result that the Sat problem in $\mathcal{SHIQ}$ is ExpTime-complete [22], where $\mathcal{SHIQ}$ is the description logic that extends $\mathcal{SH}$ with inverse roles and quantified numeric restrictions. In [22], Tobies states that his algorithm used to establish the ExpTime-bound for $\mathcal{SHIQ}$ employs the pre-completion technique together with a highly inefficient automata construction and cannot be used for efficient implementations.

In [11], Horrocks and Sattler gave a NExpTime tableau decision procedure for the $Cons$ problem in the description logic $\mathcal{SHI}$, which extends $\mathcal{SH}$ with inverse roles. In [12], Horrocks et al. gave a NExpTime tableau decision procedure for the Sat problem in $\mathcal{SHIQ}$. The point in designing these non-optimal decision procedures was to obtain algorithms that are easy to implement and optimize.

Using global caching Goré and Nguyen have developed ExpTime (optimal) tableau decision procedures for the $Cons$ problem in $\mathcal{ALC}$ [6] and $\mathcal{SHI}$ [7]. We have recently applied the global caching method [19,6,7] to develop complexity-optimal tableau decision procedures for the Sat problem in $\mathcal{ALC}$ [16] and PDL (propositional dynamic logic) [15] and for the $Cons$ problem in CPDL (PDL with converse) [17] and regular grammar logics with converse [18].

The first author has implemented a tableau prover called TGC (Tableaux with Global Caching) [14] for the *Cons* problem in $\mathcal{ALC}$. The prover is based on the decision procedure developed by himself and Goré [6] that was mentioned above. He has developed and implemented for TGC a specific set of optimizations cooperating very well with global caching and various search strategies on search spaces represented by "and-or" graphs. TGC has been tested on the sets T98-sat and T98-kb of DL'98 Systems Comparison. The results are comparable with the test results of the best systems DLP-98 and FaCT-98 that participated in that comparison (see [14]). One can say that the mentioned test sets are not representative for practical applications, but the comparison at least shows that optimization techniques in the presence of global caching can be applied to obtain decision procedures that are both complexity-optimal and efficient in practice.

For the *Sat* problem of $\mathcal{SH}$, one can encode the ABox by using "nominals" [3] or by using terminological axioms plus a concept assertion [4] and then use a translation into PDL. However, such transformation methods are highly inefficient and are therefore not used in practice. One can also use the pre-completion technique [8,22] to deal with ABoxes but, as stated in [22], this method cannot be used for efficient implementations. A very natural method for dealing with ABoxes [12] that is used in some implemented tableau provers for description logics results in decision procedures with non-optimal complexity.

In this paper we give the first direct ExpTime (optimal) tableau decision procedure for the *Sat* problem in $\mathcal{SH}$, not based on transformation or the pre-completion technique. Extending TGC [14] with this procedure would result in an efficient program for checking satisfiability of a knowledge base in $\mathcal{SH}$.

This work is an extension of our conference paper [16], which is devoted to the *Sat* problem in $\mathcal{ALC}$, and is related to the work [7] by Goré and Nguyen, which is devoted to the *Cons* problem in $\mathcal{SHI}$. Recall that the *Sat* problem deals with ABoxes and is thus more general than the *Cons* problem. Using global caching to obtain a complexity-optimal tableau decision procedure for the satisfiability problem in the presence of ABox requires a sophisticated solution and has been studied only in our works [16] for $\mathcal{ALC}$ and [15] for PDL.

The rest of this paper is structured as follows. In Section 2 we introduce notation and semantics of $\mathcal{SH}$. A tableau calculus for the considered problem is provided in Section 3. In Section 4 we prove soundness and completeness of the calculus. In Section 5, we present our decision procedure based on the calculus. Optimizations for the procedure are discussed in Section 6. Finally, Section 7 concludes the paper.

2 Notation and Semantics of $\mathcal{SH}$

We use A and B to denote *concept names*, R and S for *role names*, and a and b for *individual names*. We refer to A and B also as *atomic concepts*, to R and S as *roles*, and to a and b as *individuals*.

Definition 2.1. *Concepts* are denoted by letters like C and D, and in $\mathcal{SH}$ they are formed using the following BNF grammar:

$$C, D ::= \top \mid \bot \mid A \mid \neg C \mid C \sqcap D \mid C \sqcup D \mid \forall R.C \mid \exists R.C \qquad \lhd$$

Definition 2.2. An *interpretation* $\mathcal{I} = \langle \Delta^{\mathcal{I}}, \cdot^{\mathcal{I}} \rangle$ consists of a non-empty set $\Delta^{\mathcal{I}}$, called the *domain* of $\mathcal{I}$, and a function $\cdot^{\mathcal{I}}$, called the *interpretation function* of $\mathcal{I}$, mapping every concept name A to a subset $A^{\mathcal{I}} \subseteq \Delta^{\mathcal{I}}$, every role name R to a binary relation $R^{\mathcal{I}} \subseteq \Delta^{\mathcal{I}} \times \Delta^{\mathcal{I}}$, and every individual name a to an element $a^{\mathcal{I}} \in \Delta^{\mathcal{I}}$. $\qquad \lhd$

The interpretation function $\cdot^{\mathcal{I}}$ is extended to complex concepts as follows:

$$\top^{\mathcal{I}} = \Delta^{\mathcal{I}} \qquad\qquad \bot^{\mathcal{I}} = \emptyset \qquad\qquad (\neg C)^{\mathcal{I}} = \Delta^{\mathcal{I}} \setminus C^{\mathcal{I}}$$
$$(C \sqcap D)^{\mathcal{I}} = C^{\mathcal{I}} \cap D^{\mathcal{I}} \qquad\qquad (C \sqcup D)^{\mathcal{I}} = C^{\mathcal{I}} \cup D^{\mathcal{I}}$$
$$(\forall R.C)^{\mathcal{I}} = \left\{ x \in \Delta^{\mathcal{I}} \mid \forall y \big[(x, y) \in R^{\mathcal{I}} \text{ implies } y \in C^{\mathcal{I}} \big] \right\}$$
$$(\exists R.C)^{\mathcal{I}} = \left\{ x \in \Delta^{\mathcal{I}} \mid \exists y \big[(x, y) \in R^{\mathcal{I}} \text{ and } y \in C^{\mathcal{I}} \big] \right\}$$

Definition 2.3. An interpretation $\mathcal{I}$ *satisfies* a concept C if $C^{\mathcal{I}} \neq \emptyset$, and *validates* a concept C if $C^{\mathcal{I}} = \Delta^{\mathcal{I}}$. $\qquad \lhd$

Clearly, $\mathcal{I}$ *validates* a concept C iff it does not *satisfy* $\neg C$.

Let us now define RBox components of knowledge bases.

Definition 2.4. An $(\mathcal{SH})$ *RBox* $\mathcal{R}$ is a finite set of role axioms of the form $R \sqsubseteq S$ or $R \circ R \sqsubseteq R$. An interpretation $\mathcal{I}$ is a *model of an RBox* $\mathcal{R}$ if for every axiom $R \sqsubseteq S$ (respectively, $R \circ R \sqsubseteq R$) of $\mathcal{R}$, we have that $R^{\mathcal{I}} \subseteq S^{\mathcal{I}}$ (respectively, $R^{\mathcal{I}} \circ R^{\mathcal{I}} \subseteq R^{\mathcal{I}}$), where $\circ$ stands for the composition of relations. $\qquad \lhd$

By $ext(\mathcal{R})$ we denote the least extension of $\mathcal{R}$ such that:

- $R \sqsubseteq R \in ext(\mathcal{R})$, for all role names R
- if $R \sqsubseteq S \in ext(\mathcal{R})$ and $S \sqsubseteq T \in ext(\mathcal{R})$ then $R \sqsubseteq T \in ext(\mathcal{R})$.

By $R \sqsubseteq_{\mathcal{R}} S$ we mean $R \sqsubseteq S \in ext(R)$. If $R \sqsubseteq_{\mathcal{R}} S$ then R is a *sub-role* of S w.r.t. $\mathcal{R}$. If $R \circ R \sqsubseteq R \in \mathcal{R}$ then R is a *transitive role* w.r.t. $\mathcal{R}$. Note that if $\mathcal{I}$ is a model of $\mathcal{R}$ then it is also a model of $ext(\mathcal{R})$.

In the following definitions we introduce other components of knowledge bases, TBox consisting of terminological axioms and ABox consisting of assertions.

Definition 2.5. A *TBox* is a finite set of terminological axioms of the form $C \sqsubseteq D$ or $C = D$. An interpretation $\mathcal{I}$ is a *model of a TBox* $\mathcal{T}$ if for every axiom $C \sqsubseteq D$ (respectively, $C = D$) of $\mathcal{T}$, we have that $C^{\mathcal{I}} \subseteq D^{\mathcal{I}}$ (respectively, $C^{\mathcal{I}} = D^{\mathcal{I}}$). $\qquad \lhd$

Definition 2.6. An *ABox* is a finite set of *assertions* of the form $a : C$ (*concept assertion*) or $R(a, b)$ (*role assertion*). An interpretation $\mathcal{I}$ is a *model of an ABox* $\mathcal{A}$ if for every assertion $a : C$ (respectively, $R(a, b)$) of $\mathcal{A}$, we have that $a^{\mathcal{I}} \in C^{\mathcal{I}}$ (respectively, $(a^{\mathcal{I}}, b^{\mathcal{I}}) \in R^{\mathcal{I}}$). $\qquad \lhd$

Now we are in position to define knowledge bases.

Definition 2.7. A *knowledge base* in $\mathcal{SH}$ is a tuple $(\mathcal{R}, \mathcal{T}, \mathcal{A})$, where $\mathcal{R}$ is an RBox, $\mathcal{T}$ is a TBox, and $\mathcal{A}$ is an ABox. An interpretation $\mathcal{I}$ is a *model of a knowledge base* $(\mathcal{R}, \mathcal{T}, \mathcal{A})$ if $\mathcal{I}$ is a model of all $\mathcal{R}$, $\mathcal{T}$, and $\mathcal{A}$. A knowledge base $(\mathcal{R}, \mathcal{T}, \mathcal{A})$ is *satisfiable* if it has a model. In that case, we say that $\mathcal{A}$ is *satisfiable w.r.t.* $\mathcal{R}$ *and* $\mathcal{T}$.   ◁

Definition 2.8. An interpretation $\mathcal{I}$ *satisfies* a set X of concepts if there exists $x \in \Delta^{\mathcal{I}}$ such that $x \in C^{\mathcal{I}}$ for all $C \in X$. A set X of concepts is *satisfiable w.r.t. an RBox* $\mathcal{R}$ *and a TBox* $\mathcal{T}$ if there exists a model of $\mathcal{R}$ and $\mathcal{T}$ that satisfies X. ◁

Example 2.9. Consider the domain of web pages. Let

$$\mathcal{R} = \{link \sqsubseteq path, \ path \circ path \sqsubseteq path\}$$
$$\mathcal{T} = \{perfect \sqsubseteq interesting \sqcap \forall path.perfect\}$$
$$\mathcal{A} = \{a\!:\!perfect, link(a, b)\}$$

It can be shown that b is an instance of the concept $\forall link.interesting$ w.r.t. the knowledge base $(\mathcal{R}, \mathcal{T}, \mathcal{A})$, i.e., for every model $\mathcal{I}$ of $(\mathcal{R}, \mathcal{T}, \mathcal{A})$, we have that $b^{\mathcal{I}} \in (\forall link.interesting)^{\mathcal{I}}$. To prove this one can show that the knowledge base $(\mathcal{R}, \mathcal{T}, \mathcal{A}')$, where $\mathcal{A}' = \mathcal{A} \cup \{b\!:\!\exists link.\neg interesting\}$, is unsatisfiable.   ◁

3   Tableau Calculus for $\mathcal{SH}$

Let $(\mathcal{R}, \mathcal{T}, \mathcal{A})$ be a knowledge base in $\mathcal{SH}$. In this section we present a tableau calculus for the problem of checking satisfiability of $(\mathcal{R}, \mathcal{T}, \mathcal{A})$.

We assume that concepts and ABox assertions are represented in *negation normal form* (NNF), where $\neg$ occurs only directly before atomic concepts.[1] We denote the NNF of $\neg C$ by $\overline{C}$. For simplicity, we treat axioms of $\mathcal{T}$ as concepts representing global assumptions:

- an axiom $C \sqsubseteq D$ is treated as $\overline{C} \sqcup D$
- an axiom $C = D$ is treated as $(\overline{C} \sqcup D) \sqcap (\overline{D} \sqcup C)$.

That is, we assume that $\mathcal{T}$ consists of concepts in NNF. Thus, an interpretation $\mathcal{I}$ is a model of $\mathcal{T}$ iff $\mathcal{I}$ validates every concept $C \in \mathcal{T}$. As this way of handling TBoxes is not efficient in practice, in Section 6 we present an optimization technique called "absorption" for improving the performance of our algorithm.

Definition 3.1

- A knowledge base $(\mathcal{R}, \mathcal{T}, \mathcal{A})$ is in NNF if $\mathcal{T}$ and $\mathcal{A}$ are in NNF.

---

[1] Every formula can be transformed to an equivalent formula in NNF using the techniques of the classical first-order logic. The transformation is linear in the size of formulas.

- A *formula* is either a concept or an ABox assertion. If X and Y are sets of formulas and φ is a formula then we write X, Y to denote the set $X \cup Y$, and write X, φ to denote the set $X \cup \{\varphi\}$.   ◁

In the sequel, by a set of formulas we mean either a set of concepts or a set of ABox assertions.

Tableau rules are written downwards, with a set of formulas above the line as the *premise* and a number of sets of formulas below the line as the *(possible) conclusions*. A k-ary tableau rule has k possible conclusions and some rules have a side-condition which must be true for their application. A tableau rule is either an *"or"-rule* or an *"and"-rule*. Possible conclusions of an "or"-rule are separated by '|', while conclusions of an "and"-rule are separated by '&'. If a rule is a unary rule or an "and"-rule then its conclusions are "firm" and we ignore the word "possible". An "or"-rule has the meaning that, if the premise is satisfiable w.r.t. the RBox $\mathcal{R}$ and the TBox $\mathcal{T}$ then some of the possible conclusions are also satisfiable w.r.t. $\mathcal{R}$ and $\mathcal{T}$. On the other hand, an "and"-rule has the meaning that, if the premise is satisfiable w.r.t. $\mathcal{R}$ and $\mathcal{T}$ then all of the conclusions are also satisfiable w.r.t. $\mathcal{R}$ and $\mathcal{T}$.

Definition 3.2. The *tableau calculus* $\mathcal{CSH}$ w.r.t. an RBox $\mathcal{R}$ and a TBox $\mathcal{T}$ for the description logic $\mathcal{SH}$ is the set of the tableau rules given in Table 1, in which a letter like X denotes a set of concepts, and a letter like Y denotes a set of ABox assertions. The rules $(\exists)$ and $(\exists')$ are the only "and"-rules and the only *transitional rules*.[2] The other rules of $\mathcal{CSH}$ are "or"-rules, and are also called *static rules*. For each rule of $\mathcal{CSH}$, the distinguished formulas of the premise are called the *principal formulas* of the rule.   ◁

Example 3.3. Let $\mathcal{R} = \{R \sqsubseteq S,\ S \circ S \sqsubseteq S\}$ and $\mathcal{T} = \{C_6\}$. Instantiating the rule $(\exists)$ to have the set $\{\exists R.C_1,\ \exists R.C_2,\ \exists S.C_3,\ \forall R.C_4,\ \forall R.C_5,\ \forall S.C_5\}$ as the premise we get three conclusions: $\{C_1,\ C_4,\ C_5,\ \forall S.C_5,\ C_6\}$, $\{C_2,\ C_4,\ C_5,\ \forall S.C_5,\ C_6\}$, and $\{C_3,\ C_5,\ \forall S.C_5,\ C_6\}$.   ◁

Note that the conclusions of the transitional rule $(\exists')$ consist of only concepts (but not ABox assertions), and for each of the static rules $(\bot_0)$, (H), $(\sqcap')$, $(\sqcup')$, (H'), $(\forall')$, $(\forall'_s)$, the premise is a subset of each of the possible conclusions. We assume that these static rules are applicable only when the premise is a proper subset of each of the possible conclusions. This property of rules is called *strict monotonicity*. As is standard, we also assume that, for each rule of $\mathcal{CSH}$, the principal formulas are not members of the sets X, Y which appear in the premise of the rule.

We assume the following preferences for the rules of $\mathcal{CSH}$: the rules $(\bot_0)$, $(\bot)$, $(\bot'_0)$, and $(\bot')$ have the highest priority; unary static rules have a higher priority than non-unary static rules; all the static rules have a higher priority than the transitional rules.

---

[2] Only the rules $(\exists)$ and $(\exists')$ "realize" formulas of the form $\exists R.C$ or $a{:}\exists R.C$.

Table 1. Rules of the tableau calculus $\mathcal{CSH}$

$$(\perp_0) \ \frac{X, \perp}{\perp} \qquad (\perp) \ \frac{X, A, \neg A}{\perp} \qquad (\sqcap) \ \frac{X, C \sqcap D}{X, C, D} \qquad (\sqcup) \ \frac{X, C \sqcup D}{X, C \mid X, D}$$

$$(H) \ \frac{X, \forall S.C}{X, \forall S.C, \forall R.C} \ \text{if } R \sqsubseteq_{\mathcal{R}} S \qquad (\exists) \ \frac{X, \exists R_1.C_1, \ldots, \exists R_k.C_k}{X_1, C_1, \mathcal{T} \ \& \ \ldots \ \& \ X_k, C_k, \mathcal{T}} \ \text{if } (*)$$

$$\text{where } (*) : \begin{cases} X \text{ contains no concepts of the form } \exists R.C, \text{ and} \\ X_i = \{D \mid \forall R_i.D \in X\} \cup \\ \qquad \{\forall S.D \in X \mid R_i \sqsubseteq_{\mathcal{R}} S \text{ and } S \circ S \sqsubseteq S \in \mathcal{R}\} \end{cases}$$

$$(\perp_0') \ \frac{Y, a:\perp}{\perp} \qquad\qquad\qquad (\perp') \ \frac{Y, a:A, a:\neg A}{\perp}$$

$$(\sqcap') \ \frac{Y, a:(C \sqcap D)}{Y, a:(C \sqcap D), a:C, a:D} \qquad (\sqcup') \ \frac{Y, a:(C \sqcup D)}{Y, a:(C \sqcup D), a:C \mid Y, a:(C \sqcup D), a:D}$$

$$(H') \ \frac{X, a:\forall S.C}{X, a:\forall S.C, a:\forall R.C} \ \text{if } R \sqsubseteq_{\mathcal{R}} S \qquad (\forall') \ \frac{Y, a:\forall R.C, R(a,b)}{Y, a:\forall R.C, R(a,b), b:C}$$

$$(\forall_s') \ \frac{Y, a:\forall S.C, R(a,b)}{Y, a:\forall S.C, R(a,b), b:\forall S.C} \ \text{if } R \sqsubseteq_{\mathcal{R}} S \text{ and } S \circ S \sqsubseteq S \in \mathcal{R}$$

$$(\exists') \ \frac{Y, a_1:\exists R_1.C_1, \ldots, a_k:\exists R_k.C_k}{X_1, C_1, \mathcal{T} \ \& \ \ldots \ \& \ X_k, C_k, \mathcal{T}} \ \text{if } (\star)$$

$$\text{where } (\star) : \begin{cases} Y \text{ contains no assertions of the form } a:\exists R.C, \text{ and} \\ X_i = \{D \mid a_i:\forall R_i.D \in Y\} \cup \\ \qquad \{\forall S.D \mid a_i:\forall S.D \in Y \text{ and} \\ \qquad\qquad R_i \sqsubseteq_{\mathcal{R}} S \text{ and } S \circ S \sqsubseteq S \in \mathcal{R}\} \end{cases}$$

Definition 3.4. An *"and-or" graph for* $(\mathcal{R}, \mathcal{T}, \mathcal{A})$, also called a *tableau for* $(\mathcal{R}, \mathcal{T}, \mathcal{A})$, is a rooted "and-or" graph constructed according to the following principles:

– The graph contains nodes of two kinds: *complex nodes* and *simple nodes*. The label of a complex node consists of ABox assertions, while the label of a simple node consists of concepts. Complex nodes are expanded using the primed rules of $\mathcal{CSH}$ (i.e. $(\perp_0')$, $(\perp')$, $(\sqcap')$, $(\sqcup')$, (H'), $(\forall')$, $(\forall_s')$, $(\exists')$), while simple nodes are expanded using the other rules of $\mathcal{CSH}$.[3] The graph never contains edges from a simple node to a complex node.
– The root of the graph is a complex node with label

---

[3] Only the primed rules may be applicable to a complex node, and only the remaining rules may be applicable to a simple node.

- $\mathcal{A} \cup \{a\!:\!C \mid C \in \mathcal{T} \text{ and } a \text{ is an individual occurring in } \mathcal{A}\}$ if $\mathcal{A} \neq \emptyset$
- $\{(\tau\!:\!C) \mid C \in \mathcal{T}\}$, where τ is a special individual, if $\mathcal{A} = \emptyset$.

- For every node v of the graph, if a k-ary rule δ is applicable to (the label of) v in the sense that an instance of δ has the label of v as the premise and $Z_1, \ldots, Z_k$ as the possible conclusions, then choose such a rule accordingly to the preferences[4] and apply it to v to create k successors $w_1, \ldots, w_k$ of v respectively with labels $Z_1, \ldots, Z_k$, maintaining the following constraints:
  - if the graph already contains a node w_i' with label Z_i then instead of creating a new node w_i with label Z_i as a successor of v we just connect v to w_i' and assume $w_i = w_i'$
  - if the applied rule is $(\exists)$ or $(\exists')$ then we *label* the edge (v, w_i) by the principal formula (of the form $\exists R.C$ or $a\!:\!\exists R.C$) that corresponds to the successor w_i
  - if the rule applied to v is an "or"-rule then v is an *"or"-node*, else v is an *"and"-node* (the information about which rule is applied to v is recorded for later uses)
  - if no rule is applicable to v then v is an *end node* as well as an "and"-node.
  $\lhd$

Note that each node of the graph is "expanded" only once (using one rule), and that the graph is constructed using *global caching* [19,6,7,16,15,17,18] and its nodes have unique labels.

A set Z of formulas is *closed* w.r.t. a static rule if applying that rule to Z (used as the premise) gives back Z as one of the possible conclusions.

Remark 3.5. By the preferences of the rules of $\mathcal{CSH}$, if a node of an "and-or" graph is an "and"-node then its label is closed w.r.t. the static rules of $\mathcal{CSH}$. $\lhd$

Definition 3.6. A *marking* of an "and-or" graph G is a subgraph G' of G such that:

- the root of G is the root of G'
- if v is a node of G' and is an "or"-node of G then there exists at least one edge (v, w) of G that is an edge of G'
- if v is a node of G' and is an "and"-node of G then every edge (v, w) of G is an edge of G'
- if (v, w) is an edge of G' then v and w are nodes of G'.

A marking G' of an "and-or" graph G for $(\mathcal{R}, \mathcal{T}, \mathcal{A})$ is *consistent* if it does not contain any node with label $\{\bot\}$. $\lhd$

Theorem 3.7 (Soundness and Completeness of $\mathcal{CSH}$). *Let $(\mathcal{R}, \mathcal{T}, \mathcal{A})$ be a knowledge base in negation normal form in the logic $\mathcal{SH}$, and let G be an "and-or" graph for $(\mathcal{R}, \mathcal{T}, \mathcal{A})$. Then $(\mathcal{R}, \mathcal{T}, \mathcal{A})$ is satisfiable iff G has a consistent marking.* $\lhd$

---

[4] If there are several applicable rules of the same priority, choose any one of them.

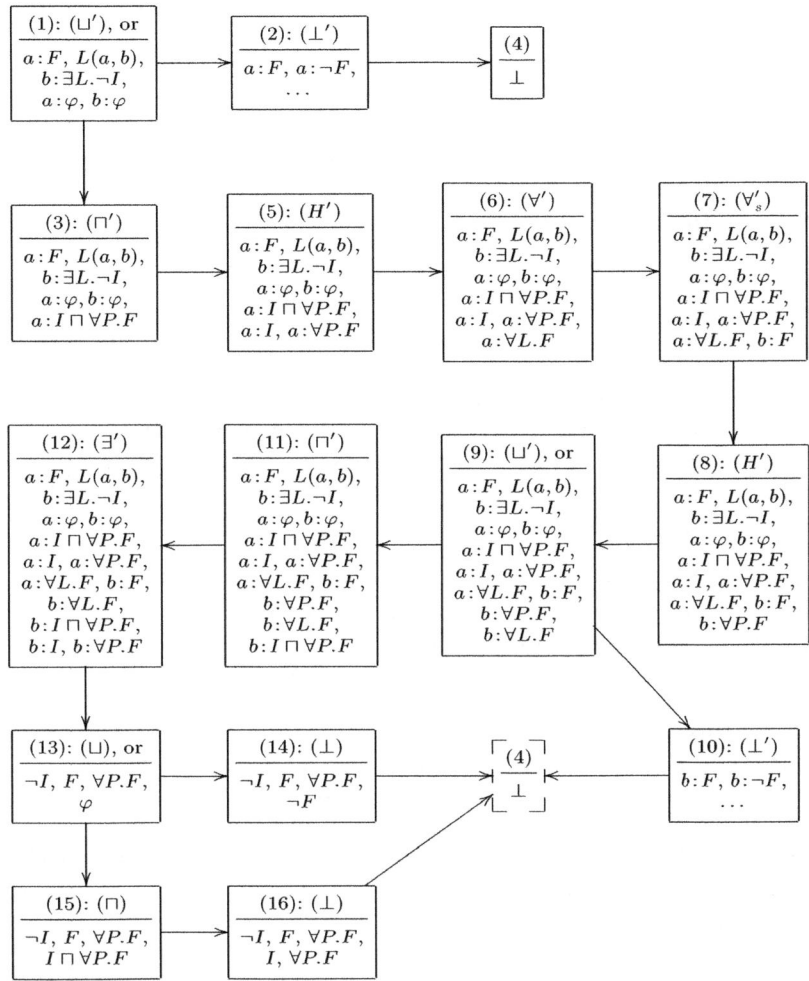

Fig. 1. An "and-or" graph for the knowledge base $(\mathcal{R}, \mathcal{T}, \mathcal{A}')$, where $\mathcal{R} = \{L \sqsubseteq P,\ P \circ P \sqsubseteq P\}$, $\mathcal{T} = \{\varphi\}$, $\mathcal{A}' = \{a\!:\!F,\ L(a,b),\ b\!:\!\exists L.\neg I\}$, and $\varphi = \neg F \sqcup (I \sqcap \forall P.F)$. The edge $((12),(13))$ is labeled by $b\!:\!\exists L.\neg I$.

The "only if" direction means soundness of $\mathcal{CSH}$, while the "if" direction means completeness of $\mathcal{CSH}$. See Section 4 for the proofs of this theorem.

Example 3.8. Reconsider Example 2.9. As abbreviations, let $L = link$, $P = path$, $I = interesting$, $F = perfect$, and $\varphi = \neg F \sqcup (I \sqcap \forall P.F)$. We have

$$\mathcal{R} = \{L \sqsubseteq P,\ P \circ P \sqsubseteq P\}$$
$$\mathcal{A}' = \{a\!:\!F,\ L(a,b),\ b\!:\!\exists L.\neg I\}$$
$$\mathcal{T} = \{\varphi\}\ \text{(in NNF)}.$$

In Figure 1, we present an "and-or" graph for $(\mathcal{R}, \mathcal{T}, \mathcal{A}')$. As the graph does not have any consistent marking, by Theorem 3.7, the knowledge base $(\mathcal{R}, \mathcal{T}, \mathcal{A}')$ is unsatisfiable.   ◁

4   Proofs of Soundness and Completeness of $\mathcal{CSH}$

4.1   Soundness

Lemma 4.1. *Let $(\mathcal{R}, \mathcal{T}, \mathcal{A})$ be a knowledge base in negation normal form in the logic $\mathcal{SH}$, and let G be an "and-or" graph for $(\mathcal{R}, \mathcal{T}, \mathcal{A})$. Suppose that $(\mathcal{R}, \mathcal{T}, \mathcal{A})$ is satisfiable. Then G has a consistent marking.*

Proof. We construct a consistent marking G' of G as follows. At the beginning, G' contains only the root of G. Then, for every node v of G' and for every successor w of v in G, if the label of w is satisfiable w.r.t. $\mathcal{R}$ and $\mathcal{T}$, then add w and the edge (v, w) to G'. To prove that G' is a consistent marking of G it suffices to show that, for every rule δ of $\mathcal{CSH}$,

- if δ is an "or"-rule and the premise is satisfiable w.r.t. $\mathcal{R}$ and $\mathcal{T}$ then one of the possible conclusions is also satisfiable w.r.t. $\mathcal{R}$ and $\mathcal{T}$
- if δ is an "and"-rule and the premise is satisfiable w.r.t. $\mathcal{R}$ and $\mathcal{T}$ then all the conclusions are also satisfiable w.r.t. $\mathcal{R}$ and $\mathcal{T}$.

We prove this only for the rule $(\exists')$ and leave the other rules to the reader. Suppose that $Y \cup \{a_1 : \exists R_1.C_1, \ldots, a_k : \exists R_k.C_k\}$ is satisfiable w.r.t. $\mathcal{R}$ and $\mathcal{T}$, and let $\mathcal{I}$ be a model of that set, $\mathcal{R}$, and $\mathcal{T}$. We show that $\mathcal{I}$ satisfies $X_i \cup \{C_i\}$ for all $1 \leq i \leq k$, where X_i are the sets specified by the rule.

Let $1 \leq i \leq k$. Since $a_i^{\mathcal{I}} \in (\exists R_i.C_i)^{\mathcal{I}}$, there exists $x_i \in \Delta^{\mathcal{I}}$ such that $R_i^{\mathcal{I}}(a_i^{\mathcal{I}}, x_i)$ holds and $x_i \in C_i^{\mathcal{I}}$. Clearly, if $a_i : \forall R_i.D \in Y$ then $a_i^{\mathcal{I}} \in (\forall R_i.D)^{\mathcal{I}}$ and $x_i \in D_i^{\mathcal{I}}$. Suppose that $a_i : \forall S.D \in Y$, $R_i \sqsubseteq_{\mathcal{R}} S$, and $S \circ S \sqsubseteq S \in \mathcal{R}$. We show that $x_i \in (\forall S.D)^{\mathcal{I}}$. Let y be an arbitrary element of $\Delta^{\mathcal{I}}$ such that $S^{\mathcal{I}}(x_i, y)$. We need to show that $y \in D^{\mathcal{I}}$. Since $R_i^{\mathcal{I}}(a_i^{\mathcal{I}}, x_i)$ and $R_i \sqsubseteq_{\mathcal{R}} S$, we have that $S^{\mathcal{I}}(a_i^{\mathcal{I}}, x_i)$. Since $S^{\mathcal{I}}(x_i, y)$ and $S \circ S \sqsubseteq S \in \mathcal{R}$, it follows that $S^{\mathcal{I}}(a_i^{\mathcal{I}}, y)$. Since $a_i : \forall S.D \in Y$, we have that $a_i^{\mathcal{I}} \in (\forall S.D)^{\mathcal{I}}$, and hence $y \in D^{\mathcal{I}}$. We have shown that $x_i \in C^{\mathcal{I}}$ for every $C \in X_i \cup \{C_i\}$. Hence $\mathcal{I}$ satisfies $X_i \cup \{C_i\}$.   ◁

4.2   Model Graphs

We prove completeness of $\mathcal{CSH}$ via model graphs. The technique has been used in [20,5,13,16,15,17,18] for other logics.

We are interested only in the individuals that occur in the considered ABox $\mathcal{A}$. For simplicity, without loss of generality we assume that the set of individual names of our language consists only of the individuals occurring in $\mathcal{A}$ in the case $\mathcal{A} \neq \emptyset$, or the special individual τ in the case $\mathcal{A} = \emptyset$.

Definition 4.2. A *model graph* is a tuple $\langle \Delta, \mathcal{C}, \mathcal{E} \rangle$, where:

- Δ is a finite set containing, amongst others, all individual names
- $\mathcal{C}$ is a function that maps each element of Δ to a set of concepts
- $\mathcal{E}$ is a function that maps each role name to a binary relation on Δ.   ◁

We use model graphs merely as data structures, but we are interested in "consistent" and "saturated" model graphs defined below. Model graphs differ from "and-or" graphs in that a model graph contains only "and"-nodes and its edges are labeled by role names. Roughly speaking, given an "and-or" graph G with a consistent marking G', to construct a model graph one can stick together the nodes in a "saturation path" of a node of G' to create a node for the model graph. Details will be given later.

Definition 4.3. A model graph $\langle \Delta, \mathcal{C}, \mathcal{E} \rangle$ is *saturated* if every $x \in \Delta$ satisfies:

(1) if $C \sqcap D \in \mathcal{C}(x)$ then $\{C, D\} \subseteq \mathcal{C}(x)$
(2) if $C \sqcup D \in \mathcal{C}(x)$ then $C \in \mathcal{C}(x)$ or $D \in \mathcal{C}(x)$
(3) if $\forall R.C \in \mathcal{C}(x)$ and $(x, y) \in \mathcal{E}(R)$ then $C \in \mathcal{C}(y)$
(4) if $\exists R.C \in \mathcal{C}(x)$ then there exists $y \in \Delta$ s.t. $(x, y) \in \mathcal{E}(R)$ and $C \in \mathcal{C}(y)$.   ◁

Definition 4.4. A saturated model graph $\langle \Delta, \mathcal{C}, \mathcal{E} \rangle$ is *consistent* if no $x \in \Delta$ has $\mathcal{C}(x)$ containing $\bot$ or containing a pair $A, \neg A$ for some atomic concept A.   ◁

Definition 4.5. Given a model graph $M = \langle \Delta, \mathcal{C}, \mathcal{E} \rangle$, the *interpretation corresponding to* M is $\mathcal{I} = \langle \Delta, \cdot^{\mathcal{I}} \rangle$ where $A^{\mathcal{I}} = \{x \in \Delta \mid A \in \mathcal{C}(x)\}$ for every concept name A, $R^{\mathcal{I}} = \mathcal{E}(R)$ for every role name R, and $a^{\mathcal{I}} = a$ for every individual name a.   ◁

Lemma 4.6. *If $\mathcal{I}$ is the interpretation corresponding to a consistent saturated model graph $\langle \Delta, \mathcal{C}, \mathcal{E} \rangle$, then for every $x \in \Delta$ and $C \in \mathcal{C}(x)$ we have that $x \in C^{\mathcal{I}}$.*

Proof. By induction on the structure of C.   ◁

4.3 Completeness

Definition 4.7. Let G be an "and-or" graph for $(\mathcal{R}, \mathcal{T}, \mathcal{A})$ with a consistent marking G' and let v be a node of G'. A *saturation path* of v w.r.t. G' is a finite sequence $v_0 = v, v_1, \ldots, v_k$ of nodes of G', with $k \geq 0$, such that, for every $0 \leq i < k$, v_i is an "or"-node and (v_i, v_{i+1}) is an edge of G', and v_k is an "and"-node.   ◁

Observe that, due to strict monotonicity of the static rules $(\bot_0)$, (H), $(\sqcap')$, $(\sqcup')$, (H'), $(\forall')$, $(\forall'_s)$ there always exists a saturation path of v w.r.t. G'.

Lemma 4.8. *Let G' be a consistent marking of an "and-or" graph, v_0 be a node of G', and $v_0, v_1, \ldots, v_k$ be a saturation path of v_0 w.r.t. G'. Then:*

1. *if v_0 is a complex node then*
   (a) the label of each v_i is a subset of the label of v_k

    (b) the label of v_k contains neither $a:\perp$ nor a pair $a:A$ and $a:\neg A$, for any a and A
2. *if v_0 is a simple node then*
    (a) all concepts of the form A, $\neg A$, $\forall R.C$, or $\exists R.C$ of the label of each v_i belong to the label of v_k
    (b) the union of the labels of $v_0, \ldots, v_k$ contains neither $\perp$ nor a pair of the form A, $\neg A$.

Proof. Recall that $v_0, v_1, \ldots, v_{k-1}$ are "or"-nodes. Thus, the assertion 1a clearly holds. For the assertion 2a, just note that if a concept of the form A, $\neg A$, $\forall R.C$, or $\exists R.C$ belongs to the premise of an "or"-rule then it also belongs to each of the possible conclusions of the rule. The assertion 1b holds because v_k is a node of the consistent marking G' and the rules $(\perp'_0)$ and $(\perp')$ have the highest priority. Consider the assertion 2b. The union of the labels of $v_0, \ldots, v_k$ does not contain $\perp$ because $v_0, \ldots, v_k$ are nodes of the consistent marking G' and the rule $(\perp_0)$ has the highest priority. If the union of the labels of $v_0, \ldots, v_k$ contained a pair of the form A, $\neg A$ then, by the assertion 2a, both A and $\neg A$ would belong to the label of v_k, which is impossible because v_k is a node of the consistent marking G' and the rule $(\perp)$ has the highest priority. $\lhd$

We now have the following lemma concerning the completeness of $\mathcal{CSH}$.

Lemma 4.9. *Let $(\mathcal{R}, \mathcal{T}, \mathcal{A})$ be a knowledge base in negation normal form in the logic $\mathcal{SH}$, and let G be an "and-or" graph for $(\mathcal{R}, \mathcal{T}, \mathcal{A})$. Suppose that G has a consistent marking G'. Then $(\mathcal{R}, \mathcal{T}, \mathcal{A})$ is satisfiable.*

Proof. We construct a model graph $M = \langle \Delta, \mathcal{C}, \mathcal{E} \rangle$ from G' as given below. During construction, each node of Δ is marked either as *unresolved* or as *resolved*, and f is constructed to map each node of $\Delta \setminus \Delta_0$ to an "and"-node of G'. Nodes of M are denoted by x or y, nodes of G are denoted by u, v or w, the label of x (in M) is denoted by $\mathcal{C}(x)$, and the label of u (in G) is denoted by $\mathcal{L}(u)$.

1. Let v_0 be the root of G' and let $v_0, \ldots, v_k$ be a saturation path of v_0 w.r.t. G'. If $\mathcal{A} \neq \emptyset$ then let Δ_0 be the set of all individuals occurring in $\mathcal{A}$, else let $\Delta_0 = \{\tau\}$. Set $\Delta := \Delta_0$. For each $a \in \Delta_0$, set $\mathcal{C}(a) := \{C \mid a:C \in \mathcal{L}(v_k)\}$ and mark a as unresolved. For each role name R, set $\mathcal{E}_0(R) := \{(a, b) \mid R(a, b) \in \mathcal{A}\}$.
2. While Δ contains unresolved nodes, take one unresolved node x and do:
    (a) For every concept $\exists R.C \in \mathcal{C}(x)$ do:
        i. If $x \in \Delta_0$ then let w_0 be the node of G' such that the edge (v_k, w_0) is labeled by $x:\exists R.C$.
        ii. Else let w_0 be the node of G' such that the edge $(f(x), w_0)$ is labeled by $\exists R.C$.
        iii. Let $w_0, \ldots, w_h$ be a saturation path of w_0 w.r.t. G' and set $X := \bigcup_{i=0}^{h} \mathcal{L}(w_i)$.
        iv. If no $y \in \Delta$ has $\mathcal{C}(y) = X$ then add a new node y to Δ, set $\mathcal{C}(y) := X$, mark y as unresolved, and set $f(y) := w_h$.

        v. Add the pair (x, y) to $\mathcal{E}_0(R)$.
  (b) Mark x as resolved.
3. For each role name T, let $\mathcal{E}(T)$ be the least extension of $\mathcal{E}_0(T)$ such that:
    – if $R \sqsubseteq_{\mathcal{R}} S$ then $\mathcal{E}(R) \subseteq \mathcal{E}(S)$
    – if $S \circ S \sqsubseteq S \in \mathcal{R}$ then $\mathcal{E}(S) \circ \mathcal{E}(S) \subseteq \mathcal{E}(S)$.

Remark 4.10. Note that:

1. At Steps 2(a)i, C belongs to $\mathcal{L}(w_0)$.
2. At Step 2(a)ii, $\exists R.C \in \mathcal{C}(x)$ belongs to $\mathcal{L}(f(x))$ (see the next item of this remark) and C belongs to $\mathcal{L}(w_0)$.
3. At Step 2(a)iv, $\mathcal{C}(y)$ is the union of the labels of nodes of a saturation path $w_0, \ldots, w_h$ that ends at $f(y) = w_h$. Intuitively, y is the result of sticking together the nodes $w_0, \ldots, w_h$ of a saturation path of w_0 w.r.t. G'. By Lemma 4.8(2a), concepts of the form $\exists R.C$ or $\forall R.C$ of $\mathcal{C}(y)$ belong to $\mathcal{L}(f(y))$.   ◁

The above construction terminates and results in a finite model graph because: for every $x, x' \in \Delta \setminus \Delta_0$, $x \neq x'$ implies $\mathcal{C}(x) \neq \mathcal{C}(x')$, and for every $x \in \Delta$, $\mathcal{C}(x)$ is a subset of the set of concepts occurring in $(\mathcal{R}, \mathcal{T}, \mathcal{A})$.

By Lemma 4.8(1b and 2b), M is a consistent model graph.

We show that M satisfies all Conditions (1)-(4) of being a *saturated* model graph. M satisfies Conditions (1) and (2) because at Step 1 (of the construction of M), the sequence $v_0, \ldots, v_k$ is a saturation path of v_0, and at Step 2a, the sequence $w_0, \ldots, w_h$ is a saturation path of w_0. M satisfies Condition (4) because: at Step 2a, C belongs to $\mathcal{L}(w_0)$ and hence also to $\mathcal{C}(y) \supseteq \mathcal{L}(w_0)$. To show that M satisfies Condition (3) we prove the following stronger assertion:

> For all $x, y \in \Delta$ and all roles R and S, if $\forall S.D \in \mathcal{C}(x)$ and $\mathcal{E}(R)(x, y)$ and $R \sqsubseteq_{\mathcal{R}} S$ then (i) $D \in \mathcal{C}(y)$, and (ii) $\forall S.D \in \mathcal{C}(y)$ if $S \circ S \sqsubseteq S \in \mathcal{R}$.

We prove this assertion by induction on the number of steps needed to derive $\mathcal{E}(R)(x, y)$ during Step 3. Suppose that $\forall S.D \in \mathcal{C}(x)$, $R \sqsubseteq_{\mathcal{R}} S$, and $\mathcal{E}(R)(x, y)$ holds. There are the following cases to consider:

– Case $\mathcal{E}_0(R)(x, y)$ holds.
  • Case $x \in \Delta_0$. Since $\forall S.D \in \mathcal{C}(x)$, we have that $x : \forall S.D \in \mathcal{L}(v_k)$.
    ∗ Case $y \in \Delta_0$. Since $(x, y) \in \mathcal{E}_0(R)$, we have that $R(x, y) \in \mathcal{A}$. Since v_k is an "and"-node, $\mathcal{L}(v_k)$ is closed w.r.t. the static rules of $\mathcal{CSH}$. Since $R \sqsubseteq_{\mathcal{R}} S$, by the rule (H'), $x : \forall R.D \in \mathcal{L}(v_k)$. By the rule $(\forall')$, it follows that $y : D \in \mathcal{L}(v_k)$, and hence $D \in \mathcal{C}(y)$. If $S \circ S \sqsubseteq S \in \mathcal{R}$ then, by the rule $(\forall'_s)$, we also have that $y : \forall S.D \in \mathcal{L}(v_k)$ and hence $\forall S.D \in \mathcal{C}(y)$.
    ∗ Case $y \notin \Delta_0$ and y is created at Step 2(a)iv. Since $x : \forall S.D \in \mathcal{L}(v_k)$, by the rule $(\exists')$, D belongs to $\mathcal{L}(w_0)$ and hence also to $\mathcal{C}(y) \supseteq \mathcal{L}(w_0)$, and additionally, if $S \circ S \sqsubseteq S \in \mathcal{R}$ then $\forall S.D$ belongs to $\mathcal{L}(w_0)$ and hence also to $\mathcal{C}(y) \supseteq \mathcal{L}(w_0)$.

- Case $x \notin \Delta_0$. Consider Step 2a at which the pair (x, y) is added to $\mathcal{E}_0(R)$. Since $\forall S.D \in \mathcal{C}(x)$, by Remark 4.10(3), we have that $\forall S.D \in \mathcal{L}(f(x))$. By the rule $(\exists)$, it follows that D belongs to $\mathcal{L}(w_0)$ and hence also to $\mathcal{C}(y) \supseteq \mathcal{L}(w_0)$, and additionally, if $S \circ S \sqsubseteq S \in \mathcal{R}$ then $\forall S.D$ belongs to $\mathcal{L}(w_0)$ and hence also to $\mathcal{C}(y) \supseteq \mathcal{L}(w_0)$.

- Case $\mathcal{E}(R)(x, y)$ is derived from $\mathcal{E}(R')(x, y)$ and $R' \sqsubseteq_{\mathcal{R}} R$. Since $R \sqsubseteq_{\mathcal{R}} S$, we have that $R' \sqsubseteq_{\mathcal{R}} S$. The derivation of $\mathcal{E}(R')(x, y)$ is shorter by one step, so it falls under the induction hypothesis (by putting R' for R in the statement of the assertion). The desired conclusions follow immediately.

- Case $\mathcal{E}(R)(x, y)$ is derived from $\mathcal{E}(R)(x, z)$, $\mathcal{E}(R)(z, y)$, and $R \circ R \sqsubseteq R \in \mathcal{R}$.

  - Case $x \in \Delta_0$. Since $\forall S.D \in \mathcal{C}(x)$, we have that $x : \forall S.D \in \mathcal{L}(v_k)$. Since $R \sqsubseteq_{\mathcal{R}} S$ and $\mathcal{L}(v_k)$ is closed w.r.t. the rule (H'), we have that $x : \forall R.D \in \mathcal{L}(v_k)$, and hence $\forall R.D \in \mathcal{C}(x)$.

  - Case $x \notin \Delta_0$. Since $\forall S.D \in \mathcal{C}(x)$, by Remark 4.10(3), we have that $\forall S.D \in \mathcal{L}(f(x))$. Since $R \sqsubseteq_{\mathcal{R}} S$ and $\mathcal{L}(f(x))$ is closed w.r.t. the rule (H), we have that $\forall R.D \in \mathcal{L}(f(x))$. Hence $\forall R.D \in \mathcal{C}(x)$, because $\mathcal{C}(x)$ is the union of the labels of nodes of a saturation path that ends at $f(x)$.

  Applying the inductive hypothesis to $\mathcal{E}(R)(x, z)$ (and putting R for S in the statement of the assertion), we obtain that $\forall R.D \in \mathcal{C}(z)$ since $R \circ R \sqsubseteq R \in \mathcal{R}$. Applying the inductive hypothesis to $\mathcal{E}(R)(z, y)$ (and putting R for S in the statement of the assertion), we obtain that $D \in \mathcal{C}(y)$. If $S \circ S \sqsubseteq S \in \mathcal{R}$ then, by the inductive assumption, $\forall S.D \in \mathcal{C}(z)$, and $\forall S.D \in \mathcal{C}(y)$.

Therefore M is a consistent saturated model graph.

Observe that $\mathcal{T} \subseteq \mathcal{C}(x)$ for all $x \in \Delta$:

- if $x = a \ \in \Delta_0$ then, for all $C \in \mathcal{T}$, $a : C \in \mathcal{L}(v_0) \subseteq \mathcal{L}(v_k)$, and hence $C \in \mathcal{C}(a)$

- if $x \in \Delta \setminus \Delta_0$ then $\mathcal{C}(x)$ is the union of the labels of nodes of a saturation path of some node u w.r.t. G', with $\mathcal{L}(u) \supseteq \mathcal{T}$ due to the rule $(\exists)$, and hence $\mathcal{T} \subseteq \mathcal{C}(x)$.

Also observe that:

- if $a : C \in \mathcal{A}$ then $a : C \in \mathcal{L}(v_0) \subseteq \mathcal{L}(v_k)$ and hence $C \in \mathcal{C}(a)$
- if $R(a, b) \in \mathcal{A}$ then $(a, b) \in \mathcal{E}_0(R) \subseteq \mathcal{E}(R)$.

Let $\mathcal{I}$ be the interpretation corresponding to M. By Lemma 4.6 and the above observations, we have that $\mathcal{I}$ is a model of $\mathcal{T}$ and $\mathcal{A}$. By the construction of $\mathcal{E}$, $\mathcal{I}$ is also a model of $\mathcal{R}$. Hence $\mathcal{I}$ is a model of $(\mathcal{R}, \mathcal{T}, \mathcal{A})$. $\triangleleft$

5   A Simple ExpTime Decision Procedure for $\mathcal{SH}$

Let $(\mathcal{R}, \mathcal{T}, \mathcal{A})$ be a knowledge base in NNF. We claim that Algorithm 1 given below is a complexity-optimal algorithm for checking satisfiability of $(\mathcal{R}, \mathcal{T}, \mathcal{A})$. In the algorithm, a node u is a parent of v and v is a child of u iff the edge (u, v)

Algorithm 1: For checking satisfiability of a knowledge base in $\mathcal{SH}$

Input: a knowledge base $(\mathcal{R}, \mathcal{T}, \mathcal{A})$ in negation normal form in $\mathcal{SH}$.
Output: *true* if $(\mathcal{R}, \mathcal{T}, \mathcal{A})$ is satisfiable, and *false* otherwise.

construct an "and-or" graph G with root v_0 for $(\mathcal{R}, \mathcal{T}, \mathcal{A})$
$UnsatNodes := \emptyset$, $V := \emptyset$
if *G contains a node $v_\perp$ with label $\{\perp\}$* **then**
    $V := \{v_\perp\}$, $UnsatNodes := \{v_\perp\}$
    while *V is not empty* **do**
        remove a node v from V
        for *every parent u of v* **do**
            if *$u \notin UnsatNodes$*
            and u is an and-node
            or u is an or-node and every child of u is in $UnsatNodes$ **then**
                add u to both $UnsatNodes$ and V

return if $v_0 \in UnsatNodes$ **then** *false* **else** *true*.

---

is in G. Optimizations for the algorithm will be discussed in the next section. To prove our claim we need some definitions and two lemmas.

For a formula φ, by $sc(\varphi)$ we denote the set of all subconcepts of φ, including φ if it is a concept. For a set X of formulas, define

$$closure\text{-}c(X) = \{C \mid C \in sc(\varphi) \text{ for some } \varphi \in X\} \cup$$
$$\{\forall R.C \mid \forall S.C \in sc(\varphi) \text{ for some } \varphi \in X \text{ and some role name } S\}$$
$$closure\text{-}f(X) = \{C, a{:}C \mid C \in closure\text{-}c(X) \text{ and } a \text{ occurs in } X\}.$$

Define the *length* of a formula to be the number of its symbols, and the *size* of a finite set of formulas to be the length of the conjunction of its formulas.

Lemma 5.1. *Let $(\mathcal{R}, \mathcal{T}, \mathcal{A})$ be a knowledge base in negation normal form in $\mathcal{SH}$, n be the size of $\mathcal{T} \cup \mathcal{A}$, and G be an "and-or" graph for $(\mathcal{R}, \mathcal{T}, \mathcal{A})$. Then G has at most $2^{O(n^2)}$ nodes and the label of each node v of G is a subset of $closure\text{-}f(\mathcal{T} \cup \mathcal{A})$, which consists of at most $O(n)$ concepts if v is a simple node, and consists of at most $O(n^2)$ assertions if v is a complex node.*

Proof. The label of each simple node of G is a subset of $closure\text{-}c(\mathcal{T} \cup \mathcal{A})$ and therefore consists of at most $O(n)$ concepts. Since the labels of simple nodes are unique, G has $2^{O(n)}$ simple nodes. The label of each complex node of G is a subset of $closure\text{-}f(\mathcal{T} \cup \mathcal{A})$ and therefore consists of at most $O(n^2)$ assertions. It can be seen that each path of complex nodes in G has length of rank $O(n^2)$ (the rank of the cardinality of $closure\text{-}f(\mathcal{T} \cup \mathcal{A})$). Hence G contains $2^{O(n^2)}$ complex nodes. ◁

Lemma 5.2. *Algorithm 1 terminates and computes the set $UnsatNodes$ in $2^{O(n^2)}$ steps, where n is the size of $\mathcal{T} \cup \mathcal{A}$.*

Proof. Lemma 5.1 guarantees that the "and-or" graph G can be built in $2^{O(n^2)}$ steps since it contains $2^{O(n^2)}$ nodes. Every node put into V is also put into *UnsatNodes*, but once a node is in *UnsatNodes*, it never leaves *UnsatNodes* and cannot be put back into V. Each iteration of the "while" removes one member of V. Since the number of nodes in G is $2^{O(n^2)}$, this means that after at most $2^{O(n^2)}$ iterations, V must become empty. Each iteration is done in $2^{O(n^2)}$ steps. Hence the algorithm terminates after $2^{O(n^2)}$ steps.   ◁

We can now prove our main theorem.

Theorem 5.3. *Algorithm 1 is an* ExpTime *(optimal) decision procedure for checking satisfiability of a knowledge base in* $\mathcal{SH}$.

Proof. It is easy to see that the "and-or" graph G with root v_0 for $(\mathcal{R}, \mathcal{T}, \mathcal{A})$ has a consistent marking iff $v_0 \notin$ *UnsatNodes*: we simply start from the root v_0 and avoid the members of *UnsatNodes*. Hence, by Theorem 3.7, Algorithm 1 is a decision procedure for checking satisfiability of $(\mathcal{R}, \mathcal{T}, \mathcal{A})$ in $\mathcal{SH}$. By Lemma 5.2, the algorithm runs in $2^{O(n^2)}$ steps.   ◁

6   Optimizations

Treating axioms of the TBox as concepts representing global assumptions is not efficient because it generates too many expansions of the kind "or". A solution for this problem is to use *absorption* techniques. A basic kind of absorption is *lazy unfolding* for acyclic TBoxes.[5] For the case the TBox is acyclic and consists of only concept definitions of the form $A = C$, by using lazy unfolding, A is treated as a reference to C and will be "unfolded" only when necessary. Using this technique, for the *Cons* problem in $\mathcal{ALC}$ TGC runs on the test set DL'98 T98-kb equally well as on the test set DL'98 T98-sat. For the case the TBox is acyclic and contains also concept inclusions of the form $A \sqsubseteq C$, a simple solution can be adopted: treat $A \sqsubseteq C$ as $A = (C \sqcap A')$ for a new atomic concept A'. For the case the TBox is cyclic, one can try to divide the TBox into two parts $\mathcal{T}_1$ and $\mathcal{T}_2$, where $\mathcal{T}_1$ is a maximal acyclic sub-TBox "not depending" on the concepts defined in $\mathcal{T}_2$, then one can apply the mentioned "replacing" and "lazy unfolding" techniques for $\mathcal{T}_1$.

Observe that Algorithm 1 first constructs an "and-or" graph and then checks whether the graph contains a consistent marking. To speed up the performance these two tasks can be done concurrently. For this we update the set *UnsatNodes* mentioned in the algorithm and check the condition $v_0 \in$ *UnsatNodes* "on-the-fly" during the construction of G.

During the construction of the "and-or" graph G, if a subgraph of G has been fully expanded (in the sense that all of its nodes and their descendants have

---

[5] If A is defined by $A = C$ or $A \sqsubseteq C$, and B occurs in C, then A *directly depends* on B. Let binary relation "depend" be the transitive closure of "directly depend". If in a TBox $\mathcal{T}$ no atomic concept depends on itself, then $\mathcal{T}$ is acyclic. For simplicity, we assume that each atomic concept is defined at most once.

been expanded) then each node of the subgraph can be determined to be unsat (unsatisfiable w.r.t. $\mathcal{R}$ and $\mathcal{T}$) or sat (satisfiable w.r.t. $\mathcal{R}$ and $\mathcal{T}$) regardlessly of the rest of G: if a node of the subgraph could not have been determined to be unsat then we can set its status to sat.

For further optimization techniques, we refer the reader to [14,9,2].

7 Conclusions

Recall that the approaches that use transformation or the pre-completion technique for dealing with ABoxes are highly inefficient. In the well-known tutorial [10], Horrocks and Sattler wrote *"direct algorithm/implementation instead of encodings"* and *"even simple domain encoding is disastrous with large numbers of roles"*. In [22, page 135], Tobies wrote *"To apply the algorithm to $\mathcal{SHIQ}$-knowledge bases, one can either use a pre-completion approach [. . .] (probably with catastrophic effects on the runtime of the algorithm), or one can integrate the ABox directly into the tableau algorithm."*.

In this work, we have given the *first* direct EXPTIME (optimal) tableau decision procedure, which is not based on transformation or the pre-completion technique, for checking satisfiability of a knowledge base in the description logic $\mathcal{SH}$. Our procedure can be implemented as an extension of the highly optimized tableau prover TGC [14] to obtain an efficient program for the mentioned satisfiability problem.

This work is a significant extension of our conference paper [16] on $\mathcal{ALC}$, as $\mathcal{SH}$ is a description logic that is considerably more expressive and complicated than $\mathcal{ALC}$. As new methods, apart from incorporating individuals into (non-prefixed) tableaux, in this paper and [16] we defined tableaux directly as "and-or" graphs with global caching, while in [6,7] Goré and Nguyen used tree-like tableaux and formulated global caching separately. Consequently, we do not have to prove soundness of global caching when having soundness and completeness of the calculus, while Goré and Nguyen [6,7] had to prove soundness of global caching separately after having completeness of their calculi.

We have recently extended our methods for PDL [15]. We intend to extend our methods also for other modal and description logics.

Acknowledgments

We would like to thank the reviewers for helpful comments and suggestions.

References

1. Baader, F., Sattler, U.: An overview of tableau algorithms for description logics. Studia Logica 69, 5–40 (2001)
2. Donini, F., Massacci, F.: ExpTime tableaux for $\mathcal{ALC}$. Artificial Intelligence 124, 87–138 (2000)

3. De Giacomo, G.: Decidability of Class-Based Knowledge Representation Formalisms. PhD thesis, Universita' di Roma "La Sapienza" (1995)
4. De Giacomo, G., Lenzerini, M.: TBox and ABox reasoning in expressive description logics. In: Aiello, L.C., Doyle, J., Shapiro, S.C. (eds.) Proc. of KR'1996, pp. 316–327. Morgan Kaufmann, San Francisco (1996)
5. Goré, R.: Tableau methods for modal and temporal logics. In: D'Agostino, et al. (eds.) Handbook of Tableau Methods, pp. 297–396. Kluwer, Dordrecht (1999)
6. Goré, R., Nguyen, L.A.: ExpTime tableaux for $\mathcal{ALC}$ using sound global caching. In: Calvanese, D., et al. (eds.) Proc. of DL 2007, pp. 299–306 (2007)
7. Goré, R., Nguyen, L.A.: ExpTime tableaux with global caching for description logics with transitive roles, inverse roles and role hierarchies. In: Olivetti, N. (ed.) TABLEAUX 2007. LNCS (LNAI), vol. 4548, pp. 133–148. Springer, Heidelberg (2007)
8. Hollunder, B.: Consistency checking reduced to satisfiability of concepts in terminological systems. Ann. Math. Artif. Intell. 18(2-4), 133–157 (1996)
9. Horrocks, I., Patel-Schneider, P.F.: Optimizing description logic subsumption. Journal of Logic and Computation 9(3), 267–293 (1999)
10. Horrocks, I., Sattler, U.: Description logics - basics, applications, and more. In: Tutorial given at ECAI 2002 (2002),
    http://www.cs.man.ac.uk/~horrocks/Slides/ecai-handout.pdf
11. Horrocks, I., Sattler, U.: A description logic with transitive and inverse roles and role hierarchies. J. Log. Comput. 9(3), 385–410 (1999)
12. Horrocks, I., Sattler, U., Tobies, S.: Reasoning with individuals for the description logic SHIQ. In: McAllester, D. (ed.) CADE 2000. LNCS, vol. 1831, pp. 482–496. Springer, Heidelberg (2000)
13. Nguyen, L.A.: Analytic tableau systems and interpolation for the modal logics KB, KDB, K5, KD5. Studia Logica 69(1), 41–57 (2001)
14. Nguyen, L.A.: An efficient tableau prover using global caching for the description logic ALC. Fundamenta Informaticae 93(1-3), 273–288 (2009)
15. Nguyen, L.A., Szałas, A.: Checking consistency of an ABox w.r.t. global assumptions in PDL. In: Czaja, L., Szczuka, M. (eds.) Proc. of CS&P'2009, pp. 431–442 (2009)
16. Nguyen, L.A., Szałas, A.: EXPTIME tableaux for checking satisfiability of a knowledge base in the description logic ALC. In: Nguyen, N.T., Kowalczyk, R., Chen, S.-M. (eds.) ICCC 2009. LNCS (LNAI), vol. 5796, pp. 437–448. Springer, Heidelberg (2009)
17. Nguyen, L.A., Szałas, A.: An optimal tableau decision procedure for Converse-PDL. In: Nguyen, N.-T., Bui, T.-D., Szczerbicki, E., Nguyen, N.-B. (eds.) Proc. of KSE'2009, pp. 207–214. IEEE Computer Society, Los Alamitos (2009)
18. Nguyen, L.A., Szałas, A.: A tableau calculus for regular grammar logics with converse. In: Schmidt, R.A. (ed.) Automated Deduction – CADE-22. LNCS (LNAI), vol. 5663, pp. 421–436. Springer, Heidelberg (2009)
19. Pratt, V.R.: A near-optimal method for reasoning about action. J. Comput. Syst. Sci. 20(2), 231–254 (1980)
20. Rautenberg, W.: Modal tableau calculi and interpolation. JPL 12, 403–423 (1983)
21. Schild, K.: A correspondence theory for terminological logics: Preliminary report. In: Mylopoulos, J., Reiter, R. (eds.) Proc. of IJCAI'1991, pp. 466–471. Morgan Kaufmann, San Francisco (1991)
22. Tobies, S.: Complexity results and practical algorithms for logics in knowledge representation. PhD thesis, RWTH-Aachen (2001)

An Efficient Ant-Based Edge Detector

Doğan Aydın

Department of Computer Engineering, Ege University, Izmir, 35100 Turkey
dogan.aydin@ege.edu.tr

Abstract. An efficient ant-based edge detector is presented. It is based on the distribution of ants on an image, ants try to find possible edges by using a state transition function based on 5x5 edge structures. Visual comparisons show that the proposed method gives finer details and thinner edges at lesser computational times when compared to earlier ant-based approaches. When compared to standard edge detectors, it shows robustness to Gaussian and Salt & Pepper noise and provides finer details than others with same parameter set in both clear and noisy images.

Keywords: Edge detection, ant-based algorithm, noisy images, ant colony optimization.

1 Introduction

Edges correspond to sharp variations of image intensity and convey vitally important information in an image. Therefore, detecting of edges is an important problem in pattern recognition, computer vision and image processing. Many edge detection methods have been proposed in the past 40 years.

The first directional derivative based detectors, such as the Sobel [1,2], Prewitt [1,2], detectors are simple to implement but they are usually inaccurate and sensitive to noise. The second derivative based methods, which are also very sensitive to noise, have fixed detection characteristics in all directions. The Canny detector [3] reduces the influence of noise by smoothing the image before detecting edges. Although the Canny detector exhibits relatively better performance, it is computationally much more complex. Recently, many proposed studies on detecting edges of the image, which is corrupted by noise, are based on different methods, such as wavelet transform method [4,5], mathematical morphological method [6,7], neural networks method [8,9], fuzzy method [10,11], etc.

Ant Colony Optimization (ACO) is a population-based meta-heuristic proposed by Dorigo [12]. ACO has been applied to a wide range of different discrete optimization problems successfully. Besides, ACO algorithms have been used to solve many image processing and computer vision problems such as multilevel thresholding [13], and image segmentation [14, 15] in recent years. To apply ACO to tackle image processing problems, two factors are needed, optimization function model to represent the image features and ACO algorithm to solve the model.

N.T. Nguyen and R. Kowalczyk (Eds.): Transactions on CCI I, LNCS 6220, pp. 39–55, 2010.

Ant-based algorithms on image analysis are modified version of Ant Colony Optimization algorithms. They don't need to formulize the problem as an optimization function model, instead they use stochastic search mechanism and pheromone information to detect some important region and edges on images. In literature, there are really few works on ant-based edge detectors which can be used with other edge detectors to improve them or try to solve the edge detection problem stand-alone. Former methods [16,17] give good results if they used to solve the problem of linking disjointed edges produced by other edge detector, albeit latter methods [18,19,20] are not yet satisfactory in terms of detailed edge detection on images corrupted by noise or not. These works aim to show that stand-alone ant-based approaches can be used to solve detect edges, which suffer from detailed detection and increasing time complexity. Moreover, necessity of more research on improvement of these works were clearly indicated by the researches [18,19].

In this paper, we propose a faster and improved ant-based edge detector that provides detail edge detection on both noisy and clean images. It is based on simple edge models defined in heuristic function, and uses ant colony search mechanism and pheromone information to detect edges.

The remainder of the paper is organized as follows; the next section describes Ant Colony Optimization, and the differences between Ant-based approaches on image analysis explained in Section 3. In Section 4, we discuss our edge detection methodology in details. Experimental results and analysis are presented in Section 5. Concluding remarks and recommendations for the future improvement are given in Section 6.

2   Ant Colony Optimization

Ant Colony Optimization (ACO) takes inspiration from the behavior of real ant colonies to solve hard optimization problems. They are based on a colony of artificial ants, that is, simple computational agents that work cooperatively and communicate through artificial pheromone trails [21, 22].

Many ant colonies have trail-laying trail-following behavior while foraging. Ants deposit a chemical substance called pheromone on the trace from where they find a food source to their nest. The amount of pheromone deposited depends on the quality and amount of the food source. They forage while wandering in the vicinity of pheromone trails. This feedback (tracing) mechanism that reinforces finding good solutions directly or indirectly is the basic idea underlying all ant-based algorithms.

In ACO algorithms, each virtual ant tries to find good solutions simultaneously and individually in a problem space. At each step of the construction of solution, they randomly choose their direction where the probability distribution associated in choosing any direction is specified. In Ant System (AS)[23], transition probability from state i to j is defined by

$$p_{ij} = \begin{cases} \dfrac{[\tau_{ij}]^{\alpha}[\eta_{ij}]^{\beta}}{\sum_{h\in\Omega}[\tau_{ih}]^{\alpha}[\eta_{ih}]^{\beta}} & if \quad j\in\Omega \\ \\ 0 & otherwise \end{cases} \tag{1}$$

where τ_{ij} is trail level of artificial pheromone between state i and j, η_{ij} is a heuristic function, Ω is the set of unvisited states, also α and β are two adjustable tuning parameters. Ant Colony System (ACS) [24] uses a different transition probability function, where the function 1 is modified to allow explicitly for exploration as follows:

$$j = \begin{cases} \arg \max_{j\in\Omega}\left\{[\tau(i,j)]\cdot[\eta(i,j)]^{\beta}\right\} & if \ q\leq q_0 \\ J & otherwise \end{cases} \tag{2}$$

where q is a random number, q_0 is a parameter $(0\leq q_0 \leq 1)$ and J is a random variable selected according to the previous probability distribution function given in eq. (1) with $\alpha = 1$. At each step, an ant in state i chooses a state j to go, according to the value of q that is randomly generated. If $q\leq q_0$ then the best edge is chosen (exploitation), otherwise an arbitrary edge is chosen according to eq. (1) (Biased exploration) [24].

Once all tour constructions (at the end of the each iteration) have been completed, the best-so-far solution is recorded/updated. Meanwhile, colony members deposit pheromone on their trail path according to the solution qualities. Pheromone depositing provides indirect communication in colony as a positive feedback. Therefore, probability of finding new good solutions is reinforced. In addition, a negative feedback is applied through the pheromone evaporation on paths. In this way, pheromone levels on previous bad paths are decreased thus preventing algorithm to stop at local optima. Generally, pheromone updating rule (for both depositing and evaporation) is defined as:

$$\tau_{new}(i,j) = (1-\rho)\tau_{old}(i,j) + \sum_{k=1}^{m}\Delta\tau^{k}(i,j) \tag{3}$$

where ρ is pheromone decay value, m is the number of ant and

$$\Delta\tau^{k}(i,j) = \begin{cases} f_k/Q & (i,j)\in T_k \\ 0 & otherwise \end{cases} \tag{4}$$

where f_k is the fitness function is the fitness function (i.e., f_k is tour length for traveling salesman problem), Q is a constant parameter usually set as 1 and T_k is the route of the kth ant.

3 Ant-Based Approaches on Image Analysis

Ant-based algorithms on image analysis use the same stochastic searching and undirected information sharing mechanism with ACO algorithms, but they differ from ACO because of four main aspects:

- The image is considered as a two-dimensional graph where the pixels are assumed as vertices.
- Pheromone is deposited on pixels (vertices) instead of on edges. Therefore, transition probability function from one pixel to another belongs to only possible unvisited pixels.
- Ant-based approaches don't need to formulize the problem as an optimization function model. Therefore, unlike original ACO approaches, each ant tries to find a part of a solution, not a solution itself. In our case, each ant tries to find an edge field, not all edges in image.
- In ACO, best-so-far ant solution is assigned as a solution after all iterations are completed. Instead, pheromone levels on image pixels carry the solution in Ant-based approaches. Pheromone levels on pixels imply the likelihood of the pixels to belong to the solution.

All previous methods [18, 19, 20] that use ant colonies to edge detection problem are based on ant-based approaches rather than ACO. Besides, Cinsdikici and Doğan [25] extracted blood vessels from background on retinal images, Huang et al. [26] segmented medical images, Arnay et al. [27] detected non-structured road boundaries by using ant-based approaches, and so on [28, 29, 30].

4   The Proposed Ant-Based Edge Detector

Informally, the proposed approach works as follows: at first, a gray level image is considered as a two-dimensional graph where the pixels are assumed as vertices as we mentioned before. At the beginning of the each iteration, ants are located on pixels randomly. Then, they wander on the graph pixel by pixel in fixed number of steps (ant memory) and deposit pheromone according to the path quality if they complete their trips successfully. The path quality indicates how closely that path belongs to an edge field. Unlike original ant-based approaches, each ant try to find a part of edge fields (a part of a solution, not a solution itself). After they complete their trips, they choose new randomly selected pixels as recent initial states and start their trips again. The algorithm is terminated after a specific number of iterations. At the end, pheromone levels indicate possibilities of each pixels that are belongs to an edge fields.

At each step of iteration, each ant selects a new neighbor pixel to visit according to the state transition function. An ant at pixel i can select the neighbor pixel j with respect to the following equation based on the function of ACS (Eq. 2):

$$
j = \begin{cases} \arg\ \max_{j \in \Omega} \left\{ [\tau(j)] \cdot [\eta(j)]^{\beta} \right\} & \text{if } q \leq q_0 \\ J & \text{otherwise} \end{cases}
$$

(5)

where $\tau(j)$ is pheromone intensity on pixel j, $\eta(j)$ is the heuristic function belongs to pixel j, and Ω is the set of unvisited pixels. Since the pixel j to be visited is determined independent of the current position of ant, η and τ become only a function of j. This function indicates that only the unvisited pixels are allowed to be visited.

The heuristic function, $\eta(j)$, plays the most critical role for ants in selecting suitable pixels to visit around the position they are at. In order to minimize occurrence of noisy edges and improve detailed edge detection, we determined $\eta(j)$ using the structures of 5×5 edge images. We used four structures of 5×5 edge images, and each had two possible variants. Fig. 1 shows these patterns for 5×5 sized edge structures.

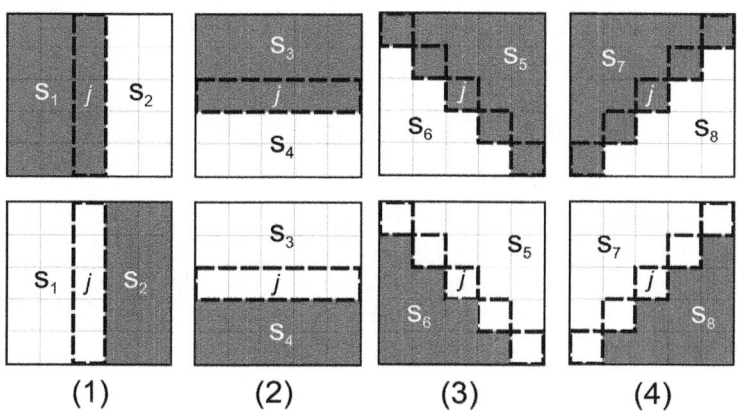

Fig. 1. 5×5 edge structures

In each pattern, edges divide the pixels into two sets, $s_1, s_2, s_3, s_4, s_5, s_6, s_7$, and s_8. If a pixel j belongs to an ideal edge region, total pixel intensity variation between two possibly divided regions should be bigger. The more the variation, the higher the probability of being an edge, and the more the pheromone. By using this assumption, we define $\eta(j)$ (j is any pixel at the center of a 5×5 image region) as

$$\eta(j) = \begin{cases} H & \text{if } \sigma_j * T < H \\ 0 & otherwise \end{cases}$$

$$, H = \frac{\arg\max\left\{\left|I_1 - I_2\right|, \left|I_3 - I_4\right|, \left|I_5 - I_6\right|, \left|I_7 - I_8\right|\right\}}{p_{max}} \quad (6)$$

where p_{max} is the maximum gray valued pixel in the entire image, σ_j is the standard deviation of pixels in 5×5 edge structure related to pixel j, T is the local threshold value and $I_i = \sum_{p \in s_i} p$, where p is the density of a pixel that is belong to set s_i. Consequently, ants move towards pixels that belong to edges on the image. Furthermore, if H is smaller than product of σ_j and local threshold coefficient T for all possible neighbors, it indicates that there are no suitable pixels to visit. In this situation, the ant does not move to any new pixel and dies.

Dying mechanism is crucial. When an ant dies, it doesn't complete its trip and can't deposit pheromone on its path. In other words, dying mechanism prevents the death ant to communicate the others and unwanted information on image. Therefore, the algorithm becomes robust almost all noisy parts and speckles on images.

After all ants complete their trip, each ant deposits some amount of pheromone on the pixels of its trip. Evaporation mechanism assists to discard mistakenly traced irrelevant pixels as edges. The pheromone intensity of a pixel becomes after pheromone updating as follows:

$$\tau_{new}(j) = (1-\rho)\tau_{old}(j) + \sum_{k=1}^{v} \Delta\tau^k(j)$$

(7)

where v is the number of ants that has visited to pixel j, and $\Delta\tau^k(j) = \eta(j)$.

After the iterations are completed, pheromone levels on pixels imply the likelihood of the pixels to belong to an edge. To determine the edge points, thresholding is applied on pheromone levels over the value of pheromone threshold Ψ and a binary image indicating the presence of edges is constructed.

5   Experimental Results

5.1   Parameters Setting

The proposed algorithm has many parameters to set and it is hard to assign them the best values. We set standard ACO parameters ρ, β, and q_0 as defined values in [24] which are 0.85, 2, and 0.98 respectively. The rest of the proposed edge detector parameters are determined by the experiments.

The number of ants and ant memory are affecting the performance depend on the varying image size. For small sizes, too many ants with large memories give more details, but lead to edge-broadening and longer computational times. For large sizes, too few ants with small memories would not produce expected synergy, giving bad results. Therefore, trade-off between ant memory and number of ants is needed. By experimental observations, we have decided to set these parameters related to size and perimeter of image as follows:

$$\text{number of ants} \approx \sqrt{A}$$
$$\text{memory of ant} \approx \sqrt{P}$$

(8)

where A and P are the area and perimeter of the image. Such parameters effects and result with selected parameters for cameraman image are shown in Fig. 2, for a 512x512 image.

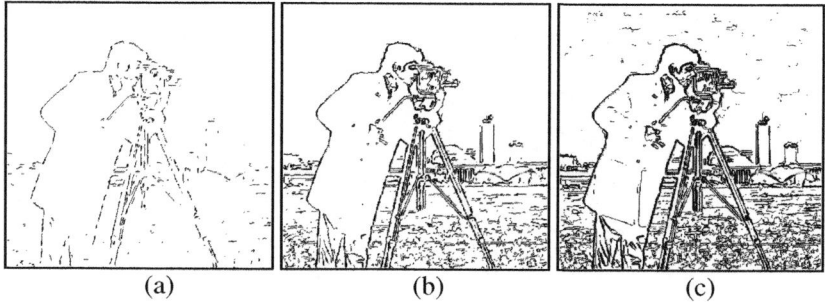

Fig. 2. Parameter effects on ant-based edge-detection of a 512x512 "Cameraman" image. (a)128 ants with 20-pixel memory (b)512 ants with 50-pixel memory (c)1024 ants with 100-pixel memory.

The rest of the algorithm parameters are local and pheromone thresholds (T and Ψ). For deciding good threshold values, we used a figure of merit to objectively evaluate the performance of edge detectors proposed by Abdou and Pratt [31]. The figure of merit is defined as

$$F = \frac{1}{\max(N_I, N_D)} \sum_{i=1}^{N_D} \frac{1}{1 + \xi d_i^2} \tag{9}$$

where d_i is the distance between pixels declared as edge point and the nearest ideal edge pixel, ξ is a penalty constant, N_I and N_D are the numbers of ideal and detected edge pixels respectively. It is a common practice to evaluate the performance of an edge detector for synthetic images by introducing random noise in the images. The value of F is less than or equal to 1. With the increase of the F value, the performance becomes better.

The experiment is based on a synthetic square image with 5 % Gaussian noise, as shown in Fig. 3. Selecting just the best parameter set for this image can be misleading. Therefore, from the experiment plotted in Fig. 4, we decided two sets of parameter values which are given the best and near the best accuracy for decided test image. Former set values are 1.6 and 7, latter set values are 0.8 and 4 for T (local threshold) and Ψ (pheromone threshold) respectively. The following comparison tests are applied using these two sets of parameters.

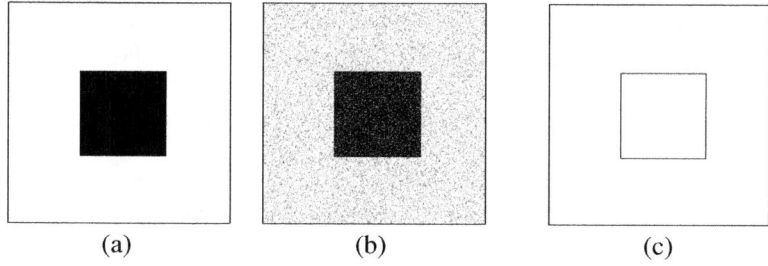

Fig. 3. Synthetic rectangle image, (b) the image with 5% Gaussian noise, and (c) edge map of the image

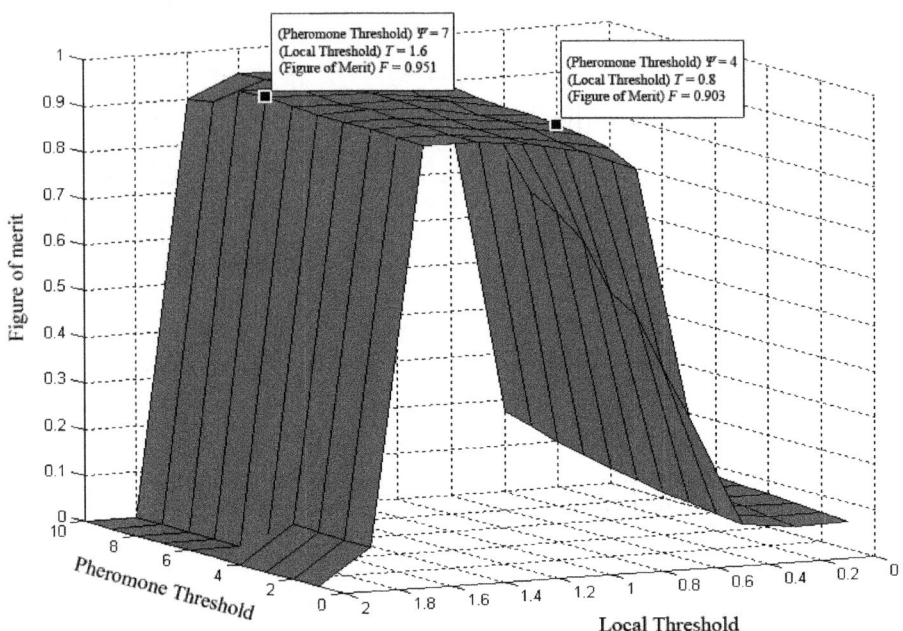

Fig. 4. Effects of the local and pheromone threshold parameters (T and Ψ) on figure of merit of edge detection

5.2   Comparisons with Conventional Edge Detectors

To demonstrate the efficiency of the proposed method, we carried out computational comparison experiments on grayscale standard images. Each image is 512x512 sized and resolution of all is 8-bit per pixel. All experiments are run on a PC with a Intel CoreTM DUO 2.6 GHz CPU and a 2 GB RAM. The algorithms are implemented using both the Matlab programming language and C#.

Sobel edge detector can be regarded as the historic 'standard', while Canny edge detector as a modern 'standard'. They are still employed quite often to compare with those proposed methods in publications today [32]. Therefore, Sobel and Canny edge detectors are employed for comparison. To obtain objective comparison, at first, figure of merit F in Eq. 9 is calculated for each method with respect to different Gaussian and Salt & Pepper noise proportion over rectangle image shown in Fig. 3(a). The results are plotted in Fig. 5. When the noise level is low, F values are over 0.9 and performances of all are very satisfactory. With the increase of noise proportion, F values decrease except in Canny edge detector with $T_{low} = 80$, $T_{high} = 160$ (T_{low}: lower threshold, T_{high}: higher threshold) and the proposed method with $T = 0.8$ $\Psi = 4$. These two results show the robustness and efficiencies clearly on that test images.

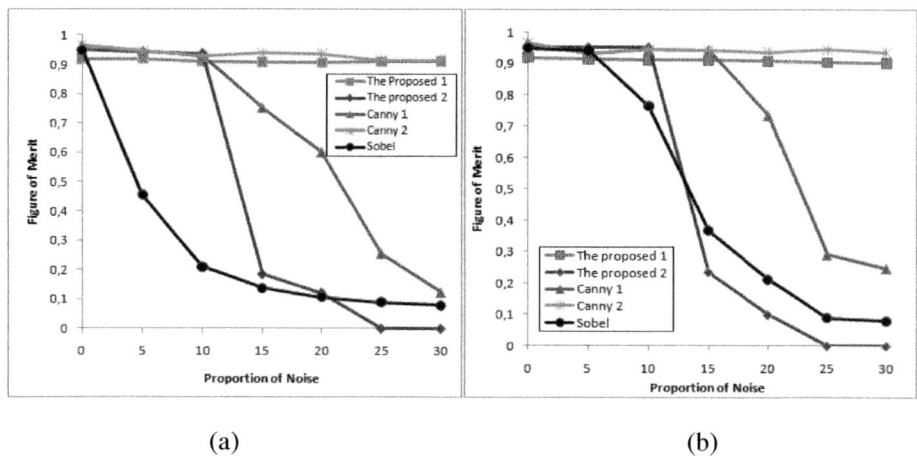

(a)   (b)

Fig. 5. The figure of merit for the synthetic square image. (a) Results for Salt & Pepper noise, (b) results for Gaussian noise (The proposed 1: $T = 0.8$ and $\Psi = 4$; The proposed 2: $T = 1.6$ and $\Psi = 7$; Canny 1: T_{low}: 40 and $T_{high} = 120$; Canny 2: T_{low}: 80 and $T_{high} = 160$; and Sobel: Threshold = 80).

Then, we compared Canny and Sobel edge detectors on standard "Lena" and "Cameraman" images. It is important to note that there is not yet any general performance index to judge the performance of the edge detection methods for standard test images [33]. Therefore, we had no choice to do statistical comparison but only visual comparison.

We added Gaussian noise (see in Fig. 6 and 7) and Salt & Pepper noise (see in Fig. 8 and 9) to images and increased the proportion of noise. Here, first rows show the tested images, the latter three rows are obtained by using Canny edge detector with different parameters (Row 2: $T_{low} = 80$, $T_{high} = 160$; Row 3: $T_{low} = 0$, $T_{high} = 40$; Row 4: $T_{low} = 40$, $T_{high} = 120$). The performance of Sobel detector under threshold 20, that gives good results in clean images, is given in fifth rows, and results of our proposed method with parameters $T = 0.8$ $\Psi = 4$ are at last rows.

Canny edge detector with parameters $T_{low} = 80$ and $T_{high} = 160$, which gives the best results aforementioned experiment, is also better in these noisy images, but fails on clear images in terms of detailed detection. Canny results in third row indicate that if the selected parameters set for clean images, the obtained results give worst results on noisy images.

In all cases, Sobel edge detector is too sensitive to noise, so it gives bad results. Results of our proposed approach shown in last rows are admissible in all cases. The selected parameter set in both clear and noisy image try to detect edges in detailed without speckles. It shows its robustness and superior to Canny and Sobel edge detectors.

Fig. 6. Results of edge detectors for Lena image. Clean, noisy with 5% and 10% Gaussian noise images are at first row. Row 2-4 edge images obtained by Canny, latter rows are results of Sobel and the proposed edge detectors respectively.

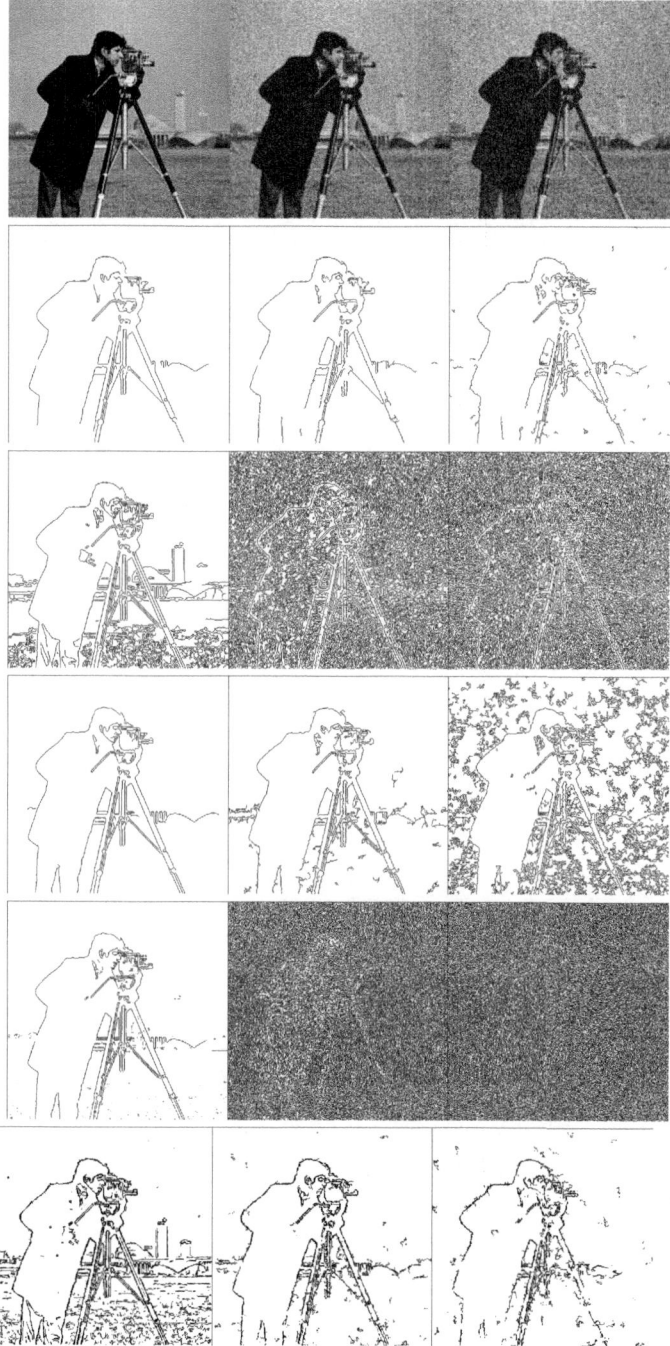

Fig. 7. Results of edge detectors for Cameraman image. Clean, noisy with 5% and 10% Gaussian noise images are at first row. Row 2-4 edge images obtained by Canny, latter rows are results of Sobel and the proposed edge detectors respectively.

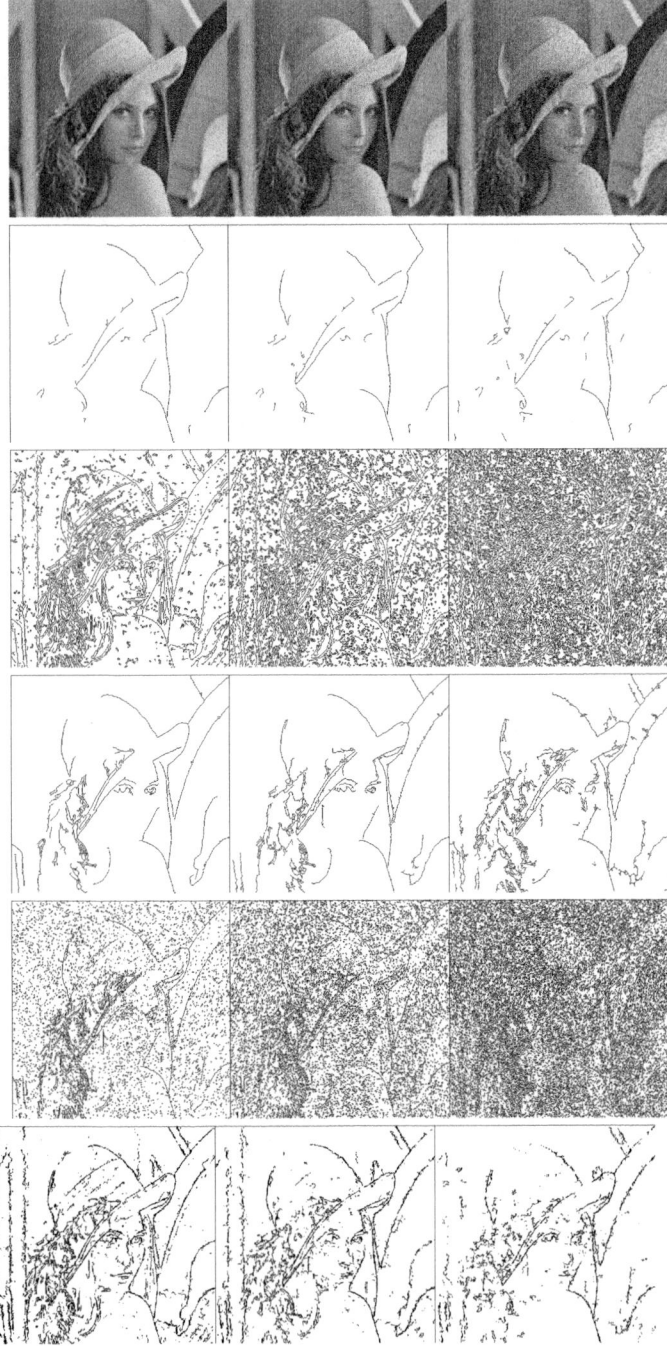

Fig. 8. Results of edge detectors for Lena image. Noisy with 2%, 5% and 10% Salt & Pepper noise images are at first row. Row 2-4 edge images obtained by Canny, latter rows are results of Sobel and the proposed edge detectors respectively.

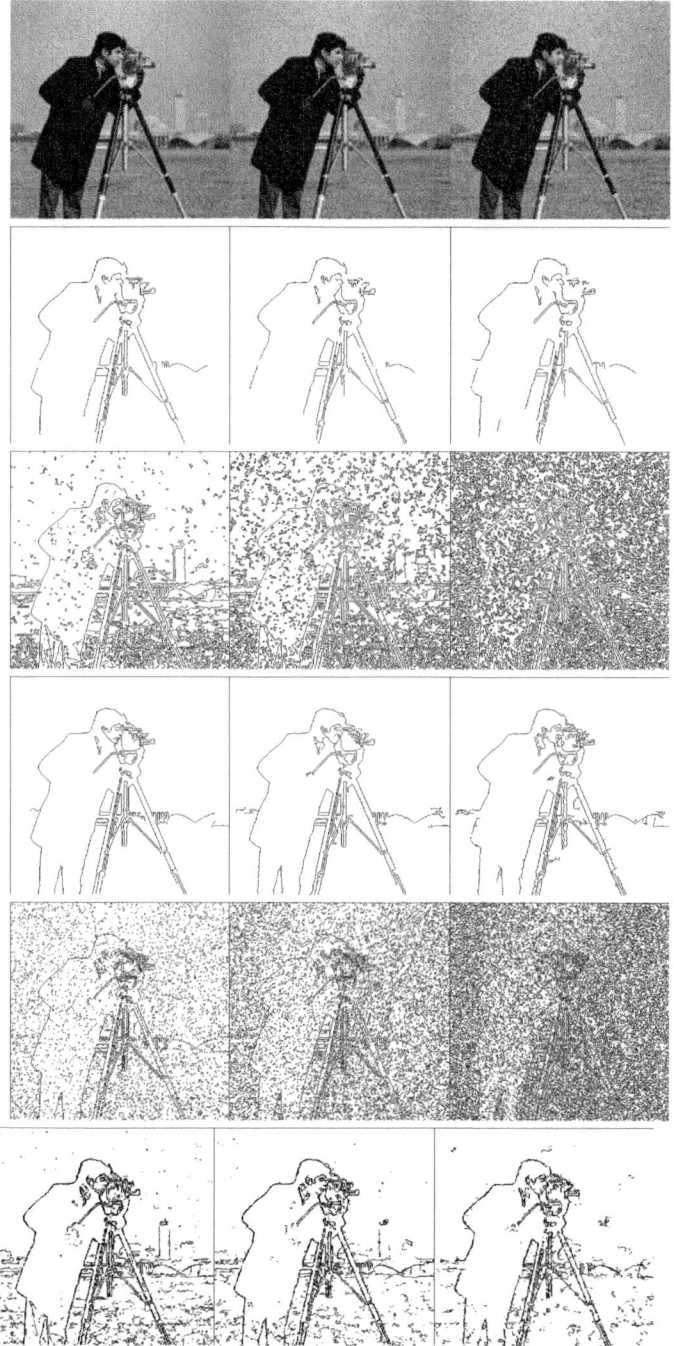

Fig. 9. Results of edge detectors for Cameraman image. Noisy with 2%, 5% and 10% Salt & Pepper noise images are at first row. Row 2-4 edge images obtained by Canny, latter rows are results of Sobel and the proposed edge detectors respectively.

Fig. 10. Comparison of ant-based edge detection algorithms. The results of Nezamabadi-pour et al. method with thinning operation is at second row, third row shows the results of Tian et al. method without thinning, and last row shows the results of our approach with T = 0.8 Ψ = 4.

5.3   Comparison with Other Ant-Based Edge Detectors

We as well compared our new ant-based edge detector with other two well-known ant-based approaches: Nezamabadi-pour et al. [19] and Tian et al. [20] edge detectors. Nezamabadi-pour et al. [19] applied ant algorithms to detect edges for the first time. They used the transition probability function in Eq.1 that caused ants to wander excessively, resulting in edge-broadening. Therefore, they had to use a morphological thinning algorithm in order to thin the binary output image. Their heuristic function operates on single pixels rather than on a region around a given pixel, making their algorithm vulnerable to noise so much. Tian et al. [20] method tries to minimize edge broadening by using a complex heuristic function. But it is computationally more expensive and fails on detailed edge detection, strictly speaking, it is inadmissible.

Fig. 10 represents the comparison results on standard images. The first row in Fig.10 shows the best results of Nezamabadi-pour et al. method, where 1500 ants with random memory lengths between 15 and 30 were used. In contrast, the third row in Fig. 5 shows our results obtained with 512 ants each with memory length of 50 with no thinning operation. The proposed ant-based approach provides finer details, and yet almost 3-times as fast. Furthermore, Tian et al. [20] method gives the worst results shown at second row in Fig. 5 according to the detailed detection in comparison. It is important to note that although the parameters as the authors suggested is used in experiment, execution time of the method is about 5 hours on 512x512 sized images.

The comparison clearly indicates that our proposed method outperforms all other ant-based edge detectors in clean images. Furthermore, well known ant-based approaches that we showed in comparison are not designed for noisy images. Therefore, for showing our methods superiority, we did not need to do any statistical comparison with the others on noisy test images.

6   Conclusion

This paper introduces an efficient ant-based edge detector that gives satisfactory results both in clean and noisy images. It uses effective and simple to implement heuristic function leading ants towards to pixels that are belong to edge fields. Unlike the other approaches, dying mechanism, with the heuristic function, assist to forget mistakenly traced pixel and the resulted edge image is robust to noise, and the colony members detect edge fields in detailed.

In making runs with Sobel, Canny and our proposed edge detector, we found that Sobel is really sensitive to noise and selecting different parameter set is required to obtain satisfactory results with Canny for each image. But our proposed method gives better results than the others both in clean and noisy images without resetting the parameter set.

When we compare our proposed edge detector with other ant-based approaches, our edge detector gives finer details and thinner edges at lesser computation times. It is important to note that as a course of the ant-based approaches' nature, the proposed method is still slower than the convenient edge detectors. Fortunately, ant-based approaches are amenable to parallelization, and we will try to reduce of the proposed method with parallelization as a future work.

References

1. Bovik, A.: Handbook of image and video processing. Acedemic Press, New York (1998)
2. Umbaugh, S.E.: Computer Vision and Image Processing. Prentice-Hall Int. Inc., Englewood Cliffs (1998)
3. Canny, J.: A computational approach to edge detection. IEEE Transaction on Pattern Analysis and Machine Intelligence 8, 679–698 (1986)
4. Zhang, L., Bao, P.: Edge detection by scale multiplication in wavelet domain. Pattern Recognition Letters 23, 1771–1784 (2002)
5. Aydin, T., Yemez, Y., Anarim, E., Sankur, B.: Multidirectional and multiscale edge detection via M-band wavelet transform. IEEE Transaction on Image Processing 5(9), 1370–1377 (1996)
6. Lee, J.S.J., Haralick, R.M., Shapiro, L.G.: Morphological edge detection. IEEE Journal of Robotics and Automation 3, 142–156 (1897)
7. Chen, T., Wu, Q.H., Rahmani-Torkaman, R., Hughes, J.: A pseudo top-hat mathematical morphological approach to edge detection in dark regions. Pattern Recognition 35, 199–210 (2002)
8. Rajab, M.I., Woolfson, M.S., Morgan, S.P.: Application of region based segmentation and neural network edge detection to skin lesions. Comput. Med. Imag. Graphics 28, 61–68 (2004)
9. Zhao, J., Wang, H., Yu, D.: A new approach to edge detection of noisy image based on CNN. International Journal of Circuit Theory and Applications 31, 119–131 (2003)
10. Liang, L.R., Looney, C.G.: Competitive fuzzy edge detection. Applied Soft Computing 3, 123–137 (2003)
11. Hu, L., Cheng, H.D., Zhang, M.: A high performance edge detector based on fuzzy inference rules. Information Sciences 177, 4768–4784 (2007)
12. Dorigo, M., Di Caro, G.: Ant colony optimization: A new metaheuristic. In: Proc. of the Congress on Evolutionary Computation, vol. 2, pp. 1470–1477 (1999)
13. Liang, Y.-C., Chen, A.H.-L., Chyu, C.-C.: Application of a hybrid ant colony optimization for the multilevel thresholding in image processing. In: King, I., Wang, J., Chan, L.-W., Wang, D. (eds.) ICONIP 2006. LNCS, vol. 4233, pp. 1183–1192. Springer, Heidelberg (2006)
14. Tao, W., Jin, H., Liu, L.: Object segmentation using ant colony optimization algorithm and fuzzy entropy. Pattern Recognition Letters 28(7), 788–796 (2007)
15. Zhuang, X.: Image segmentation with ant swarm - A case study of digital signal processing with biological mechanism of intelligence. In: 11th Digital Sig. Proc. Workshop'04, pp. 143–146 (2004)
16. Wong, Y.-P., Soh, V.C.-M., Ban, K.-W., Bau, Y.-T.: Improved Canny Edges Using Ant Colony Optimization. In: 5th Int. Conf. on Computer Graphics, Imaging and Visualisation, pp. 197–202 (2008)
17. Lu, D.-S., Chen, C.-C.: Edge detection improvement by ant colony optimization. Pattern Recognition Letters 29(4), 416–425 (2008)
18. Rezaee, A.: Extracting edge of images with ant colony. Journal of Electrical Engineering 59(1), 57–59 (2008)
19. Nezamabadi-pour, H., Saryazdi, S., Rashedi, E.: Edge detection using ant algorithms. Soft Computing 10, 623–628 (2006)
20. Tian, J., Yu, W., Xie, S.: An Ant Colony Optimization Algorithm For Image Edge Detection. In: IEEE Congress on Evolutionary Computation 2008 (CEC 2008), pp. 751–756 (2008)

21. Dorigo, M., Stützle, T.: Ant Colony Optimization. MIT Press, Cambridge (2004)
22. Martínez, C.G., Cordón, O., Herrera, F.: A taxonomy and an empirical analysis of multiple objective ant colony optimization algorithms for the bi-criteria TSP. European Journal of Operational Research 180(1), 116–148 (2007)
23. Dorigo, M., Maniezzo, V., Colorni, A.: The ant system: Optimization by a colony of cooperating agents. IEEE Trans. on Systems Man and Cyber. Part-B 26, 29–41 (1996)
24. Dorigo, M., Gambardella, L.M.: Ant colonies for the traveling salesman problem. Bio. Systems 43, 73–81 (1997)
25. Cinsdikici, M.G., Aydın, D.: Detection of blood vessels in ophthalmoscope images using MF/ant (matched filter/ant colony) algorithm. Computer Methods and Programs in Biomedicine 96, 85–95 (2009)
26. Huang, P., Cao, H., Luo, S.: An artificial ant colonies approach to medical image segmentation. Computer Methods and Programs in Biomedicine 92(3), 267–273 (2008)
27. Arnay, R., Acosta, L., Sigut, M., Toledo, J.: Ant colony optimization algorithm for detection and tracking of non-structured roads. Electronics Letters 44(12), 725–727 (2008)
28. Fernandes, C., Ramos, V., Rosa, A.C.: Self-Regulated Artificial Ant Colonies on Digital Image Habitats. International Journal of Lateral Computing 2(1), 1–8 (2005)
29. Lee, M.-E., Kim, S.-H., Cho, W.-H., Park, S.Y., Lim, J.S.: Segmentation of Brain MR Images using an Ant Colony Optimization Algorithm. In: Ninth IEEE International Conference on Bioinformatics and Bioengineering, pp. 366–369 (2009)
30. Khajehpour, P., Lucas, C., Araabi, B.N.: Hierarchical Image Segmentation Using Ant Colony and Chemical Computing Approach. In: Wang, L., Chen, K., Ong, Y.S. (eds.) ICNC 2005. LNCS, vol. 3611, pp. 1250–1258. Springer, Heidelberg (2005)
31. Abdou, I.E., Pratt, W.K.: Quantitative design and evaluation of enhancement thresholding edge detectors. Proc. IEEE 69, 753–763 (1979)
32. Heath, M., Sarkar, S., Sanocki, T., Bowyer, K.: Comparison of edge detectors: a methodology and initial study. Computer Vision and Image Understanding 69(1), 38–54 (1998)
33. Kanga, C.-C., Wang, W.-J.: A novel edge detection method based on the maximizing objective function. Pattern Recognition 40(2), 609–618 (2007)

Stochastic Local Search for Core Membership Checking in Hedonic Games

Helena Keinänen

Turku School of Economics, Department of Economics

Abstract. Hedonic games have emerged as an important tool in economics and show promise as a useful formalism to model multi-agent coalition formation in AI as well as group formation in social networks. We consider a *coNP*-complete problem of core membership checking in hedonic coalition formation games. No previous algorithms to tackle the problem have been presented. In this work, we overcome this by developing two stochastic local search algorithms for core membership checking in hedonic games. We demonstrate the usefulness of the algorithms by showing experimentally that they find solutions efficiently, particularly for large agent societies.

1 Introduction

In recent years, coalition formation has been the focus of extensive research in multi-agent systems. Coalition formation has also been a main research area in various social, political and economical studies concerning voting, trade, environmental and legislative issues. Whenever distinct agents group together to form coalitions, one of the most important questions is to determine stability of the resulting disjoint coalitions. Essentially, this amounts to checking that no group of agents has an incentive to break away from their coalitions, given the individual preferences of all the agents.

Hedonic coalitional games provide a suitable framework for modeling these issues: a stable division of agents into coalitions essentially corresponds to a coalition structure residing in core (a set of all stable partitions of agents into disjoint coalitions) of a hedonic game. Moreover, in hedonic coalitional games the preference an agent assigns to a coalition depends solely on the members of her own coalition and not on the composition of the other coalitions. For this reason, hedonic games are a suitable model for many real-life environments where agents behave rather self-interestedly instead of cooperatively while pursuing their own goals.

Hence, the problem of core membership checking in hedonic games is so important that developing special purpose algorithms for the problem is worthwhile. It is recently shown that the core membership checking in hedonic games is a *coNP*-complete problem [1]. Yet no algorithms have been presented in the literature to tackle the problem. In this paper we thus contribute to the literature by developing two novel algorithms to check core membership in hedonic games. Both of them are stochastic local search algorithms but are based on a very

N.T. Nguyen and R. Kowalczyk (Eds.): Transactions on CCI I, LNCS 6220, pp. 56–70, 2010.

different heuristics. Through extensive numerical experiments, we show that our core membership checking algorithms are practically efficient on hedonic games. Our experiments show that we can easily check core membership on multi-agent societies that are orders of magnitudes larger than reported up till now, involving agents beyond tens up to 5000.

Much previous research effort has been directed at related questions. The concept of core has been studied extensively in cooperative game theory starting from [2]. Recently, the computability of core related questions have been studied in coalitional games [3, 4]. Games with hedonic preferences were introduced in [5]. For hedonic games it was shown that deciding the non-emptiness of the core is NP-complete [6]. Hedonic coalitional games have been studied mostly in the context of economics with the main focus on models and stability concepts (see, e.g.,[7–10]). Also, hedonic games can be used to model multi-agent coordination and group formation in social networks [11]. Stochastic local search algorithms are often considered as the state-of-the-art for finding high quality solutions to various combinatorial problems but they have been only occasionally applied to combinatorial problems arising in game theoretic settings.

2 Preliminaries

2.1 Hedonic Games

We study coalition formation in hedonic games [1, 8, 9]. Hedonic games are defined as follows.

Definition 1. *A hedonic game is denoted by* $G = \langle N, \succeq \rangle$ *where* $N = \{1, 2, \ldots, n\}$ *is a finite set of agents and* $\succeq = (\succeq_1, \succeq_2, \ldots, \succeq_n)$ *is a preference profile. For all* $i \in N$, *relation* $\succeq_i$ *defines a preference order of agent* i *over set* $\mathcal{A}^i = \{S \subseteq N \mid i \in S\}$.

In hedonic games, a coalition S is any nonempty subset of agents N. A coalition structure CS is a partition of N into mutually disjoint coalitions in which, for all $S, S' \in CS$, we have $S \cap S' = \emptyset$ and $\bigcup_{S \in CS} = N$. Let $\mathcal{C}(N)$ denote the set of all possible coalition structures over N. Let $CS(i)$ denote the coalition in CS which contains agent i.

The preferences of each agent $i \in N$ over $\mathcal{C}(N)$ are completely determined by the preference relation of i, such that for all coalition structures $CS, CS' \in \mathcal{C}(N)$, i weakly prefers CS to CS' if and only if $CS(i) \succeq_i CS'(i)$.

As in [1, 8, 9] we assume that the agents' preferences $\succeq = (\succeq_1, \succeq_2, \ldots, \succeq_n)$ are additive, meaning that for each agent $i \in N$, there exists valuation function $v_i : N \to \mathbb{R}$ characteristic $S \succeq_i S'$ such that for all $S, S' \in \mathcal{A}^i$, $S \succeq_i S'$ if and only if

$$\sum_{j \in S} v_i(j) \geq \sum_{j \in S'} v_i(j).$$

We will denote $\sum_{j \in S} v_i(j)$ by $v_i(S)$ for every $i \in N$ and for every $S \in \mathcal{A}^i$. Additive preferences provides a concise representation to store a hedonic game in computers' memory as this requires only a space quadratic in the number of agents $|N|$.

2.2   Core Membership

In this paper, the main focus is not on how agents group together to form coalition structures. Instead we are mainly interested in evaluating whether or not a given coalition structure is stable. For this purpose, we now define the concepts of stability of coalition structure and core of a game. We call a coalition structure CS stable, if $CS(i) \succeq_i S$ holds for all $S \subseteq N$ and for all $i \in S$. A core of game G is the set of all stable coalition structures of G. We call coalition S a blocking coalition, if for all $i \in S$, $S \succ_i CS(i)$. Intuitively, a stable coalition structure is such that no group of agents benefits from leaving their coalitions and forming a new (blocking) coalition.

In this paper, we are concerned with the following problem which is known to be $coNP$-complete [1].

Definition 2 (Core Membership Checking Problem). *Given a coalition structure $CS \in \mathcal{C}(N)$ and hedonic game $G = (N, \succeq)$, the core membership checking problem is to decide whether CS is in the core of G, and to give a blocking coalition if one exists.*

In general, additive preferences do not guarantee the non-emptiness of the core. However, the core is always non-empty for preferences based on aversion to enemies [1] which are defined as follows. In hedonic games with additive preferences, agents' coalition partners can be either friends, enemies or neutral partners. We call agent j a friend (enemy) of agent i if and only if $v_i(j) > 0$ ($v_i(j) < 0$). If $v_i(j) = 0$ agent i considers agent j as a neutral partner. The additive preferences are based on aversion to enemies, if for each $i \in N$, $v_i(\cdot) \in \{-n, 1\}$ and $v_i(i) = 1$. A hedonic game with aversion to enemies preferences provides us with a structured example for the experiments in this paper.

2.3   Examples

Let us consider some examples of hedonic games which illustrate the related concepts such as core and blocking coalitions.

Example 1. Consider a hedonic game with $N = \{1, 2, \ldots, 6\}$ and generic, additively separable preferences defined in the below matrix (for all $i, j \in N$ the value $v_i(j)$ is shown in line i and column j):

0	6	4	4	4	-20
6	0	5	-12	-20	-12
4	5	0	-20	4	6
6	-12	-20	0	5	-12
4	-20	4	5	0	6
-20	-12	5	-12	6	0

The core of this game is non-empty. The core consists of a single member, namely the coalition structure $\{\{1, 2\}, \{3, 5, 6\}, \{4\}\}$. There is no blocking coalition for this coalition structure.

Example 2. Consider a hedonic game with $N = \{1, 2, \ldots, 6\}$ and generic, additively separable preferences defined in the below matrix (for all $i, j \in N$ the value $v_i(j)$ is shown in line i and column j):

0	10	-20	1	1	1
1	0	10	-20	1	1
1	1	0	10	-20	1
1	1	1	0	10	-20
-20	1	1	1	0	10
10	-20	1	1	1	0

The core of this game is empty. All coalition structures admit a blocking coalition in this game. The reason is that the preferences are cyclic similar to the examples considered in [8] and [9].

Example 3. Let us consider a hedonic game with aversion to enemies preferences. Let $N = \{1, 2, \ldots, 6\}$ and consider the preferences defined in the matrix below (for all $i, j \in N$ the value $v_i(j)$ is shown in line i and column j).

1	-6	1	-6	1	-6
-6	1	-6	1	-6	1
1	1	1	-6	-6	-6
-6	-6	1	1	-6	-6
1	1	-6	-6	1	1
-6	-6	-6	1	1	1

As with all hedonic games with aversion to enemies preferences, the core of this game is non-empty. The core of the game consists of two coalition structures: $\{\{1,3\}, \{2\}, \{4\}, \{5,6\}\}$ and $\{\{1,5\}, \{2\}, \{3\}, \{4\}, \{6\}\}$. Notice that the coalition structure involving only singletons $\{\{1\}, \{2\}, \{3\}, \{4\}, \{5\}, \{6\}\}$ is blocked by, e.g., coalition $\{1,3\}$ since both players 1 and 3 prefer each other more than staying alone.

We now turn to the algorithmics of testing the core membership.

3 Algorithms for Core Membership Checking

We design two distinct stochastic local search algorithms for the core membership checking problem in hedonic games. These algorithms are essentially based on iterative improvement technique but both of them use very different search heuristics to escape local minima. Given a coalition structure and agents' preferences, we aim to check whether the coalition structure is stable by searching for a blocking coalition from the set of all possible coalitions. One can view this problem as an combinatorial minimisation task as follows.

The algorithms search for a blocking coalition from the set of all coalitions by working on coalitions and selecting thereof agents who will be either removed or added to current coalition S. The objective is to minimize the number of agents in the coalition S who prefer the given coalition structure CS over S. The number of agents in S which prefer coalition structure CS over S is denoted by $Goodness(S)$. If $Goodness(S)$ converges to 0, then a blocking coalition is found and the coalition structure CS is not in the core.

In other words, both algorithms search the space of all coalitions by selecting in each step an agent i in N, and proceed to modify the current coalition S by removing from or adding i in S, such that $Goodness(S)$ decreases.

Consequently, for both algorithms we use a neighbourhood which maps coalitions to the set of their neighbour coalitions such that the set of neighbours S' of coalition S are defined as $\{S' \in 2^N \setminus \emptyset \mid S' = S \setminus \{i\}$ or $S' = S \cup \{i\}$ where $i \in N\}$. Note that this neighbourhood provides the algorithms with a search landscape where solutions may be reached by at most $|N|$ search steps through the landscape.

3.1   Adapted Metropolis Search

We first introduce a simple stochastic local search algorithm obtained by adapting the heuristic of a basic Metropolis dynamics [12]. We call the resulting algorithm outlined below Adapted Metropolis Search (AMS). AMS is parameterised by an integer iterationLimit, a real valued parameter $p \in [0,1]$, input coalition structure CS and the agents' preferences of the corresponding hedonic game G. The AMS begins with some initial coalition S. At each iteration it chooses a random neighbouring coalition S' which aims to decrease the value of $Goodness(S)$. Here, p determines the probability of accepting a candidate coalition S' that would lead to increasing values of $Goodness(S)$. The probability to accept worsening solutions depends both on p and on the decline in the quality of the objective function.

Algorithm 1. Adapted Metropolis Search (AMS)

```
Input: iterationLimit, p, CS, G
Output: a blocking coalition

determine initial coalition S;
iterations = 0;
while iterations < iterationLimit  do
  if for all i in S, S >_i CS(i) then return S, else:
    S' = a random neighbour of S;
    if Goodness(S') <= Goodness(S) then S = S', else:
      S = S' with probability p^(Goodness(S')-Goodness(S))
  iterations = iterations+1;
```

Notably, if the value of $p^{(Goodness(S')-Goodness(S))}$ is considerably small, then the algorithm uses essentially a so-called first improvement neighbour selection strategy which always chooses the first seen improving neighbour coalition.

3.2 Randomised Iterative Improvement

In this subsection we introduce a more complicated algorithm which is essentially based on randomised iterative improvement (RII) heuristic. Our RII algorithm can be summarized as follows. The RII algorithm is parameterised by an integer

---

Algorithm 2. Randomised Iterative Improvement (RII)

```
Input: iterationLimit, p, CS, G
Output: a blocking coalition

determine initial coalition S;
iterations = 0;
while iterations < iterationLimit  do
  if for all i in S, S >_i CS(i) then return S, else:
  Improves = {};
  for all agents i in N
    S' = S;
    if i is in S and |S|>1 then remove i from S', else:
      add i in S'
    if Goodness(S') <= Goodness(S) then add i in Improves
  if Improves is non-empty, then
    pick a random agent i in Improves;
    if i is in S and |S|>1 then remove i from S, else:
      add i in S;
  else:
    with probability p:
      pick a random agent i in N;
      if i is in S and |S|>1 then remove i from S, else:
      add i in S
    with probability (1-p):
      min = 0;
      bestseen = |N|+1;
      for all agents i in N
        S' = S;
        if i is in S and |S|>1 then remove i from S', else:
        add i in S'
        if Goodness(S') < bestseen then
          min = i;
          bestseen = Goodness(S');
      if min is in S and |S|>1 then remove min from S, else:
      add min in S;
  iterations = iterations+1;
```

---

iterationLimit, a real valued noise parameter $p \in [0, 1]$, input coalition structure CS and the agents' preferences of the corresponding hedonic game G. In addition, the algorithm uses as temporary storages a set Improves as well as integer variables min and bestseen.

The RII algorithm starts with an initial candidate coalition S, and then performs greedy and random moves with a fixed probability, guided by a dedicated heuristic. The functionality of the RII is that, at each iteration, the agent to be added/removed from coalition S is determined by which agent selection yields a decrease in the objective function $Goodness(S)$. If no decrease is possible, then either random coalition neighbour is chosen or a neighbour coalition yielding the smallest increase in $Goodness(S)$.

An essential behaviour of the RII is that a worsening neighbour coalition S' of coalition S is accepted only if a neighbour improving $Goodness(S)$ does not exist. A random worsening neighbour coalition is chosen according to the noise parameter p such that with probability $(1 - p)$ the RII algorithm selects a neighbour with the lowest increase in the value of the objective function $Goodness$. Notably, the iterations of the RII algorithm require only time $O(n)$, with $n = |N|$ the number of agents in input game G, which makes the algorithm practically efficient.

4   Experimental Setup

We have implemented in the C programming language [13] the AMS and the RII algorithms proposed in this paper as well as several problem instance generators for additive hedonic games. To the best of our knowledge, the AMS and the RII are the only algorithms in the literature to check the core membership in hedonic games. Thus, there is no other algorithms that can be used for a numerical comparison in this setting.

To evaluate the AMS and the RII algorithms, we use two classes of randomly generated instances of hedonic coalition formation games. One class is generic hedonic games with additive preferences. Another class of benchmark instances is hedonic games with aversion to enemies preferences.

Problems are generated as follows.

1. A random integer matrix *values* of size $n \times n$ (with $n = |N|$) is produced to represent the agents' additive preferences. The i-th line of matrix *values* represents agent's $i \in N$ payoffs for the other agents inclusion in the same coalition with i. For every agent $i \in N$, and for every coalition $S \in \mathcal{A}^i$ containing i, i's value $v_i(S)$ for coalition S is $\Sigma_{j \in S} values[i, j]$.

2. We iterate over each agent's preference list as follows. For agent $i \in N$ and another agent $j \in N \setminus \{i\}$ in i's preference list, we generate a random number $-n \leq k \leq n$ in generic case, and a random number $k \in \{-n, 1\}$ in aversion to enemies case.

3. The diagonal values for the preference matrix are generated as follows. For every agent $i \in N$, the value of i in the preference list of i is a random

number $-n \leq k \leq n$ in the generic additive case, and constant 1 in the case of aversion to enemies preferences.

4. A random coalition structure CS is generated by assigning each agent integer $1 \leq l \leq n$ uniformly at random which represents the coalition where the agent resides in the coalition structure.

To get a clear and detailed picture of the performance of the algorithmics, we have instrumented the implemented source codes in order to measure operation counts and run-lengths that are needed to solve the problem instances. Essentially, for both AMS and RII heuristics the operations counted are the number of coalitions needed to find a blocking coalition. All of the experiments were run on a 1.60GHz Mobile Intel Celeron CPU running Linux Red Hat 7.3 with sufficient main memory, and we used over two weeks of CPU time to obtain the following results.

5   Results and Discussion

5.1   Noise Parameter Determination

Our first initial experiment aims to find optimal values of the noise parameter p for both algorithms. For this purpose, we run the algorithms on a representative hedonic game instance with generic additive preferences and with the size of 150 agents. Both algorithms are run 10 times on this instance, starting the search from a random initial coalition. For the AMS heuristic we use the values $0.1, 0.3, 0.5, 0.7$ of p, and for the RII the values $0.2, 0.4, 0.6, 0.8$ of p. For both algorithms, the run-time limit is set to 50000 seen coalitions in this experiment.

Figures 1 and 2 show the results, where the run-lengths (minima and maxima of 10 runs) are given as a function of the number of agents who prefer the given coalition structure CS over the currently checked coalition. A blocking coalition is found as soon as the number of such agents declines to 0.

As can be seen from the results in Fig. 1, the AMS with the noise parameter value $p = 0.1$ finds a blocking coalition almost immediately, but for the greater values of p than 0.1 the AMS times out without finding a blocking coalition. In this example, the AMS algorithm works most effectively when the probability to take worsening steps is close to 0. In contrast to AMS, the RII algorithm does not time out so often in this example.

As shown in Fig. 2, the RII algorithm works effectively when the noise parameter p lies between 0.4 and 0.6. This experiment shows that the noise parameter p has clearly effect on the performances of both algorithms, and thus must always be tuned to obtain optimal run-times.

5.2   Initial Starting Coalitions

The starting point of both algorithms AMS and RII is to determine an initial coalition to begin with the iteration. In our second series of experiments, we aim

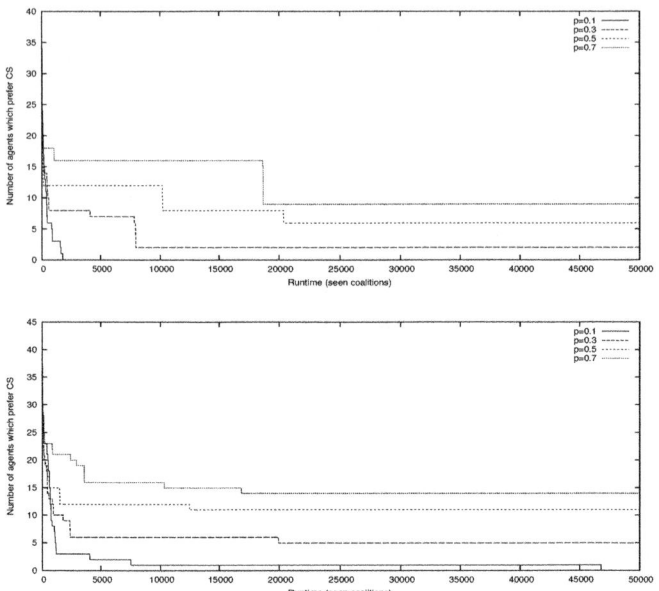

Fig. 1. Run-lengths for the AMS with different values of p, minima (top) and maxima (down) of 10 runs on an instance with 150 agents

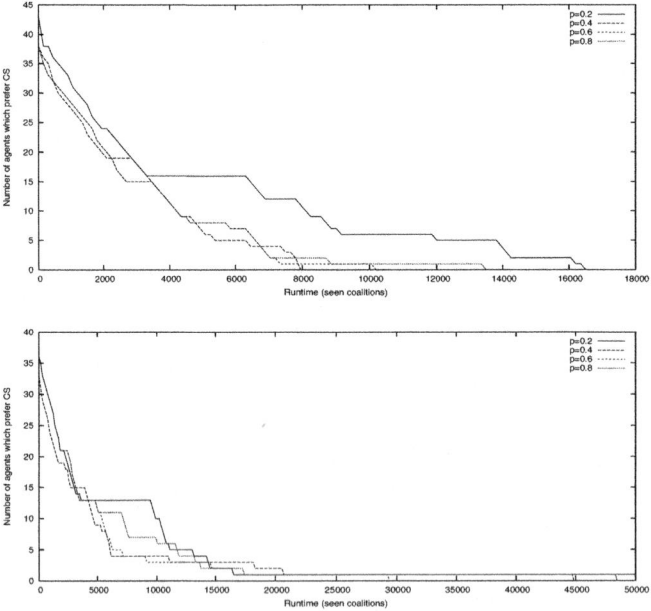

Fig. 2. Run-lengths for the RII with different values of p, minima (top) and maxima (down) of 10 runs on an instance with 150 agents

to find out what is the most beneficial way of determining initial coalitions for both algorithms.

As initial coalitions for the algorithms we use either any coalition selected uniformly at random or a singleton coalition consisting of 1 agent selected at random. To compare the run-lengths of the algorithms with the two different starting coalitions, we investigate the execution times to find a blocking coalition on 1000 randomly generated 150-agent game instances. The run-time limits are set to 100000 seen coalitions, and the algorithms are run with approximately optimal parameters, the AMS with $p = 0.1$ and the RII with $p = 0.5$.

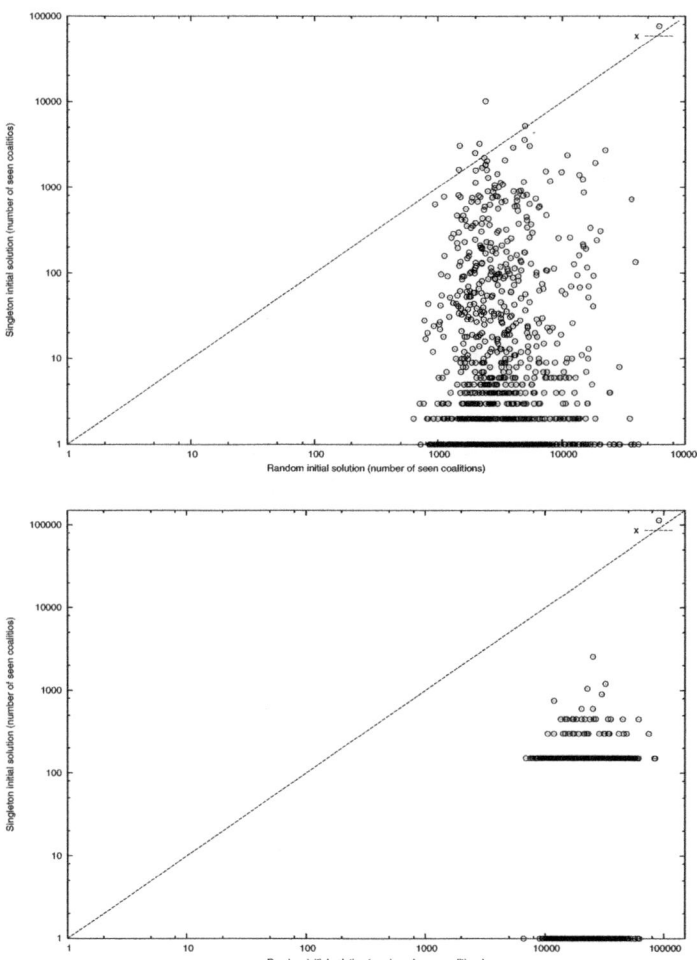

Fig. 3. AMS run-times to find a blocking coalition (top) and RII run-times to find a blocking coalition (down), 1000 instances with generic additive preferences, singleton coalition vs. random coalition as a starting point

Figure 3 shows the correlation between different algorithm variants on game instances with generic additive preferences. Figure 4 shows similar results on instances with aversion to enemies preferences. The results clearly show that the AMS with initial singleton coalition outperforms the AMS with a random initial coalition. The same observation holds for the RII, too. Consequently, choosing a singleton coalition as a starting point speeds up considerably both algorithms.

We conjecture that a blocking coalition is most likely to be found quickly with the AMS and RII algorithms, if the search for a blocking coalition starts from a very small coalition and a noise parameter p is used which keeps the checked coalitions rather small. This is due to the definition of the blocking

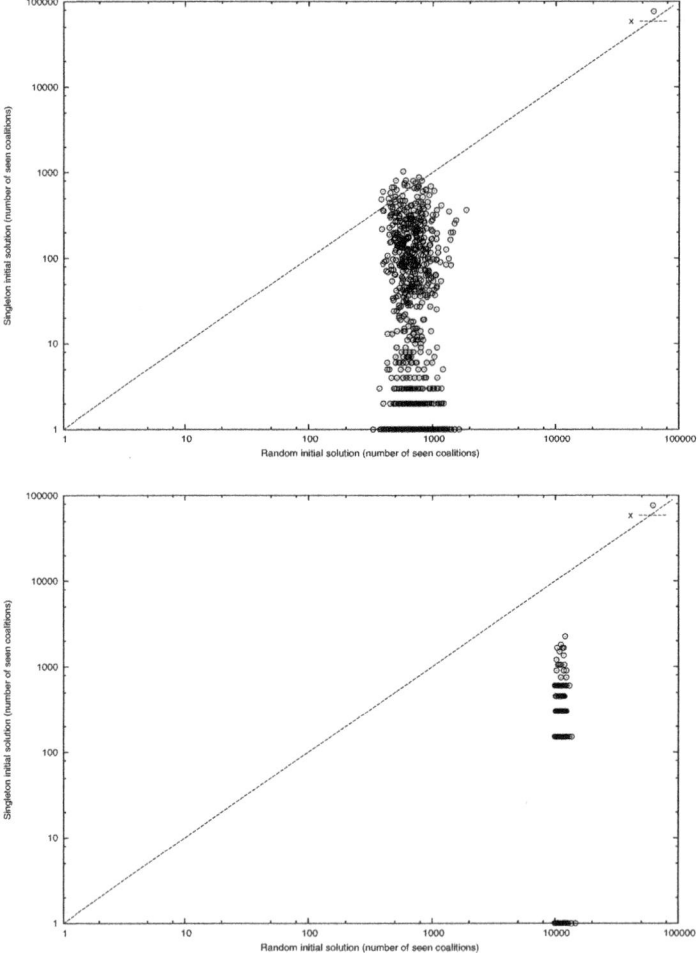

Fig. 4. AMS run-times to find a blocking coalition (top) and RII run-times to find a blocking coalition (down), 1000 instances with aversion to enemies preferences, single-ton coalition vs. random coalition as a starting point

coalition which requires that every coalition member of a blocking coalition has to prefer the coalition over the given coalition structure. Any small coalition involves naturally only a few agents who need to comply with this requirement.

5.3   Runtime and Robustness Comparisons

To systematically compare the AMS algorithm with the RII algorithm on large agent societies, we conducted further experiments on problems with sizes 1000/ 2000/ 3000/ 4000/ 5000 agents, 100 instances per size for both random and aversion to enemies preferences. The run-time limit for both algorithms is set to 100000 coalitions. For both algorithms with a singleton initial coalition and both preference profile classes, Table 1 summarises run-time characteristics achieved in these tests. For each problem size ($|N|$ number of agents), we show the minimum, median and maximum run-lengths for both algorithms, on 100 instances, each instance run 11 times per algorithm. For both algorithms, minimum run-times are very small considering the large sizes of the agent societies and astronomical sizes of the underlying search spaces ($2^{|N|}$). Notice that median run-times are significantly lower for the AMS than for the RII because the latter always checks the whole neighbourhood. As shown in Table 1, in the case of games with generic additive preferences the AMS often times out already for 1000 agent games while the RII always finds a blocking coalition. Hence, the RII algorithm is more robust on these problems.

Table 1. Statistics for AMS and RII run-lengths, 11 runs on 100 instances per size (number of agents), - stands for time-out with limit 100000 seen coalitions

Size	Aversion to Enemies preferences						Generic preferences					
	AMS			RII			AMS			RII		
	min	med	max	min	med	max	min	med	max	min	med	max
1000	1	4	4932	1	1001	26001	1	3	-	1	1001	19001
2000	1	3	10430	1	2001	26001	1	3	-	1	2001	10001
3000	1	27	22074	1	3001	42001	1	4	-	1	3001	39001
4000	1	4	25302	1	4001	72001	1	3	-	1	4001	36001
5000	1	4	41322	1	5001	50001	1	4	-	1	5001	-

Finally, we have studied variation of run-lengths in terms of probability to find a blocking coalition using the AMS and the RII algorithms. For this purpose we run 100 times both algorithms on two hard 1000-agent hedonic game instances, one instance with generic additive preference profiles the other with aversion to enemies preferences.

Figures 5 and 6 show the probabilities to find a blocking coalition over running times, the AMS is run with $p = 0.6$ and the RII with $p = 0.005$ which are approximately optimal for these particular instances. As can be seen from these plots, run-length variation is quite small for 100 runs of the RII on 1 instance. We observe that in games with generic additive preferences the variation of

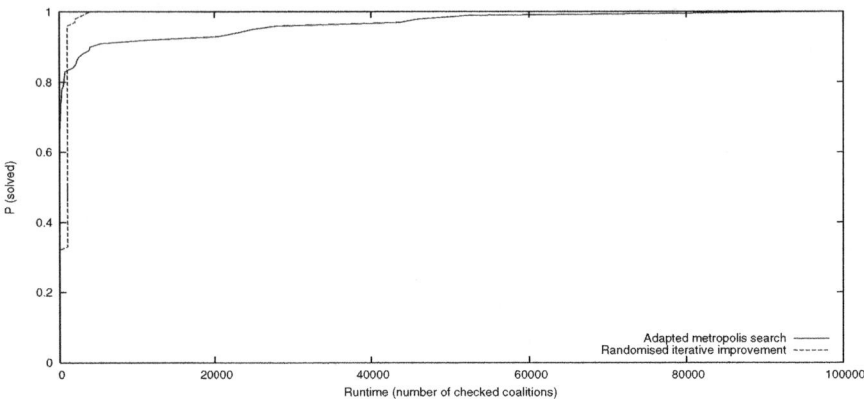

Fig. 5. Probability to find a blocking coalition, 100 runs on a hard instance with 1000 agents and generic additive preferences

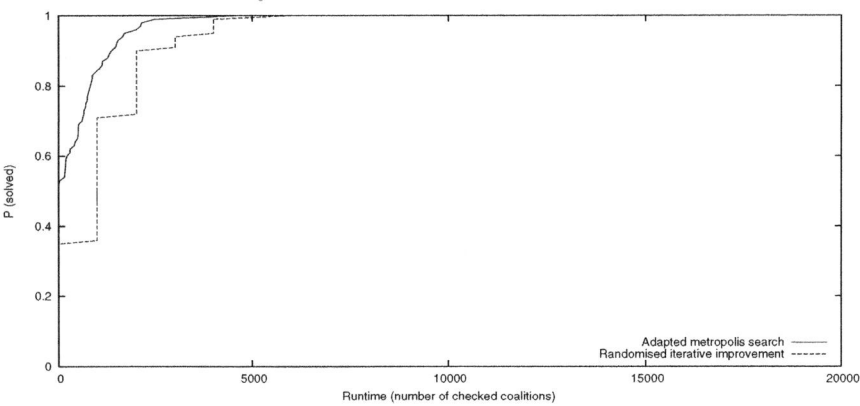

Fig. 6. Probability to find a blocking coalition, 100 runs on a hard instance with 1000 agents and aversion to enemies preferences

running times is significantly greater for the AMS than for the RII algorithm, as illustrated in Fig. 5. One may thus prefer to use the RII instead of the AMS in checking the core membership in additive hedonic games.

6   Related Work

Originally, hedonic coalitional games have mainly been studied by economists. More recently, these games have been studied also in the multi-agent systems and artificial intelligence research area. Initial research on hedonic games in

[5, 8, 9] focused mainly on defining the formal model for hedonic games as well as on determining the sufficient conditions for the existence of stable coalition structures in hedonic settings.

There are various succinct or complete representations for hedonic preferences in the literature. The two main lines of research representing hedonic preferences are as follows. Firstly, we can represent the hedonic preferences such that the representation scheme is a always concise. One way to do this is to represent the hedonic preferences as additively separable preferences [1, 8, 9] which requires only a space quadratic in the number of agents. Also, one can represent the preferences succinctly by B- and W-preferences introduced in [14, 15]. A drawback to these kinds of representations is that they are incomplete, meaning that not all preference profiles can be captured. Secondly, there exist representations for hedonic preferences that are complete but not necessarily always succinct. An example is the individually rational coalition list representation in [6]. Hedonic nets [16] provide an alternative, complete representation scheme for preferences in hedonic games. The main difficulty with these kinds of complete representation schemes is that the lengths of the preference lists can be exponential in the number of agents in the worst case.

There exists several computational complexity results related to hedonic games. The core membership is known to be decidable in polynomial time, if the preferences are represented as individually rational coalition lists [6]. However, as the lengths of the preference lists can be exponential in the number of agents, this representation scheme is not very attractive in all contexts. Also, it is known that the problem of core membership checking of a given partition with additively separable preferences is $coNP$-complete [1]. Furthermore, the core membership checking problem is shown $coNP$-complete for hedonic nets [16].

Stochastic local search techniques have successfully been used to solve many decision and optimisation problem occurring in artificial intelligence and in operation research. However, in game theoretic settings these methods have not been applied very often. For example, an application of a stochastic local search algorithm to combinatorial auctions is reported in [17].

7   Conclusions

We have presented two algorithms for the core membership checking problem in hedonic games. The algorithms are based on different stochastic local search heuristics which aim to find rapidly an agent coalition which serves as a counterexample for the stability of a given coalition structure in a hedonic game instance. We show through extensive practical experiments how the presented algorithms can be used most effectively to solve hard core membership checking problems. In future work, we plan to devise special purpose algorithms to generate from a given hedonic game a coalition structure residing in the core.

References

1. Sung, S.C., Dimitrov, D.: On core membership testing for hedonic coalition formation games. Operations Research Letters 35, 155–158 (2007)
2. Gillies, D.: Solutions to general non-zero-sum games. In: Tucker, A.W., Luce, R.D. (eds.) Contributions to the Theory of Games, vol. 4, pp. 47–85. Princeton University Press, Princeton (1959)
3. Conitzer, V., Sandholm, T.: Complexity of constructing solutions in the core based on synergies among coalitions. Artificial Intelligence 170, 607–619 (2006)
4. Malizia, E., Palopoli, L., Scarcello, F.: Infeasibility certificates and the complexity of the core in coalitional games. In: Veloso, M.M. (ed.) IJCAI, pp. 1402–1407 (2007)
5. Drèze, J.H., Greenberg, J.: Hedonic optimality and stability. Econometrica 4, 987–1003 (1980)
6. Ballester, C.: NP-completeness in hedonic games. Games and Economic Behavior 49, 1–30 (2004)
7. Alcalde, J., Romero-Medina, A.: Coalition formation and stability. Social Choice and Welfare 27, 365–375 (2006)
8. Banerjee, S., Konishi, H., Sonmez, T.: Core in a simple coalition formation game. Social Choice and Welfare 18, 135–153 (2001)
9. Bogomolnaia, A., Jackson, M.O.: The stability of hedonic coalition structures. Games and Economic Behavior 38, 201–230 (2002)
10. Iehlé, V.: The core partition of hedonic games. Mathematical Social Sciences 54, 176–185 (2007)
11. Elkind, E., Wooldridge, M.: Hedonic coalition nets. In: AAMAS '09: Proceedings of The 8th International Conference on Autonomous Agents and Multiagent Systems, Richland, SC, International Foundation for Autonomous Agents and Multiagent Systems, pp. 417–424 (2009)
12. Metropolis, N., Rosenbluth, A., Rosenbluth, M., Teller, A., Teller, E.: Equations of state calculations by fast computing machines. J. Chem. Phys. 21, 1087–1092 (1953)
13. Kernighan, B.W., Ritchie, D.M.: The C Programming Language. Prentice Hall, Englewood Cliffs (1988)
14. Cechlárová, K., Hajduková, J.: Computational complexity of stable partitions with B-preferences. International Journal of Game Theory 31(3), 353–364 (2002)
15. Cechlárová, K., Hajduková, J.: Stable partitions with W-preferences. Discrete Applied Mathematics 138, 333–347 (2004)
16. Elkind, E., Chalkiadakis, G., Jennings, N.R.: Coalition structures in weighted voting games. In: Proc. of the 18th European Conf. on Artificial Intelligence, pp. 393–397. IOS Press, Amsterdam (2008)
17. Hoos, H.H., Boutilier, C.: Solving combinatorial auctions using stochastic local search. In: Proc. of the 7th National Conf. on Artificial Intelligence, pp. 22–29. AAAI Press, Menlo Park (2000)

A Different Perspective on a Scale for Pairwise Comparisons

J. Fülöp[1], W.W. Koczkodaj[2,*], and S.J. Szarek[3]

[1] Research Group of Operations Research and Decision Systems
Computer and Automation Research Institute
Hungarian Academy of Sciences
1518 Budapest, P.O. Box 63, Hungary
[2] Computer Science, Laurentian University
Sudbury, Ontario P3E 2C6, Canada
[3] Department of Mathematics
Case Western Reserve University
Cleveland, Ohio 44106-7058, USA &
Université Pierre et Marie Curie-Paris 6
75252 Paris, France

Abstract. One of the major challenges for collective intelligence is inconsistency, which is unavoidable whenever subjective assessments are involved. Pairwise comparisons allow one to represent such subjective assessments and to process them by analyzing, quantifying and identifying the inconsistencies.

We propose using smaller scales for pairwise comparisons and provide mathematical and practical justifications for this change. Our postulate's aim is to initiate a paradigm shift in the search for a better scale construction for pairwise comparisons. Beyond pairwise comparisons, the results presented may be relevant to other methods using subjective scales.

Keywords: Pairwise comparisons, collective intelligence, scale, subjective assessment, inaccuracy, inconsistency.

1 Introduction

Collective intelligence (CI) practitioners face many challenges as collaboration, especially involving highly trained intellectuals, is not easy to manage. One of the important aspects of collaboration is inconsistency arising from different points of view on the same issue. According to [33], "Inconsistent knowledge management (IKM) is a subject which is the common point of knowledge management and conflict resolution. IKM deals with methods for reconciling inconsistent content of knowledge. Inconsistency in the sense of logic has been known for a long time. Inconsistency of this kind refers to a set of logical formulae which have no common model." and "The need for knowledge inconsistency resolution arises in many practical applications of computer systems. This kind of inconsistency

---

* The corresponding author, wkoczkodaj at cs laurentian ca.

N.T. Nguyen and R. Kowalczyk (Eds.): Transactions on CCI I, LNCS 6220, pp. 71–84, 2010.

results from the use of various sources of knowledge in realizing practical tasks. These sources often are autonomous and they use different mechanisms for processing knowledge about the same real world. This can lead to inconsistency."

Unfortunately, inconsistency is often taken for a synonym of inaccuracy but it is a "higher level" concept. Inconsistency indicates that inaccuracy of some sort is present in the system. Certainly, inaccuracy by itself would not take place if we were aware of it. We will illustrate it in a humorous way. When a wrong phone call is placed, the caller usually apologizes by "I am sorry, I have the wrong number" and may hear in reply: "if it is a wrong number, why have you dialed it?" Of course we would have not dialed the number if we had known that it was wrong. In fact, the respondent is the one who detects the incorrectness, not the caller.

However, a self correction may also take place in some other cases, for example, via an analysis of our own assessments for inconsistency by comparing them in pairs. Highly subjective stimuli often are present in the assessment of public safety or public satisfaction. Similarly, decision making, as an outcome of mental processes (cognitive process), is also based on mostly subjective assessments for the selection of an action among several alternatives. We can compute the inconsistency indicator of our assessments (subjective or not) rarely getting zero which stands for fully consistent assessments.

As the membership function of a fuzzy set is a generalization of the indicator function in classical sets, the inconsistency indicator is related to the degree of contradictions existing in the assessments. In fuzzy logic, the membership function represents the degree of truth. Similarly, the inconsistency indicator is related to both the degree of inaccuracy and contradiction. Degrees of truth are often confused with probabilities, although they are conceptually distinct. Fuzzy truth represents membership in vaguely defined sets but not the likelihood of some event or condition. Likewise, the inconsistency indicator is not a probability of contradictions but the degree of contradiction.

In our opinion, pairwise comparisons method is one of the most feasible representations of collective intelligence. It also allows one to measure it, for example, by comparing CI with individual intelligence. (According to the online *Handbook of Collective Intelligence*, hosted at the website of MIT Center of Collective Intelligence `http://cci.mit.edu/research/index.html`, measuring CI is one of two main projects for developing theories of CI.) Pairwise comparisons are easy to use, but may require complex computations to interpret them properly. This is why we address the fundamental issue of scales of measure, which – in particular – may have an effect on feasibility of some computational schemes.

2   Pairwise Comparisons Preliminaries

Comparing objects and concepts in pairs can be traced to the origin of science or even earlier – perhaps to the stone age. It is not hard to imagine that our ancestors must have compared "chicken and fish", holding each of them in a separate hand, for trading purposes. The use of pairwise comparisons is still considered as one of the most puzzling, intriguing, and controversial scientific method although the first published use of pairwise comparisons (PC) is attributed to Condorcet in 1785 (see [12], four years before the French Revolution). Ramon Llull, or Raimundus Lullus designed an election method around 1275 in [30]. His approach promoted the use of pairwise comparisons. However, neither Llull nor Condorcet used a scale for pairwise comparisons.

Condorcet was the first who used a kind of binary version of pairwise comparisons to reflect the preference in the voting by the won-lost situation. In [37], a psychological continuum was defined by Thurstone in 1927 with the scale values as the medians of the distributions of judgments on the psychological continuum.

In [34], Saaty proposed a finite (nine point) scale in 1977. In [26], Koczkodaj proposed a smaller five point scale with the distance-based inconsistency indicator. This smaller scale better fits the heuristic *"off by one grade or less"* for the acceptable level of inconsistency proposed in [26]. We will show here that a new convexity finding for the first time supports the use of an even smaller scale.

Mathematically, an $n \times n$ real matrix $A = [a_{ij}]$ is a pairwise comparison (PC) matrix if $a_{ij} > 0$ and $a_{ij} = 1/a_{ji}$ for all $i, j = 1, \ldots, n$. Elements a_{ij} represent a result of (often subjectively) comparing the ith alternative (or stimuli) with the jth alternative according to a given criterion. A PC matrix A is consistent if $a_{ij}a_{jk} = a_{ik}$ for all $i, j, k = 1, \ldots, n$. It is easy to see that a PC matrix A is consistent if and only if there exists a positive n-vector w such that $a_{ij} = w_i/w_j, i, j = 1, \ldots, n$. For a consistent PC matrix A, the values w_i serve as priorities or implicit weights of the importance of alternatives.

3   The Pairwise Comparisons Scale Problem

Thurstone's approach was extensively analyzed and elaborated on in the literature, in particular by Luce and Edwards [28] in 1958. The bottom line is that subjective quantitative assessments are not easy to provide. Not only is the dependence between the stimuli and their assessments usually nonlinear, but the exact nature of the nonlinearity is in general unclear. In this context, a smaller scale is expected to generate a smaller error, for example by mitigating the deviation from nonlinearity.

On page 236 in [28], authors wrote: W.J. McGill is currently attempting to find a better way of respecting individual differences while still obtaining a "universal scale". Authors of this study have not been able to trace any publication of the late W.J. McGill on the "universal scale" construction. However, the proposed smaller scale may be at least some kind of temporary solution as a reflection of "the small is beautiful" movement inspired by Leopold Kohr by his opposition to the "cult of bigness" in social organization. The smaller five-point scale better fits the heuristic "off by one grade or less" for the acceptable level of the distance-based inconsistency (as proposed in [26]). We will show here that the new convexity finding, for the first time, supports the use of an even smaller scale.

There are strong opponents of the pairwise comparisons method going as far as opposing the use of pairwise comparisons altogether. However, they forget that every measurement, e.g., of length, is based on pairwise comparisons since we compare the measured object with some assumed unit. For example, one meter is the basic unit of length in the International System of Units (SI). It was literally defined as a distance between two marks on a platinum-iridium bar. Evidently, we are unable to eliminate pairwise comparisons from science hence we need to improve them. As we will demonstrate, it is the issue of scale (in other words the input data) and, as such, it cannot be ignored.

4   In Search of the Nearest Consistent Pairwise Comparisons Matrix

Several mathematical methods have been proposed for finding the nearest consistent pairwise comparisons matrix for a given inconsistent pairwise comparisons matrix. In [34], the eigenvector method was proposed in which w is the principal eigenvector of A. Another class of approaches is based on optimization methods and proposes different ways of minimizing (the size of) the difference between A and a consistent PC matrix. If the difference to be minimized is measured in the least-squares sense, i.e. by the Frobenius norm, then we get the Least Squares Method presented by Chu et al. [10]. The problem can be written in the mathematical form (we present the normalized version, see [20]):

$$\min \sum_{i=1}^{n} \sum_{j=1}^{n} \left(a_{ij} - \frac{w_i}{w_j} \right)^2$$

$$\text{s.t.} \sum_{i=1}^{n} w_i = 1, \tag{1}$$

$$w_i > 0, \quad i = 1, \dots, n.$$

Since the $n \times n$ matrices in the form of columnwise ordering can also be considered as n^2-dimensional vectors, (say, by stacking the columns over each other), problem (1) determines a consistent PC matrix closest to A in the sense of the Euclidean norm. Unfortunately, problem (1) may be a difficult nonconvex optimization problem with several possible local optima and with possible multiple isolated global optimal solutions [24, 25].

Some authors state that problem (1) has no special tractable form and is difficult to solve [10, 21, 31, 11]. In order to elude the difficulties caused by the nonconvexity of (1), several other, more easily solvable problem forms are proposed to derive priority weights from an inconsistent pairwise comparison matrix. The Weighted Least Squares Method [10, 3] in the form of

$$\min \sum_{i=1}^{n} \sum_{j=1}^{n} (a_{ij} w_j - w_i)^2$$

$$\text{s.t.} \sum_{i=1}^{n} w_i = 1, \tag{2}$$

$$w_i > 0, \quad i = 1, \dots, n$$

applies a convex quadratic optimization problem whose unique optimal solution is obtainable by solving a set of linear equations. The Logarithmic Least Squares Method [16, 13] in the form

$$\min \sum_{i=1}^{n} \sum_{i<j} \left[\log a_{ij} - \log\left(\frac{w_i}{w_j}\right) \right]^2$$

$$\text{s.t.} \quad \prod_{i=1}^{n} w_i = 1, \tag{3}$$

$$w_i > 0, \quad i = 1, \ldots, n$$

is (because of constraints being linearizable) a simple optimization problem whose unique solution is the geometric mean of the rows of matrix A. For further approaches, see [5, 17, 20] and the references therein. However, we have to emphasize that the main purpose of many (if not most) optimization approaches was to exclude the difficulties caused by the possible nonconvexity of problem (1). It was usually done by sacrificing the natural approach of the Euclidean distance minimization.

As with many other real-life situations, there is no possibility to decide which solution is the best without a clear objective function. For example, a "Formula One" car is not the best vehicle for a family with five children but it may be hard to win a Grand Prix race with a family van. In fact, pairwise comparisons could be used for solving the dilemma of which approximation solution is the best for PC (and for the family transportation problem).

The distance minimization approach (1) is so natural that one may wonder why it was only recently revived in [5]. The considerable computational complexity (100 hours CPU time for $n = 8$) and the possibility of having multiple solutions (and/or multiple local minima) may be the reasonable explanation for not becoming popular in the past. Problem (1) has recently been solved in [1] by reducing 100 hours of CPU (or more likely, 150 days of the CPU time) to milliseconds. It was asserted in [4, 24, 25] that the multiple solutions are far enough from the ones that appear in the real-life situations. However, it appears that these assertions are mostly based on anecdotal evidence. More (numerical and/or analytical) research to elucidate this point would be helpful.

As proved by Fülöp [20], the necessary condition for the multiple solutions to appear is that the elements of the matrix A are large enough. In [20], using the classic logarithmic transformation

$$t_i = \log w_i, \quad i = 1, \ldots, n,$$

and the univariate function

$$f_a(t) = \left(e^t - a\right)^2 + \left(e^{-t} - 1/a\right)^2 \tag{4}$$

depending on the real parameter a, problem (1) can be transformed into the equivalent form

$$\min \ \sum_{i=1}^{n-1} f_{a_{in}}(t_i) + \sum_{i=1}^{n-2} \sum_{j=i+1}^{n-1} f_{a_{ij}}(t_{ij}) \tag{5}$$
$$\text{s.t.} \ \ t_i - t_j - t_{ij} = 0, \ i = 1, \ldots, n-2, \ j = i+1, \ldots, n-1.$$

It was also proved in [20], there exists an $a_0 > 1$ such that for any $a > 0$ the univariate function f_a of (4) is strictly convex if and only if $1/a_0 \le a \le a_0$. Consequently, in the case when the condition $1/a_0 \le a_{ij} \le a_0$ is fulfilled for all i, j, then (1) can be transformed into the convex programming problem (5) with a strictly convex objective function to be minimized (see [20], Proposition 2). In other words, problem (1) and the equivalent problem (5) have a unique solution which can be found using standard local search methods. The above-mentioned constant equals to $a_0 = ((123 + 55\sqrt{(5)})/2)^{1/4} = \sqrt{\frac{1}{2}\left(11 + 5\sqrt{5}\right)} \approx 3.330191$, which is a reasonable bound for many real-life problems. The above a_0 is not necessarily a strict threshold since its proof is based on the convexity of univariate functions (see [20], Proposition 2, or see the Appendix of the present paper for a compact low-tech argument) and it is conceivable that the exact threshold for the sum of univariate functions is greater than a_0. We know, however, that this threshold must be less than $a_1 \approx 3.6$ since, as shown by Bozóki [4], for any $\lambda > a_1$ it is easy to construct a 3×3 PC matrix with λ as the largest element and with multiple local minima. Finally, even if some elements of a PC matrix are relatively large, it may still happen that (1) has a single local minimum; a sample sufficient condition is given in Corollary 2 of [20].

A nonlinear programing solver (available in Excel and described in [1]) is good enough if (1) has a single local minimum for a given a PC matrix A. Our incentive for postulating a restricted ratio scale for pairwise comparisons comes both from the guaranteed uniqueness in the interval determined in [20] and from demonstrably possible (by [4]) non-uniqueness outside of a just slightly larger interval.

There have been several inconsistency indicators proposed. The distance-based inconsistency (introduced in [26]) is the maximum over all triads $\{a_{ik}, a_{kj}, a_{ij}\}$ of elements of A (with all indices i, j, k distinct) of their inconsistency indicators defined as:

$$\min \left(|1 - \frac{a_{ij}}{a_{ik}a_{kj}}|, |1 - \frac{a_{ik}a_{kj}}{a_{ij}}| \right)$$

Convergence of this inconsistency was finally provided in [27] (an erlier attempt in [22] had a hole in the proof of Theorem 1). A modification of the distance-based inconsistency was proposed in 2002 in [18]. Analysis of the eigenvalue-based and distance-based inconsistencies was well presented in [6]. Paying no attention to what we really process to get the best approximation, brings us what GIGO, the informal rule of "garbage in, garbage out", so nicely illustrates. This is why localizing the inconsistency and reducing it is so important.

5 The Scale Size Problem

As of today, the scale size problem for the PC method has not been properly addressed. We postulate the use of a smaller rather than larger scale and more research to validate it.

As mentioned earlier, an interesting property of PC matrices has been recently found in [20]. Namely, (1) has a unique local (thus global) optimal solution and it can be easily obtained by local search techniques if $1/a_0 \leq a_{ij} \leq a_0$ holds for all $i, j = 1, \ldots, n$, where the value a_0 is at least 3.330191 (but can not be larger than $a_1 \approx 3.6$, see [4]). In our opinion, this finding has a fundamental importance for construction of any scale and we postulate the scale 1 to 3 (1/3 to 1 for inverses) should be carefully looked at before a larger scale is considered. In the light of the property from [20], finding the solution of (1) would be easier and faster. This fact should shift the research of pairwise comparisons back toward (1) for approximations of inconsistent PC matrices. This is a starting point for the distance minimization approaches. It is worth to note that PC method is for processing subjectivity expressed by quantitative data. For purely quantitative data (reflecting objectively measurable even if possibly uncertain quantities), there are usually more precise methods (e.g., equations, systems of linear equations, PDEs just to name a few of them). In general, we are better prepared for processing quantitative data (e.g., real numbers) than for qualitative data.

A comparative scale is an ordinal or rank order scale that can also be referred to as a non-metric scale. Respondents evaluate two or more objects at a time and objects are directly compared with one to another as part of the measuring process. In practice, using a moderate scale for expressing preferences makes perfect sense. When we ask someone to express his/her preference on the 0 to 100 scale, the natural tendency is to use numbers rounded to tens (e.g., 20, 40, 70,...) rather than by using finer numbers. In fact, there are situations, such as being pregnant or not, with practically nothing between. The theory of scale types was proposed by Stevens in [36]. He claimed that any measurement in science was conducted using four different types of scales that he called "nominal", "ordinal", "interval", and "ratio".

Measurement is defined as "the correlation of numbers with entities that are not numbers" by the representational theory in [32]. In the additive conjoint measurement (independently discovered by the economist Debreu in [15] and by the mathematical psychologist Luce and statistician Tukey in [29]), numbers are assigned based on correspondences or similarities between the structure of number systems and the structure of qualitative systems. A property is quantitative if such structural similarities can be established. It is a stronger form of representational theory than of Stevens, where numbers need only be assigned according to a rule. Information theory recognizes that all data are inexact and statistical in nature. Hubbard in [23], characterizes measurement as: "A set of observations that reduce uncertainty where the result is expressed as a quantity."

In practice, we begin a measurement with an initial guess as to the value of a quantity, and then, by using various methods and instruments, try to reduce the uncertainty in the value. The information theory view, unlike the positivist representational theory, considers all measurements to be uncertain. Instead of assigning one value, a range of values is assigned to a measurement. This approach also implies that there is a continuum between estimation and measurement.

The Rasch model for measurement seems to be the relevant to PC with the decreased scale. He uses a logistic function (or logistic curve, the most common sigmoid curve): $P(t) = \frac{1}{1+e^{-t}}$. Coincidentally, the exponential function was used in [20] for his estimations of the upper bound of a_{ij}.

We mentioned that the phenomenon of the scale reduction appears implicitly in the Logarithmic Least Squares Method [16, 13] as well. It is easy to see that in problem (3), it is not the original PC matrix A which is approximated but $\log A$ which consists of the entries $\log a_{ij}$.

6   An Example of a Problem Related to Using Two Scales

Let us look at two scales: 1 to 5 and 1 to 3:

Bigger scale	1	2	**3**	4	5
Smaller scale	1	1.5	**2**	2.5	3

The inconsistent pairwise comparisons table for the 1 to 5 scale generated by the triad $[3, 5, 3]$ is:

1	3	5
$\frac{1}{3}$	1	3
$\frac{1}{5}$	$\frac{1}{3}$	1

The inconsistency of this table is computed by $(\min(|1 - \frac{5}{3*3}|, |1 - \frac{3*3}{5}|)$ as 4/9.

The triad $[3, 5, 3]$ consists of the top scale value in the middle and the middle scale value as the first and last values of the triad. Similarly, the inconsistent pairwise comparisons table for the 1 to 3 scale generated by the triad $[2, 3, 2]$ is:

1	2	3
$\frac{1}{2}$	1	2
$\frac{1}{3}$	$\frac{1}{2}$	1

The inconsistency of this table is computed by $(\min(|1 - \frac{3}{2*2}|, |1 - \frac{2*2}{3}|))$ as 0.25.

The middle value in the triad $[2, 3, 2]$ is the upper bound of the scale 1 to 3. The other two values (2) are equal to the middle point value of the scale 1 to 3. The same goes for all values of the triad $[3, 5, 3]$ on the scale 1 to 5 hence we can see that they somehow correspond to each other yet the inconsistencies are drastically different from each other and clearly unacceptable for the heuristic assumed in [26] of $\frac{1}{3}$ for the first table and acceptable for the second table. Needless to say, there is no canonical mapping from the scale 1 to 5 to the scale 1 to 3. The table proposed above is admittedly ad hoc and we present it for demonstration purposes only.

Evidently, more research is needed for this not so recent problem. In all likelihood, it was mentioned for the first time in [28] in 1958. Most real-life projects using the pairwise comparisons method are impossible to replicate or compute for the new scale as the costs of such exercise would be substantial. It may take some time before a project with a double scale is launched and completed.

7   The Power of the Number Three

The "use of three" for a comparison scale has a reflection in real life. Probably the greatest support for the use of three as the upper limit for a scale comes from the grammar. Our spoken and written language has evolved for thousands of years and grammar is at the core of each modern language. In his 1946 textbook [8] (which also nicely describes the degree of comparisons as they may be used in PC), Bullions defines comparisons of adjectives in as:

> Adjectives denoting qualities or properties capable of increase, and so of existing in different degrees, assume different forms to express a greater or less degree of such quality or property in one object compared with another, or with several others. These forms are three, and are appropriately denominated the positive, comparative, and superlative. Some object to the positive being called a degree of comparison, because in its ordinary use it does not, like the comparative and superlative forms, necessarily involve comparison. And they think it more philosophical to say, that the degrees of comparison are only two, the comparative and superlative. This, however, with the appearance of greater exactness is little else than a change of words, and a change perhaps not for the better. If we define a degree of comparison as a form of the adjective which necessarily implies comparison, this change would be just, but this is not what grammarians mean, when they say there are three degrees of comparison. Their meaning is that there are three forms of the adjective, each of which, when comparison is intended, expresses a different degree of the quality or attribute in the things compared: Thus, if we compare wood, stone, and iron, with regard to their weight, we would say "wood is heavy, stone heavier, and iron is the heaviest."
>
> Each of these forms of the adjective in this comparison expresses a different degree of weight in the things compared, the positive heavy expresses one degree, the comparative heavier, another, and the superlative heaviest, a third, and of these the first is as essential an element in the comparison as the second, or the third. Indeed there never can be comparison without the statement of at least two degrees, and of these the positive form of the adjective either expressed or implied, always expresses one. When we say "wisdom is more precious than rubies," two degrees of value are compared, the one expressed by the comparative, "more precious," the other necessarily implied. The meaning is "rubies are precious, wisdom is more precious." Though, therefore, it is

true, that the simple form of the adjective does not always, nor even commonly denote comparison, yet as it always does indicate one of the degrees compared whenever comparison exists, it seems proper to rank it with the other forms, as a degree of comparison. This involves no impropriety, it produces no confusion, it leads to no error, it has a positive foundation in the nature of comparison, and it furnishes an appropriate and convenient appellation for this form of the adjective, by which to distinguish it in speech from the other forms.

8   Conclusions and Final Remarks

Expressing subjective assessments with a high accuracy is really impossible, therefore a small comparison scale is appropriate. For example, expressing our pain on the scale of 1 to 100, or even 1 to 10, seems more difficult – and arguably less meaningful – than on the scale of 1 to 3. In the past, the scale 1 to 9 was proposed in [34] and 1 to 5 in [26]. In this study, we have demonstrated that the use of the smaller 1 to 3 scale, rather than larger ones, has good mathematical foundations.

More research needs to be conducted along the measurement theory lines of [36], but with emphasis on PC. In our opinion, playing endlessly with numbers and symbols to find a precise solutions for inherently ill-defined problems should be replaced by more research towards utilization of the choice theory in pairwise comparisons. The presented strong mathematical evidence supports the use of a more restricted scale. We would like to encourage other researchers to conduct Monte Carlo simulations with the proposed scale and to compare the results with those yielded by other approaches. In particular, it would be useful to investigate more closely the relationship between the degree of inconsistency of a PC matrix, the size of the scale and the possible existence of multiple local or global optima for the Least Squares Method (cf. [4, 24, 25]).

The use of large scales (e.g., 1 to 10 in medicine for the pain level specification routinely asked in all Canadian hospitals upon admitting an emergency patient if he/she is still capable of talking) is a crown example of how important this problem may be for the improvement of daily life. Making inferences on the basis of meaningless numbers might have pushed other patients further in usually long emergency lineups.

Although the theoretical basis for suggesting the scale 1 to 3 hinges on the value of the constant $a_0 = \sqrt{\frac{1}{2}\left(11 + 5\sqrt{5}\right)} \approx 3.330191$, the importance of which was established in [20] in the context of pairwise comparisons, its applicability to the universal subjective scale is a vital possibility worth further scientific examination.

Acknowledgments

This research has been supported in part by OTKA grants K 60480, K 77420 in Hungary. Acting in the spirit of collective intelligence, we acknowledge that there are so many individuals involved in the development of our approach and in the publication process that naming them could bring us beyond the publisher's page limit.

References

[1] Anholcer, M., Babiy, V., Bozóki, S., Koczkodaj, W.W.: A simplified implementation of the least squares solution for pairwise comparisons matrices. Central European Journal of Operations Research (to appear)

[2] Basile, L., D'Apuzzo, L., Marcarelli, G., Squillante, M.: Generalized Consistency and Representation of Preferences by Pairwise Comparisons. In: Panamerican Conference of Applied Mathematics, Huatulco, Mexico (2006)

[3] Blankmeyer, E.: Approaches to consistency adjustments. Journal of Optimization Theory and Applications 54, 479–488 (1987)

[4] Bozóki, S.: A method for solving LSM problems of small size in the AHP. Central European Journal of Operations Research 11, 17–33 (2003)

[5] Bozóki, S.: Solution of the least squares method problem of pairwise comparisons matrices. Central European Journal of Operations Research 16, 345–358 (2008)

[6] Bozóki, S., Rapcsák, T.: On Saaty's and Koczkodaj's inconsistencies of pairwise comparison matrices. Journal of Global Optimization 42(2), 157–175 (2007)

[7] Brunelli, M., Fedrizzi, M.: Fair Consistency Evaluation in Fuzzy Preference Relations and in AHP. In: Apolloni, B., Howlett, R.J., Jain, L. (eds.) KES 2007, Part II. LNCS (LNAI), vol. 4693, pp. 612–618. Springer, Heidelberg (2007)

[8] Bullions, P.: The Principles of English Grammar, 16th edn. Pratt, Woodford, & Co. (1846)

[9] Cavallo, B., D'Apuzzo, L.: A general unified framework for pairwise comparison matrices in multicriterial methods. International Journal of Intelligent Systems 24(4), 377–398 (2009)

[10] Chu, A.T.W., Kalaba, R.E., Spingarn, K.: A comparison of two methods for determining the weight belonging to fuzzy sets. Journal of Optimization Theory and Applications 4, 531–538 (1979)

[11] Choo, E.U., Wedley, W.C.: A common framework for deriving preference values from pairwise comparison matrices. Computers and Operations Research 31, 893–908 (2004)

[12] Condorcet, M.: Essai sur l'Application de l'Analyse à la Probabilité des Décisions Rendues à la Pluralité des Voix, Paris (1785)

[13] Crawford, G., Williams, C.: A note on the analysis of subjective judgment matrices. Journal of Mathematical Psychology 29, 387–405 (1985)

[14] D'Apuzzo, L., Marcarelli, G., Squillante, M.: Generalized consistency and intensity vectors for comparison matrices. International Journal of Intelligent Systems 22(12), 1287–1300 (2007)

[15] Debreu, G.: Topological methods in cardinal utility theory. In: Arrow, K.J., Karlin, S., Suppes, P. (eds.) Mathematical Methods in the Social Sciences, pp. 16–26. Stanford University Press, Stanford (1960)

[16] De Jong, P.: A statistical approach to Saaty's scaling method for priorities. Journal of Mathematical Psychology 28, 467–478 (1984)

[17] Farkas, A., Lancaster, P., Rózsa, P.: Consistency adjustment for pairwise comparison matrices. Numer. Linear Algebra Applications 10, 689–700 (2003)

[18] Fedrizzi, M., Fedrizzi, M., Marques Pereira, R.A.: On the issue of consistency in dynamical consensual aggregation. In: Bouchon Meunier, B., Gutierrez Rios, J., Magdalena, L., Yager, R.R. (eds.) Technologies for Constructing Intelligent Systems. Studies in Fuzziness and Soft Computing, vol. 1, 89, pp. 129–137. Springer, Heidelberg (2002)

[19] Fedrizzi, M., Giove, S.: Incomplete pairwise comparison and consistency optimization. European Journal of Operational Research 183(1), 303–313 (2007)

[20] Fülöp, J.: A method for approximating pairwise comparison matrices by consistent matrices. Journal of Global Optimization 42, 423–442 (2008)

[21] Golany, B., Kress, M.: A multicriteria evaluation method for obtaining weights from ratio-scale matrices. European Journal of Operational Research 69, 210–220 (1993)

[22] Holsztynski, W., Koczkodaj, W.W.: Convergence of inconsistency algorithms for the pairwise comparisons. Information Processing Letters 59(4), 197–202 (1996)

[23] Hubbard, D.: How to measure anything. Wiley, Chichester (2007)

[24] Jensen, R.E.: Comparison of eigenvector, least squares, chi squares and logarithmic least squares methods of scaling a reciprocal matrix, working paper 153, Trinity, University (1983)

[25] Jensen, R.E.: Alternative scaling method for priorities in hierarchical structures. Journal of Mathematical Psychology 28, 317–332 (1984)

[26] Koczkodaj, W.W.: A new definition of consistency of pairwise comparisons. Mathematical and Computer Modelling 18(7), 79–84 (1993)

[27] Koczkodaj, W.W., Szarek, S.J.: On distance-based inconsistency reduction algorithms for pairwise comparisons. Logic Journal of IGPL (2010) (advance access published January 17, 2010)

[28] Luce, R.D., Edwards, W.: The derivation of subjective scales from just noticeable differences. Psychological Review 65(4), 222–237 (1958)

[29] Luce, R.D., Tukey, J.W.: Simultaneous conjoint measurement: a new scale type of fundamental measurement. Journal of Mathematical Psychology 1, 1–27 (1964)

[30] Llull, R.: Artifitium electionis personarum (before 1283)

[31] Mikhailov, L.: A fuzzy programming method for deriving priorities in the analytic hiarerchy process. Journal of the Operational Research Society 51, 341–349 (2000)

[32] Nagel, E.: Measurement. Erkenntnis 2(1), 313–335 (1931)

[33] Nguyen, N.T.: Advanced method in Inconsistency Knowledge Management, p. 356. Springer, Heidelberg (2008)

[34] Saaty, T.L.: A scaling method for priorities in hierarchical structures. Journal of Mathematical Psychology 15, 234–281 (1977)

[35] Saaty, T.L.: The Analytic Hierarchy Process. McGraw-Hill, New York (1980)

[36] Stevens, S.S.: On the theory of scales of measurement. Science 103, 677–680 (1946)

[37] Thurstone, L.L.: A law of comparative judgement. Psychological Review 34, 278–286 (1927)

Appendix

After a change of variables to $t_j = \log w_j, j = 1, \ldots, n$, and a change in normalization to $\prod_{j=1}^n w_j = 1$, the problem (1) can be rewritten as

$$\min\{\sum_{i<j} \left(e^{t_i - t_j} - a_{ij}\right)^2 + \left(e^{-t_i + t_j} - 1/a_{ij}\right)^2 : t_1, \ldots, t_n \in \mathbb{R}, \sum_{i=1}^n t_i = 0\} \quad (6)$$

Our goal is to provide a streamlined version of the argument from [20] for showing that if a_{ij}'s are not "too large", then this minimization problem has a unique solution.

The existence part is easy: if the norm of $\mathbf{t} = (t_1, \ldots, t_n)$ tends to ∞, then – because of the constraint $\sum_{i=1}^n t_i = 0$ – we must have both $\max_i t_i \to +\infty$ and $\min_j t_j \to -\infty$, hence $t_i - t_j \to \infty$ for some i, j, which forces the objective function to go to ∞. This allows to reduce the problem to a compact subset of $\mathbb{R}^n$, where existence of a minimum follows from continuity of the objective function.

The uniqueness will follow if we show that the objective function in (6) – denote it by $\Phi = \Phi(t_1, \ldots, t_n)$ – is globally convex, and strictly convex when restricted to the hyperplane given by the constraint.

For $a > 0$ and $x \in \mathbb{R}$, we set $f_a(x) := (e^x - a)^2 + (e^{-x} - 1/a)^2$, then $\Phi = \sum_{i<j} f_{a_{ij}}(t_i - t_j)$. Our next goal is to show that if $a_0 := \sqrt{\frac{1}{2}\left(11 + 5\sqrt{5}\right)} \approx 3.33019$ and $a \in [1/a_0, a_0]$, then f_a is convex. Since a composition of a linear function with a convex function (in that order) is convex, it follows that if $\max_{ij} a_{ij} \le a_0$, then each term $f_{a_{ij}}(t_i - t_j)$ is convex, and so is Φ, the entire sum.

To that end, we calculate the second derivative of f_a and obtain

$$f_a''(x) = -2\left(a^2 e^x - 2a(e^{-2x} + e^{2x}) + e^{-x}\right)/a.$$

Roughly, f_a will be convex whenever the expression in the outer parentheses is negative (note that $a > 0$ by hypothesis). Given that the expression is a quadratic function in a, this will happen when a is between the roots of this function, which are easily calculated to be $\varphi(w) = (1 + w^4 - \sqrt{1 + w^4 + w^8})/w^3$ and $\psi(w) = (1 + w^4 + \sqrt{1 + w^4 + w^8})/w^3$, where $w = e^x > 0$. The graphs of the functions $a = \varphi(w)$ and $a = \psi(w)$ can be easily rendered (see Fig. 1). In particular, it is apparent that there is a nontrivial range of values of a, for which $\varphi(w) < a < \psi(w)$ for all $w > 0$, which implies that the corresponding f_a's are strictly convex on their entire domain $-\infty < x < \infty$. In view of symmetries of the problem, that range must be of the form $1/a_0 < a < a_0$, and it is clear from the picture that $a_0 > 3$. For the extreme values $a = a_0$ and $a = 1/a_0$, the second derivative of f_a will be strictly positive except at one point, which still implies strict convexity of f_a.

It is not-too-difficult to obtain more precise results, both numerically and analytically. For the latter, we check directly (or deduce from symmetries of f_a or f_a'') that $\varphi(1/w) = 1/\psi(w)$; this confirms that $a_0 := \inf \psi(w) = 1/\sup \varphi(w)$,

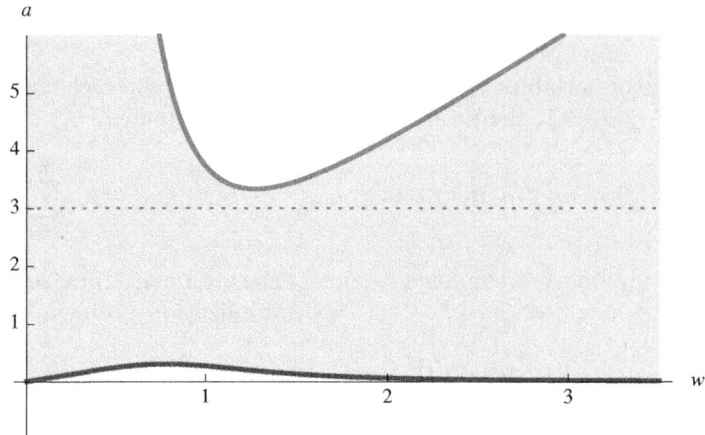

Fig. 1. The graphs of $a = \varphi(w)$, $a = \psi(w)$ and $a = 3$. The shaded region $\varphi(w) \leq a \leq \psi(w)$ corresponds to "regions of convexity" of the functions f_a.

and so it is enough to determine a_0. To apply the first derivative test to ψ, we calculate

$$w^4\,\psi'(w) = \frac{-3 - w^4 + w^8}{\sqrt{1 + w^4 + w^8}} + w^4 - 3.$$

While this looks slightly intimidating, it is not hard to check that the only positive zero of ψ' is $w_0 = \sqrt{\frac{1}{2} + \frac{\sqrt{5}}{2}} \approx 1.27202$, which also shows rigorously that ψ decreases on $(0, w_0)$ and increases on (w_0, ∞) (both strictly). Consequently, $a_0 = \psi(w_0) = \sqrt{\frac{1}{2}\left(11 + 5\sqrt{5}\right)}$, as asserted. All these calculations can be done by hand, or – much faster – using a computer algebra system such as *Mathematica*, *Maple*, or *Maxima*.

The above argument proves global convexity of Φ, it remains to show strict convexity on the hyperplane $\mathcal{H} = \{t = (t_i)_{i=1}^n \ : \ \sum_{i=1}^n t_i = 0\}$, which is equivalent to strict convexity of the restriction to any line contained in $\mathcal{H}$. Given such line $\lambda \to t + \lambda u$ (with $t, u \in \mathcal{H}, u \neq 0$ and $\lambda \in \mathbb{R}$), consider any pair of coordinates i, j such that $u_i - u_j \neq 0$ and the corresponding term in the sum defining Φ, namely $f_{a_{ij}}\big((t_i - t_j) + \lambda(u_i - u_j)\big) =: \phi(\lambda)$. Clearly $\phi''(\lambda) = (u_i - u_j)^2 f''_{a_{ij}}\big((t_i - t_j) + \lambda(u_i - u_j)\big) \geq 0$, and it can vanish for at most one value of λ (and only if $a_{ij} = a_0$ or $a_{ij} = 1/a_0$). Thus ϕ is strictly convex, and since all the other terms appearing in Φ are convex, it follows that the restriction of Φ to the line, and hence to $\mathcal{H}$, are strictly convex. It is also clear that if $\max_{i,j} a_{ij} < a_0$, the above argument yields a non-trivial lower bound on the positive-definiteness of the Hessian of the restriction of Φ to $\mathcal{H}$ (this issue has been elaborated upon in [20]), which in particular has consequences for the speed of convergence of algorithms solving (6).

An Awareness-Based Learning Model to Deal with Service Collaboration in Cloud Computing

Mauricio Paletta[1] and Pilar Herrero[2]

[1] Centro de Investigación en Informática y Tecnología de la Computación (CITEC)
Universidad Nacional Experimental de Guayana (UNEG)
Av. Atlántico, Ciudad Guayana, 8050, Venezuela
mpaletta@uneg.edu.ve
[2] Facultad de Informática, Universidad Politécnica de Madrid (UPM)
Campus de Montegancedo S/N; 28660; Madrid, Spain
pherrero@fi.upm.es

Abstract. Cloud computing addresses the use of scalable and often virtualized resources. It is based on service-level agreements that provide external users with services under request. Cloud computing is still evolving. New specific collaboration models among service providers are needed for enabling effective service collaboration, allowing the process of serving consumers to be more efficient. This paper presents AMBAR-C, an adaptation of AMBAR (Awareness-based learning Model for distriButive collAborative enviRonment) designed to allow nodes in a distributed environment to accomplish an effective collaboration among service providers in a "cloud" by means of a multi-agent architecture in which agents are aware of its surroundings throughout a parametrical and flexible use of this information. As occurs in AMBAR, AMBAR-C makes use of heuristic strategies to improve effectiveness and efficiency in collaborations of these particular environments.

Keywords: Collaboration, multi-agent system, awareness, learning, cloud computing.

1 Introduction

Cloud computing [1] is emerging as a new distributed system that works toward providing reliable, customized and QoS guaranteed dynamic computing environments for end-users. The success of achieving this goal in proper time (efficiency) and/or to obtain higher quality results (effectiveness) in these dynamic and distributed environments depends on implementing an appropriate collaboration model between service providers in the *cloud*. Moreover, this collaboration mechanism should include learning abilities necessary for the use of the previous experience acquired (from situations that occurred in the past) in order to improve newly required collaborations. Learning-based heuristic techniques seem to be a good alternative to achieve this goal.

N.T. Nguyen and R. Kowalczyk (Eds.): Transactions on CCI I, LNCS 6220, pp. 85–100, 2010.
© Springer-Verlag Berlin Heidelberg 2010

On the other hand, according to CSCW (Computer Supported Cooperative Work) awareness is a useful concept employed to achieve cooperation and collaboration in distributed environments because it increases communication opportunities [2]. A collaborative process is leaded by five processes [3, 4]: 1) co-presence, that gives the feeling that the user is in a shared environment with some other user at the same time; 2) awareness, a process where users recognize each other´s activities on the premise of co-presence; 3) communication; 4) collaboration, that together with communication permits users to collaborate with each other to accomplish the tasks and common goals; and 5) coordination which is needed to solve the conflicts towards effective collaborations.

In the same order of ideas, in CSCL (Computer Supported Collaborative Learning), awareness plays an important role as it promotes collaboration opportunities in a natural and efficient way [5] and improves the effectiveness of collaborative learning. Related to this, Gutwin et al identified the following types of awareness [6]: social, task, concept, workspace, and knowledge.

Moreover, SMI (Spatial Model of Interaction) [7] is one of the awareness models proposed as a way to obtain knowledge from the immediately closer world in collaborative virtual environments. It is based primarily on the use of a variety of mechanisms that were defined for this model and in addressing the interaction of nodes in a virtual environment. These are the concepts of medium, aura, focus, nimbus and awareness. The concept of awareness in this context, more explicitly awareness of interaction, is defined by quantifying the degree, nature and quality of the interaction between the elements of the environment.

By using an specific interpretation of the SMI-based awareness concept, AMBAR (Awareness-based learning Model for distriButive collAborative enviRonment) [8] was defined as a MAS-based learning collaboration model for distributed environments endowed with heuristic-based strategies. This model aims to approach the information of awareness in collaborations occurring in the environment for achieving the most appropriate future awareness situations. In this regard, this paper presents AMBAR-C, an adaptation of AMBAR aiming to be applied in *Cloud* environments.

The remainder of this paper is organized as follows. Some details of the AMBAR model are showed in section 2. Section 3 describes the adjustments that were made to AMBAR aiming to define AMBAR-C proposed in this paper. Details of the implementation and the validation of the model are showed in Section 4. Finally, the last section includes the conclusions and outgoing future research related to this work.

2   AMBAR: An Awareness-Based Learning Model for Collaborative Distributive Systems

This section presents some details of the AMBAR model. As can be seen in Fig. 1 AMBAR is structured by the following elements (more details are explained below in this section):

1) The awareness representation and the collaboration process associated with this representation.

2) An architecture used for designing the IA-Awareness intelligent agents (SOFIA).

3) A negotiation mechanism designed to deal with saturated conditions.

4) A mutual exclusion strategy to synchronize the use of critical sections.

5) A load-balancing strategy (CAwaSA).

6) Heuristic-based learning strategies (CAwANN).

7) A communication protocol that allows agents to exchange messages and therefore interact with each other.

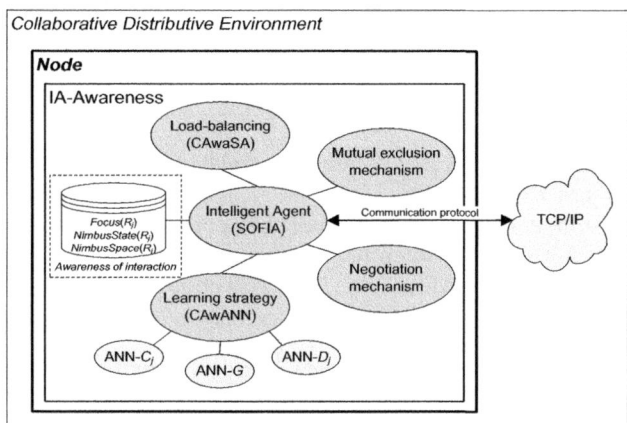

Fig. 1. The AMBAR structure

2.1 Awareness Representation and Collaboration Process

The collaborative process used in AMBAR and whose first results can be found in [9, 10, 11] uses the key awareness concepts originally proposed in [12, 13]. It has a distributed environment E containing a set of n nodes N_i ($1 \leq i \leq n$) and r different types of resources R_j ($1 \leq j \leq r$) that nodes can indifferently give to each other. These resources can be shared as a collaborative mechanism among different nodes. It has the following concepts:

1) $N_i.Focus(R_j)$: It is a set of resources which is interpreted as the subset of the distributed environment on which the agent in N_i has focused his attention aiming to interact or collaborate, according to the resource R_j.

2) $N_i.NimbusState(R_j)$: This indicates the current grade of collaboration that N_i can give over R_j. It could have three possible values: *Null, Medium* or *Maximum*. If the current grade of collaboration N_i that is given about R_j is not high, and this node could collaborate more over this resource, then $N_i.NimbusState(R_j)$ will get the *Maximum* value. If the current grade of collaboration N_i that is given over R_j is high but N_i could improve the collaboration over this service, then $N_i.NimbusState(R_j)$ would be *Medium*. Finally, $N_i.NimbusState(R_j)$ will be *Null* if N_i cannot offer R_j or if it cannot collaborate with this service any more.

3) $N_i.NimbusSpace(R_j)$: This represents the subset of the distributed environment where N_i aims to establish the collaboration over R_j.

4) $R_j.AwareInt(N_a, N_b)$: This concept quantifies the degree of collaboration over R_j between a pair of nodes N_a and N_b. It is manipulated via *Focus* and *Nimbus* (*State* and *Space*). Following the awareness classification introduced by Greenhalgh [14], values of this concept could be *Full*, *Peripheral* or *Null*. It is calculated according to (1).

$$R_j.AwareInt(N_a,N_b) = \begin{cases} Full, & N_b \in N_a.Focus(R_j) \wedge \\ & N_a \in N_b.NimbusSpace(R_j) \\ Peripheral, & (N_b \in N_a.Focus(R_j) \wedge \\ & N_a \notin N_b.NimbusSpace(R_j)) \vee \\ & (N_b \notin N_a.Focus(R_j) \wedge \\ & N_a \in N_b.NimbusSpace(R_j)) \\ Null, & \text{other case} \end{cases} \quad (1)$$

5) $N_i.TaskResolution(R_1,...,R_p)$: N_i requires collaboration with all R_j ($1 \le j \le p$) to solve a specific task T.

6) $N_i.CollaborativeScore(R_j)$: Determines the score to collaborate over R_j in N_i. It is represented with a value between [0, 1]. The closer the value is to 0 the hardest it will be for N_i to collaborate with the needed R_j. The higher the value is (closer to 1) the completer will the willingness to collaborate be.

Any node N_a in the distributive environment is endowed with an IA-Awareness agent, that has the corresponding information about E, i.e.: $N_a.Focus(R_j)$, $N_a.NimbusState(R_j)$ and $N_a.NimbusSpace(R_j)$ for each R_j. The collaborative process in the system is as follows:

1) N_b must solve a task T by means of a collaborative task-solving process making use of the resources $R_1,...,R_p$, and it generates a $N_b.TaskResolution(R_1,...,R_p)$.

2) N_b looks for the current conditions to calculate the values associated to the key concepts of the model (*Focus/Nimbus* related to the other nodes), given by $N_i.Focus(R_j)$, $N_i.NimbusState(R_j)$ and $N_i.NimbusSpace(R_j)$ ($1 \le i \le n$; $1 \le j \le r$). This information is used to decide the most suitable node with which to collaborate related with any resource R_j (by using the load-balancing strategy CAwaSA). Nodes in this particular environment respond to requests for information made by N_b. This is done through the exchange of messages between agents (by using the communication protocol). As a final result of this information exchange the model will calculate the current awareness levels given by $R_j.AwareInt(N_i, N_b)$ as well as the collaboration score given by $N_b.CollaborativeScore(R_j)$.

3) For each resource R_j ($1 \le j \le p$) included in $N_b.TaskResolution(R_1,...,R_p)$, N_b selects the node N_a whose $N_a.CollaborativeScore(R_j)$ is the most suitable to start the collaboration process (greatest score). Then, N_a will be the node in which N_b should collaborate on resource R_j.

4) Once N_a receives a request for cooperation, it updates its *Nimbus* (given by $N_a.NimbusState(R_j)$ and $N_a.NimbusSpace(R_j)$). In like manner, once N_a has finished collaborating with N_b it must update its *Nimbus*.

Each node in the system has an IA-Awareness agent designed to take into account the following features:

1) While each node may have different agents / processes, the IA-Awareness is the one that handles and manages the collaboration process; moreover, it learns to collaborate. In this sense, any need for cooperation from some source that is currently running on the node, communicates through the IA-Awareness service *TaskResolution*($R_1,...,R_p$). In response to this service, IA-Awareness returns a list of p nodes, one for each resource R_j, better suited to collaborate with the current node in relation with the corresponding R_j.

2) There are services (abilities) that report on current levels of *Focus*(R_j), *NimbusState*(R_j) and *NimbusSpace*(R_j) for a specific resource R_j.

3) Once all the necessary information is achieved, the search for the most suitable nodes to collaborate related with any R_j is done by using the service *FindSuitableNodes*($R_1,...,R_p$).

4) When conditions on the environment are not appropriated enough to establish a collaboration process ($N_i.NimbusState(R_j) = Null$ for most of the N_i, R_j), the nature of the node N_b initiating a collaborative process to answer a $N_b.TaskResolution(R_1,...,R_p)$ can lead to having no options, so that N_b can start a negotiation process that allows for N_b to identify new candidates to collaborate with. The detection of this saturated conditions is accomplished by using the service *IsOverloaded*(N, R).

5) The initiation and completion of the collaboration associated with the resource R is achieved through the implementation of services *StartCollaboration*(R) and *EndCollaboration*(R).

2.2 Agent Architecture

SOFIA (SOA-based Framework for Intelligent Agents) [10, 15] is the architecture used to design the IA-Awareness agents ("IA" stands for "Intelligent Agent"). It focuses on the design of a common framework for intelligent agents with the following characteristics: 1) it merges interdisciplinary theories, methods and approaches, 2) it is extensible and open as to be completed with new requirements and necessities, and 3) it highlights the agent´s learning processes within the environment. SOFIA's general architecture contains four main components (see Fig. 2):

1) The Embodied Agent (IA-EA) or the "body": It is a FIPA-based structure [16] because it has a Service Directory element which provides a location where specific and correspondent services descriptions can be registered. The IA-EA encloses the set of services related to the abilities of sensing stimuli from the environment and interacting with it.

2) The Rational Agent (IA-RA) or the "brain": This component represents the agent's intelligent part and therefore, it encloses the set of services used by the agent to implement the processes associated with these abilities. It is also a FIPA-based structure.

3) The Integrative/Facilitator Agent (IA-FA) or the "facilitator": It plays the role of simplifying the inclusion of new services into the system as well as the execution of each of them when they are needed. The basic function of the IA-FA is to coordinate the integration between the IA-SV and the rest of the IA components. This integration is needed when a new service is integrated with the IA and therefore it is registered into the corresponding Service Directory, even when an existing service is being executed.

4) The IA Services or "abilities" (IA-SV): It is a collection of individual and independent software components integrated to the system (the IA) which implements any specific ability either to the IA-EA or to the IA-RA.

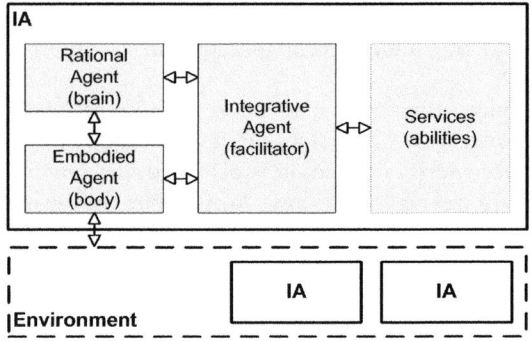

Fig. 2. The SOFIA general architecture

2.3 The Negotiation Mechanism

The negotiation mechanism included in AMBAR whose first results can be found in [17, 18] consists of three elements: 1) a heuristic algorithm used for deciding the most suitable node to initiate negotiation based on current conditions; 2) a heuristic method developed to accept/decline a need for collaboration during a negotiation; 3) a protocol for exchanging messages between agents.

For deciding the most suitable node to negotiate with, the idea is to define an unsupervised-based learning strategy aiming to correlate current information of the nodes in the distributive environment based on clusters. It is worth taking into account that "most suitable node" means a candidate that accepts the requirement established to collaborate with it, so that the negotiation is successful.

The basic idea is to find / identify a node N that is a potential candidate to negotiate with, taking into account the possibility to make changes in its *Nimbus* in relation with the resource R. N can then collaborate with this node in relation with R. "Potential" in this case means that N accepts to negotiate with the requesting node i.e. the negotiation is successful.

To achieve this goal a Neural-Gas (NGAS) [19] based strategy is used. The decision is to identify the closest node to the hyper-plane defined by the space given by the current environment conditions. In other words, it is necessary to determine the winning unit by testing the NGAS with the environment. The goal of this learning process is 1) to cluster the input data into a set of partitions such as the intra-cluster variance which remains small compared with the inter-cluster variance, and 2) to estimate the probability density function. This clustering scheme seems possible as we expect a strong correlation among the awareness information involved.

This learning strategy is a part of the mechanism that has been identified as CAwANN (Collaborative distributive environment by means of an Awareness & Artificial Neural Network model) [20]. In AMBAR the NGAS-based neural networks are identified as ANN-G (see Fig. 1).

Regarding accepting/declining collaboration, as with the decision of the most suitable node to negotiate with, this is also an Artificial Neural Network (ANN) based strategy. In this case there are s supervised ANN called ANN-D_j, one for each resource R_j in the system. All ANNs are defined in the same way and trained by using both Multi-Layer Perceptron (MLP) [21] and Radial Based Function Network (RBFN) [22] strategies.

2.4   The Mutual Exclusion Mechanism

The nature of a node initiating a collaborative process to answer a *TaskResolution*($R_1,...,R_p$), provokes a change in the conditions of the collaboration levels of the environmental nodes involved in the process. Since this information is required by the process of taking action, the levels of collaboration between the nodes turn to a critical section, so that a mutual exclusion mechanism is required. The strategy used in AMBAR is a variation of the Naimi-Tréhel's token-based algorithm [23]. In the AMBAR token-based approach [24], the token travels with a queue Q which has the nodes that require the exclusive use of the critical section and haven't been able to satisfy that need.

2.5   The Load-Balancing Strategy

It has a set of p resources R_j ($1 \leq j \leq p$). For each resource it must identify the most suitable node in the environment with which to collaborate according to the corresponding resource. "Most suitable" means that it should considers the following assumptions:

1) The node N_b that seeks collaboration should be on the *Focus* of the node N_a to be able to identify it, i.e. $N_b \in N_a.Focus(R_j)$.
2) The score of collaboration given by $N_a.CollaborativeScore(R)$ must indicate the full readiness to collaborate over R (value equal or close to 1).
3) The selection must be done so that there would be a load-balancing mechanism distributed equally among all possible nodes with which to collaborate. This should take into account the current environment conditions given by $N_i.NimbusState(R_j)$ and $N_i.NimbusSpace(R_j)$ $\forall i,j$ $1 \leq i \leq n$, $1 \leq j \leq r$.
4) The answer must be given in a reasonable time after the request is generated.

Strategy used to solve this problem is based in the Simulated Annealing (SA) [25, 26] technique which is a generalization of a Monte Carlo method that searchs for a minimum in a more general system forming the basis of an optimization technique to solve combinatorial and other problems. This strategy is called CAwaSA (Collaborative Distributive Environment by means of Awareness and SA) and its first results can be found in [27].

2.6   Heuristic-Based Learning Strategies

In addition to the unsupervised-based method for selecting a potential candidate to negotiate on saturated conditions and the supervised-based method to learn the decision of whether or not a node must change the information that describes its current conditions related with collaboration, AMBAR also incorporates a supervised-based method for learning collaborations based on levels of awareness. This process is about learning the association between the current status of the environment and the levels of collaboration obtained from that specific situation given by the $N_i.CollaborativeScore(R_j)$ ($\forall i$, $1 \le i \le n$ y $\forall j$, $1 \le j \le r$). The ANNs used in this solution are called ANN-C and, as happens with the ANN-D_j, the ANN-C are defined by using both MLP and RBFN strategies.

To differentiate one resource from another, given the fact that each service can have a different treatment in the levels of collaboration, the IA-Awareness has a different ANN-C_j network for each resource R_j. This is an important aspect of the strategy because:

1) Each resource can be trained separately from the rest.

2) The training process is less complex and, therefore, it is expected to obtain a higher quality in the response given by each ANN-C_j.

3) The model is expansible because new ANNs can be added when a new resource has to be incorporated into the environment.

4) Each node has a particular set of ANN-C_j, i.e. the IA-Awareness of each node trains and uses this ANNs according to the particular treatment a node wants to give to each resource R_j, making the collaboration model more flexible.

2.7 The Communication Protocol

Messages for AMBAR-based agent interaction are defined according to the FIPA performative and used for: 1) querying the current conditions of each node in the environment given by its *Focus/Nimbus*; 2) performing the mutual exclusion mechanism; 3) performing the negotiation mechanism; and 4) informing the initiation and completion of the collaboration associated with a particular resource. There are in total ten different messages.

The seven elements previously identified and briefly explained are those in which AMBAR is structured and IA-Awareness agents are defined, which are the basic components of the simulation tool proposed in this paper. The next section describes the proposed changes that were made to AMBAR to adapt this model to *cloud* environments in order to obtain the proposed AMBAR-C.

3 AMBAR-C: An Awareness-Based Learning Model for Service Collaboration in Cloud Computing

This section presents the differences between AMBAR and AMBAR-C explained here in order to offer a learning model for service collaboration in *cloud* environments. In this regard, the most important change is related to the use of services rather than resources. Therefore, in AMBAR-C there are s different types of services S_j ($1 \le j \le s$) that nodes can indifferently give to each other so that, concepts of $N_i.Focus(S_j)$, $N_i.NimbusState(S_j)$, $N_i.NimbusSpace(S_j)$ and $S_j.AwareInt(N_a, N_b)$ are redefined according to the given service S_j.

Any node N_a in the *cloud* is endowed with an intelligent agent who has the corresponding information about E, i.e.: $N_a.Focus(S_j)$, $N_a.NimbusState(S_j)$ and $N_a.NimbusSpace(S_j)$ for each S_j. The MAS-based collaborative process in the *cloud* follows these steps:

1) N_b solves a task T by means of a collaborative task-solving process by making use of the services $S_1,…,S_p$.

2) N_b looks for the *cloud* current conditions given by $N_i.Focus(S_j)$, $N_i.NimbusState(S_j)$ and $N_i.NimbusSpace(S_j)$ $\forall i$, $1 \leq i \leq n$ and $\forall j$, $1 \leq j \leq s$. This information is used to decide the most suitable node with which to collaborate related with any service S_j. Service $N_i.GetCurrentState(S_j)$ is used to inquiring over node N_i for this information.

3) For each service S_j ($1 \leq j \leq p$) and by using the heuristic-based learning strategies that the intelligent agents in AMBAR-C have (see Section 2), N_b selects the node N_a which is the most suitable to start the collaborative process. Then, N_a will be the node in which N_b should focus on asking collaboration related on service S_j.

4) Service $N_a.S_j(data)$ is used for N_a to collaborate with N_b based on the needs of N_b to collaborate; *data* is the additional information N_a requires to execute S_j. As a consequence of receiving this service, N_a should update its *Nimbus* (given by $N_a.NimbusState(S_j)$ and $N_a.NimbusSpace(S_j)$). In like manner, once N_a has finished collaborating with N_b it must update its *Nimbus*.

5) In case of saturated conditions related with a service S_j and therefore no node N_a is selected as a candidate to collaborate with N_b, the AMBAR-C negotiation mechanism could be used as a variant of the AMBAR mechanism (Section 2.3). In AMBAR-C after deciding the most suitable node N_c to negotiate with, N_b executes the service $N_c.Negotiate(S_j)$ whose answer determines whether or not N_c accepts to collaborate with N_b related to S_j.

3.1 The Mutual Exclusion Mechanism

As occurs in AMBAR (Section 2.4), the levels of collaboration between the nodes in AMBAR-C turn also into a critical section, so that a mutual exclusion mechanism is also required. In AMBAR-C there is a different token for each service involved in a collaborative process. This difference has a positive impact on the efficiency and effectiveness of the model since it is now possible to start a number of collaborative processes in parallel, one for each service involved in the task and not on a unique collaborative process for all resources, as in the case of AMBAR.

The mutual exclusion mechanism of AMBAR-C makes use of the following services:

1) $N_a.AskToken(N_b, S_j)$ which is used for a node N_b to ask if another node N_a has the token associated with the service S_j. If N_a has the token it puts N_b in the corresponding queue Q; otherwise N_a does nothing.

2) $N_b.SetToken(S_j, Q)$ which is used for a node N_a, that is supposed to have the token associated to S_j, to send the token to N_b that is supposed to be the first node in Q.

3.2 Agent Communication

Instead of using message exchange for agent communication which is the case on AMBAR, AMBAR-C makes use of service exchange. As was seen previously in this section it can be done by using the list of services indicated in Table 1.

Table 1. Services for agent communication

Service	Description
$GetCurrentState(S_j)$	Ask current state related to S_j.
$Negotiate(S_j)$	Negotiate on saturated conditions related to S_j.
$AskToken(N_b, S_j)$	Require the token N_b be able to collaborate related to S_j.
$SetToken(S_j, Q)$	Assign the token related to S_j with its corresponding Q.

Next Section presents some details related with the implementation of AMBAR-C as well as a case of study to validate its applicability.

4 Implementation and Validation

As was mentioned in Section 2, IA-Awareness is the SOFIA-based agent used for implementing AMBAR. This IA-Awareness has been implemented in JADE [28] because it is FIPA-compliant as well as an open-source (based on Java). IA-Awarennes-C which is a specialization of IA-Awareness has been implemented to design AMBAR-C. IA-Awarennes-C uses the same nucleus of IA-Awarennes although there is a difference with the component "Embodied Agent" or IA-EA (see Fig. 2) which in the case of IA-Awarennes-C uses Web Service[1] technology for agent communication.

On the other hand, aiming to measure the effectiveness (θ) and efficiency (ξ) of the collaboration process, expressions (2) and (3) were defined respectively. Note that both measures (θ, ξ) are positive values in [0, 1] where 1 is the maximum value for effectiveness and efficiency. Variables in expressions are the following:

- *PSN*: It is the percentage of successful negotiations made in saturated conditions, based on the number of negotiations that receive a positive response from a node requesting to change its current saturated conditions in relation to the total attempts made.

- *MDN*: It is the mean duration in seconds of the negotiation process under saturated conditions. The process starts at the moment the node requires the cooperation until it receives an answer, whether affirmative or negative. For both answers the possible retries to be made are taken into account.

- *ATC*: It is the average time of collaboration in seconds.

- *PSC*: It is the percentage of successful collaborations based on the number of services in which there was positive response from a node to collaborate with, in relation to the total quantity of services in which collaboration was required.

---

[1] http://www.w3.org/2002/ws/

- *TOT*: It is the number of times in which any timeout expires.
- *AMT*: It is the average number of queries sent in the request for the token.
- *ATT*: It is the average waiting time in seconds for the token.
- *ATB*: It is the mean duration in seconds of CAwaSA method in solving the load-balancing problem.
- *ATL*: It is the mean duration in seconds of the learning process.

Moreover, to differentiate the context in which effectiveness or efficiency is calculated, individual expressions for the entire model (MOD), the mutual exclusion mechanism (MEM), the load-balancing problem (LBP), the negotiation mechanism (NEG), and the learning process (LPR) are given. Factors α, β, χ and δ, all of them in [0, 1] which sum is exactly equal to 1, determine the importance of each component of the model (MEM, LBP, NEG and LPR) for measuring θ and ξ.

$$\theta(MOD) = \alpha\theta(MEM) + \beta\theta(LPB) + \chi\theta(NEG) + \delta\theta(LPR)$$
$$\theta(MEM) = 3/AMT$$
$$\theta(LBP) = PSC/100 \tag{2}$$
$$\theta(NEG) = PSN/100$$
$$\theta(LPR) = (PSC + PSN)/200$$

$$\xi(MOD) = \alpha\xi(MEM) + \beta\xi(LPB) + \chi\xi(NEG) + \delta\xi(LPR)\text{-}0.05 * TOT$$
$$\xi(MEM) = \begin{cases} ATT/ATC, & ATT <= ATC \\ ATC/ATT, & ATT > ATC \end{cases}$$
$$\xi(LBP) = 1 - ATB/ATC \tag{3}$$
$$\xi(NEG) = 1 - MDN/ATC$$
$$\xi(LPR) = 1 - ATL/ATC$$

4.1 A Case Study

In order to validate the use of AMBAR-C a case of study related with the design of packages of combined trips is presented. It proposes to attend a reservation that is made implicit in a trip and also to attend all the possible items involved, such as transport, room and board, and tourism. This case is related to a distributed system that possesses nodes that collaborate with each other to offer a combined package that satisfies the necessities of the traveler.

The application is developed searching to design a package of combined trips made for diverse purposes (tourism, business, pleasure and others). Businesses that work in and with the travelling area are benefited from this application. Generally, a package of combined travels involves a series of items such as: room and board, hotel, transportation, vehicle rental, tickets to shows or tourist attractions among others. Occasionally, clients that chose this type of businesses to request a travelling package are offered an incomplete package because the business finds it impossible to include some of the items in the package. As a consequence the client must work on some of the remaining arrangements separately from the business.

It is necessary then an application that allows businesses that work within the travelling area to collaborate with each other to complete the requested travelling packages. If this happened then a company that could not complete a package because it cannot offer a certain item can then complete the package by asking the missing item to some other companies that can offer it. Companies benefit from this because their profits rise by participating as a whole in combined packages that are requested in any of them and their clients receive a complete package without having to work on some of the missing items individually.

The nodes N_i of the collaborative distributive environment E in this case are formed by those businesses that posses one or more services related to the elements that can be a part of a combined travelling package and that wish to participate in this collaboration system. The quantity of nodes allowed to be in the system at the beginning is unlimited. The services S_j are related in this case to the services or elements that can be a part of a combined travelling package and the related operations such as: making reservations, cancelling reservations, changing a reservation or purchase and purchase and payment of an item. For example, for an item related with transportation the following services are at hand: making reservations for a certain kind of transportation, cancelling a reservation, changing a previously made reservation or purchase, purchasing tickets for a certain kind of transportation, and so on.

The apparition of a new element that could be a part of a combined travelling package implies the incorporation of four new services in the environment. These services are associated to one of the operations previously described. The quantity of elements to be considered in this application to be a part of a combine travelling package is unlimited. Specific parameters such as the company in charge of the final service (for example: airlines, vehicle rental companies and hotels), the evaluation given from users, the number of stars of a hotel, the price and so forth, can be used to define new resources in such a way that the collaboration in this specific parameter might become focused.

Based on this representation of the environment, the interpretation that is given to expression $N_1.Focus(S_1) = \{N_2, N_3, N_4\}$, for example, is that the business represented by N_1 can, whenever there is a necessity of including in a combined travelling package the element represented by S_1 (for example make a reservation for any kind of transportation), search collaboration from the businesses N_2, N_3 and N_4 that are supposed to be habilitated to make this kind of operation. An equivalent expression to, for example, $N_1.NimbusState(S_2) = Null$ indicated that the business N_1 offers the service represented by S_2, and that N_1 is or is not collaborating in relation with the service S_2 at present. Finally, an expression equal to $N_4.NimbusSpace(S_4) = \{N_2, N_3\}$ indicates that at present N_4 is, for example, making transactions to acquire tickets for a particular transportation (S_4) due to different collaboration requests made by N_2 and N_3.

4.2 Experimental Results

Experiments were conducted with AMBAR-C in a TCP/IP-based local network which assumes that each node can directly communicate with any other node. Different scenarios were simulated aiming to rate the capability for managing the growth of the nodes in the different environment conditions. The scenarios were defined by changing the quantity of nodes/PCs n (agents) as well as the number of services s according to $n \in \{4, 8\}$ and $s \in \{2, 6, 10\}$. Therefore 6 different scenarios were simulated: 1) $n = 4$, $s = 2$; 2) $n = 4$, $s = 6$; 3) $n = 4$, $s = 10$; 4) $n = 8$, $s = 2$; 5) $n = 8$, $s = 6$; and 6) $n = 8$, $s = 10$. Moreover:

1) The initial condition of the *cloud* for each scenario ($N_i.Focus(S_j)$, $N_i.NimbusState(S_j)$ and $N_i.NimbusSpace(S_j)$; $1 \le i \le n$; $1 \le j \le s$) was randomly defined by considering the following: one node belongs to the *Focus* of another node with a probability of 0.75 and to the *NimbusSpace* with a probability of 0.85.

2) All N_b nodes execute an automatic process that randomly selects a need to collaborate in relation with a particular service.

3) The simulation time was 120 minutes for each scenario.

4) A timeout of one minute to a node for waiting the information of the current state of each node and a timeout of two minutes given for negotiation of resources under saturated conditions were configured.

5) By setting $\alpha = 0.1$, $\beta = 0.25$, $\chi = 0.3$ and $\delta = 0.35$ we give more importance to the learning process aiming to analyze differences in efficiency and effectiveness of the model before and after the model has learned to collaborate.

Table 2. Measures obtained from experimentation

Measure	$n=4$ $s=2$	$n=4$ $s=6$	$n=4$ $s=10$	$n=8$ $s=2$	$n=8$ $s=6$	$n=8$ $s=10$
PSN	100.00	68.13	64.29	93.75	78.13	100.00
MDN	0.00	2.14	1.23	0.13	2.16	0.44
ATC	3.40	3.46	3.34	7.47	14.87	19.28
PSC	98.96	94.24	97.70	99.89	78.08	57.90
TOT	0.00	0.00	0.00	0.00	0.00	0.00
AMT	3.05	3.01	3.02	3.04	3.28	3.64
ATT	2.47	5.86	9.58	6.73	167.38	445.15
ATB	0.00	0.02	0.05	0.06	0.68	2.03
ATL	0.01	0.02	0.02	0.01	0.03	0.02
θ(MEM)	0.98	1.00	0.99	0.99	0.92	0.83
θ(LBP)	0.99	0.94	0.98	1.00	0.78	0.58
θ(NEG)	1.00	0.68	0.64	0.94	0.78	1.00
θ(LPR)	0.99	0.81	0.81	0.97	0.78	0.79
θ(MOD)	0.99	0.82	0.82	0.97	0.79	0.80
ξ(MEM)	0.72	0.60	0.35	0.89	0.13	0.05
ξ(LBP)	1.00	0.99	0.98	0.99	0.95	0.89
ξ(NEG)	1.00	0.38	0.64	0.98	0.85	0.98
ξ(LPR)	1.00	0.99	0.99	1.00	1.00	1.00
ξ(MOD)	0.97	0.77	0.82	0.98	0.86	0.87

Table 2 shows the measures obtained after the simulations. Fig. 3 shows the effectiveness and efficiency of the model related with these measures. According to these results it is possible to make the following observations and/or conclusions:

1) The average effectiveness is 0.86 and the average efficiency is 0.88.
2) Both effectiveness and efficiency have a similar trend of behaviour.
3) Nor the variation in the number of nodes or the variations in the number of services resources have a particular tendency to improve or worsen the effectiveness and efficiency.
4) The effectiveness and efficiency tends to improve with the time and therefore the learning process becomes better. Moreover, due to the fact that it is a learning-based mechanism from past situations, it is assumed that as there is much more to learn, the metrics associated with it must be improved.

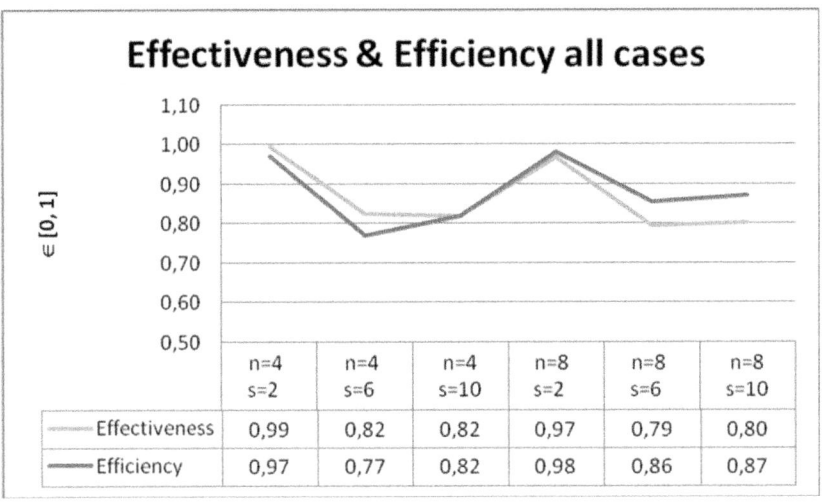

Fig. 3. Effectiveness and efficiency obtained from experimentation

5   Conclusion and Future Work

This paper presents AMBAR-C a new collaboration model used for a multi-agent based system in collaborative *cloud* computing environments. It has been designed as an adaptation of AMBAR (Awareness-based learning Model for distriButive collAborative enviRonment). The method proposed in this paper is endowed with heuristic techniques to: 1) solve the load-balancing problem, 2) decide for the most suitable node to collaborate with, and 3) to decide whether or not to collaborate.

AMBAR-C has been designed for *cloud* environments that includes nodes that are aware of the existence of others notes that can establish a collaborative process. Results show that AMBAR-C is 86% effective and 88% efficient according to the proposed functions of effectiveness and efficiency. Therefore, this model ensures collaboration in these environments in short time.

Although this method has not been tested in real case scenarios, it has been designed to be suitable for real *cloud* computing environments. In fact the experimentation and validation were carried out to demonstrate that this method could be extended to real case scenarios with no problems. Moreover, there are no limitations for the use of this collaboration model. This model in most likely to work with no problems in environments that are not necessarily *cloud*-based where collaboration/cooperation is needed.

We are currently working on testing this method in real environments as well as using the model in actual end-use applications.

References

1. Weiss, A.: Computing in the Clouds. NetWorker 11(4), 16–25 (2007)
2. Matsushita, Y., Okada, K. (eds.): Collaboration and Communication. Distributed collaborative media series 3. Kyoritsu Press (1995)
3. Kuwana, E., Horikawa, K.: Coordination Process Model - based Design for Synchronous Group Task Support System. Technical Reports of Information Processing Society of Japan, No. 13, pp. 1–6. Groupware (1995)
4. Malone, T.W., Crowston, K.: The interdisciplinary study of coordination. ACM Computing Surveys 26(1), 87–119 (1994)
5. Ogata, H., Yano, Y.: Knowledge Awareness: Bridging Learners in a Collaborative Learning Environment. International Journal of Educational Telecommunications 4(2), 219–236 (1998)
6. Gutwin, C., Stark, G., Greenberg, S.: Support for Workspace Awareness in Educational Groupware. In: Proc. Computer Supported Collaborative Learning (CSCL '95), pp. 147–156 (1995)
7. Benford, S.D., Fahlén, L.E.: A Spatial Model of Interaction in Large Virtual Environments. In: Proc. 3rd European Conference on Computer Supported Cooperative Work, pp. 109–124. Kluwer Academic Publishers, Dordrecht (1993)
8. Paletta, M., Herrero, P.: Collaboration in Distributed Systems by means of an Awareness-based Learning Model. Accepted to be published in Recent Patents on Computer Science (CSENG). Bentham Science Publishers (to be published, 2010)
9. Paletta, M., Herrero, P.: Learning cooperation in collaborative grid environments to improve cover load balancing delivery. In: Proc of IEEE/WIC/ACM Joint Conferences on Web Intelligence and Intelligent Agent Technology, vol. E3496, pp. 399–402. IEEE Computer Society, Los Alamitos (2008)
10. Paletta, M., Herrero, P.: Towards fraud detection support using grid technology. Multiagent and Grid Systems - An International Journal 5, 311–324 (2009)
11. Paletta, M., Herrero, P.: Foreseeing cooperation behaviors in collaborative grid environments. In: Proc. of 7th International Conference on Practical Applications of Agents and Multi-Agent Systems (PAAMS'09), vol. 50, pp. 120–129. Springer, Heidelberg (2009)
12. Herrero, P., Bosque, J.L., Pérez, M.S.: An agents-based cooperative awareness model to cover load balancing delivery in grid environments. In: Meersman, R., Tari, Z., Herrero, P. (eds.) OTM-WS 2007, Part I. LNCS, vol. 4805, pp. 64–74. Springer, Heidelberg (2007)
13. Herrero, P., Bosque, J.L., Pérez, M.S.: Managing dynamic virtual organizations to get effective cooperation in collaborative grid environments. In: Meersman, R., Tari, Z. (eds.) OTM 2007, Part II. LNCS, vol. 4804, pp. 1435–1452. Springer, Heidelberg (2007)

14. Greenhalgh, C.: Large Scale Collaborative Virtual Environments. Ph.D. Thesis, University of Nottingham, UK (1997)
15. Paletta, M., Herrero, P.: Awareness-based learning model to improve cooperation in collaborative distributed environments. In: Håkansson, A., Nguyen, N.T., Hartung, R.L., Howlett, R.J., Jain, L.C. (eds.) KES-AMSTA 2009. LNCS, vol. 5559, pp. 793–802. Springer, Heidelberg (2009)
16. Foundation for Intelligent Physical Agents: FIPA Abstract Architecture Specification. SC00001, Geneva, Switzerland (2002), http://www.fipa.org/specs/fipa00001/index.html
17. Paletta, M., Herrero, P.: A MAS-based Negotiation Mechanism to deal with Service Collaboration in Cloud Computing. In: Proc. International Conference on Intelligent Networking and Collaborative Systems (INCoS 2009), pp. 147–153. IEEE Computer Society, Los Alamitos (2009)
18. Paletta, M., Herrero, P.: A MAS-based Negotiation Mechanism to deal with saturated conditions in Distributed Environments. In: Proc. Second International Conference on Agents and Artificial Intelligence (ICAART 2010) (to be published, 2010)
19. Martinetz, T.M., Schulten, K.J.: A neural gas network learns topologies. In: Kohonen, T., Mäkisara, K., Simula, O., Kangas, J. (eds.) Artificial Neural Networks, pp. 397–402 (1991)
20. Paletta, M., Herrero, P.: An awareness-based artificial neural network for cooperative distributed environments. In: Cabestany, J., Sandoval, F., Prieto, A., Corchado, J.M. (eds.) IWANN 2009. LNCS, vol. 5517, pp. 114–121. Springer, Heidelberg (2009)
21. Haykin, S.: Neural Networks: A Comprehensive Foundation. Prentice Hall, Englewood Cliffs (1998)
22. Jin, R., Chen, W., Simpson, T.W.: Comparative studies of metamodelling techniques under multiple modeling criteria. Struct. Multidiscip. Optim. 23, 1–13 (2001)
23. Naimi, M., Trehel, M., Arnold, A.: A log (N) distributed mutual exclusion algorithm based on path reversal. J. Parallel Distributed Computing 34(1), 1–13 (1996)
24. Paletta, M., Herrero, P.: A Token-Based Mutual Exclusion Approach to Improve Collaboration in Distributed Environments. In: Nguyen, N.T., Kowalczyk, R., Chen, S.-M. (eds.) ICCCI 2009. LNCS (LNAI), vol. 5796, pp. 118–127. Springer, Heidelberg (2009)
25. Kirkpatrick, S.: Optimization by simulated annealing: Quantitative Studies. J. Statistical Phy. 34(5-6), 975–986 (1984)
26. Metropolis, N., Rosenbluth, A.W., Rosenbluth, M.N., Teller, A.H., Teller, E.: Equations of state calculations by fast computing machines. J. Chem. Phy. 21(6), 1087–1091 (1953)
27. Paletta, M., Herrero, P.: An awareness-based simulated annealing method to cover dynamic load-balancing in collaborative distributed environments. In: Baeza-Yates, R., et al. (eds.) Proc. 2009 IEEE/WIC/ACM International Conference on Intelligence Agent Technology (IAT 2009), pp. 371–374. IEEE Computer Society, Los Alamitos (2009)
28. Bellifemine, F., Poggi, A., Rimassa, G.: JADE-A FIPA-compliant agent framework. Telecom Italia internal technical report. In: Proc. International Conference on Practical Applications of Agents and Multi-Agent Systems (PAAM'99), pp. 97–108 (1999)

Ontology-Based Administration of Web Directories

Marko Horvat, Gordan Gledec, and Nikola Bogunović

Faculty of Electrical Engineering and Computing, University of Zagreb
Unska 3, HR-10000 Zagreb, Croatia
{Marko.Horvat2,Gordan.Gledec,Nikola.Bogunovic}@fer.hr

Abstract. Administration of a Web directory and maintenance of its content and the associated structure is a delicate and labor intensive task performed exclusively by human domain experts. Subsequently there is an imminent risk of a directory structures becoming unbalanced, uneven and difficult to use to all except for a few users proficient with the particular Web directory and its domain. These problems emphasize the need to establish two important issues: *i)* generic and objective measures of Web directories structure quality, and *ii)* mechanism for fully automated development of a Web directory's structure. In this paper we demonstrate how to formally and fully integrate Web directories with the Semantic Web vision. We propose a set of criteria for evaluation of a Web directory's structure quality. Some criterion functions are based on heuristics while others require the application of ontologies. We also suggest an ontology-based algorithm for construction of Web directories. By using ontologies to describe the semantics of Web resources and Web directories' categories it is possible to define algorithms that can build or rearrange the structure of a Web directory. Assessment procedures can provide feedback and help steer the ontology-based construction process. The issues raised in the article can be equally applied to new and existing Web directories.

Keywords: Ontology, Ontology Alignment, Artificial Intelligence, Semantic Web, Web directory.

1 Introduction

The Semantic Web vision and related spectrum of technologies have enjoyed rapid development during the last ten years. The initial and often cited paper by Tim Berners-Lee [1] introduced a rather abstract notion of universally described semantics of information and services on the Web. The vision of a Web as a shared common medium for data, information and knowledge exchange, and collaboration, fostered a wealth of research and pragmatic development. The idea itself was simple but appropriately far reaching. The Semantic Web brought the power of managed expressivity provided by ontologies to the World Wide Web (WWW) [2]. Today research in Semantic Web applications is very diverse but not particularly focused on the problem of ontologically-based Web directories. So far only a handful or papers have been published on the topic of combining ontologies and Web directories [3][4][5]. Furthermore, as yet a lot of the effort is unfinished and more computer systems utilizing

N.T. Nguyen and R. Kowalczyk (Eds.): Transactions on CCI I, LNCS 6220, pp. 101–120, 2010.

ontologies are in the phase of research and development (R&D) than in everyday production [6].

However, Web directories have simple hierarchical structures which are effective in data storage and classification. This makes Web directories important applications for storing information and its taxonomy, but also motivates research in the assessment of their semantic qualities and automatic management of their hierarchical structures. Solutions to both problems can also be useful in the more general and commonplace problem of ontology sorting.

It should be mentioned that Web directories are important but often overlooked means of resource integration and implementation of collective intelligence on the Web. The construction and maintenance of Web directories are both asymmetrical and collectively executed tasks where the contributors provide resources (i.e. information) to the directory and its administrators decide if the resources can be accepted and where should they be placed within the directory's structure. The third party in these processes, the general users, can extract semantically ordered data from the directories and freely use them in their own business processes. It can be said that Web directories are public frameworks for information sharing and collaboration. As such they are designed for hierarchical data storage and retrieval by means of browsing. Furthermore, in the context of the Semantic Web vision, Web directories are taxonomies of semantically and formally annotated data. The information stored in the directories is formatted in machine and human readable form, and thus becomes extractable by intelligent agents and can be used in distributed intelligent systems.

The remainder of the paper is organized as follows; the next section describes the categories and the structure of Web directories. Mutual associations between the Semantic Web and Web directories, as well as the semantic dimension of categories, are all presented in the third section. Web directories construction scenarios are presented in the fourth section, while the fifth chapter describes an algorithm for their ontology-based construction. Semantic quality measures of Web directories are discussed in the sixth section. Related publications and our conclusion with an outlook for future work are presented at the end of the paper.

2   Categories and the Structure of Web Directories

In order to explain how Web directories can be positioned within the Semantic Web vision, it is necessary to formally define a Web directory, its constituent components and their organization. It is also important to add semantic annotations to these building elements.

A web directory (web catalog or link directory, as it is also called) is a structured and hierarchically arranged collection of links to other web sites. Web directories are divided into categories and subcategories with a single top category, often called the root category, or just the root. Each category has a provisional number of subcategories with each subcategory further subsuming any number of other subcategories, and so on. Furthermore, every category has a unique name with an accompanying Uniform Resource Locator (URL), and can also carry other associated information.

Each category of a Web directory contains a set of links to various sites on the WWW and another set of links to other categories within the web directory. These two sets of links represent the most important characteristic of any Web directory. Links to categories within the same directory are called cross-links.

Each Web directory has to have a start page, i.e. a home page, which represents its root category, and every other category of a Web directory has its own adjoined web page. The start page displays subcategories that belong to the root. By following a link to a subcategory, user opens that category's page and browses through its links and subcategories. This process continues until the user finds a link to a web resource that s/he is looking for. In essence, the user can be described as an intelligent agent that traverses the structure of a Web directory looking for specific information.

Since Web directories are always rooted and the order of categories is strictly maintained, it is possible to assign level numbers to categories. The subcategories of the root are the 2nd level categories, and in turn their subcategories are the 3rd level categories, and so on. As a convention the root is always a 1st level category. The maximum level of a Web directory is called depth.

Each category, except the root, has one category above it, which is called its parent. The categories below a certain category (i.e. with a greater level number than the category) are called its children, while categories on the same level as a node are called its siblings. Categories with no children are called terminal categories, and a category with at least one child is sometimes called nonterminal category. Associations between categories are arbitrary, but there must be at least one path between any pair of categories. Disjoint sets of categories are not allowed, as well as parallel links and self-loops. Each nonterminal category must have links to all its children, but can also have links to other categories in the Web directory which are semantically similar, or otherwise analogous to the category.

2.1 Formal Definition of Web Directories

We shall formally designate with C the set of all categories in a Web directory, and R will be the set of all Web resources in a Web directory. One category with unique identification number n is denoted c_n. Category has its own characteristic URL url. The category c_n must be a member of C. C_n is a subset of C that belongs to the category c_n, and R_n the subset of R with Web resources that belong to the category c_n. In order to be more informative, the categories can also be written as c_n^l with their member level l, where l is a natural number smaller than or equal to the depth of a Web directory L [7]. The first level, or the root level, is always $l=1$. Category is a tuple $c_n = \{n, l, url, C_n, R_n\}$ and can be schematically annotated as in the figure below.

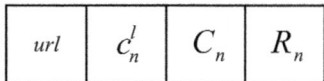

Fig. 1. Vector representation of a single category within a Web directory

We can define a Web directory wd to be an element of the WWW. With C and R being members of wd the algebraic definitions of the elements of a Web directory and their mutual relationships are

$$C_n \in c_n \subset C$$
$$R_n \in c_n \subset R$$
$$l \in [1, L] \in N \qquad (1)$$
$$C \in wd \subset \text{WWW}$$
$$R \in wd \subset \text{WWW}$$

The set of all children categories to c_n^l is C_n . If the root is the top node (l=1) then the set of all children one level below is C_n^{l+1} or (for the sake of brevity) C_n^{+1}, two levels below C_n^{l+2} or C_n^{+2}, etc. As can be seen in (1), category is also a Web resource ($c_n \subset R$), as it should be expected since it has unique URL and carries specific information. Furthermore, Web directory itself also becomes a tuple $wd = \{C, R\}$. The semantic information attached to resources and their related categories derives from the documents (e.g. Web pages, articles, blog posts, various textual documents, etc.) that are linked to the category. Also, the categories may have their own keywords and description defined by the directory's administrators. All this data collectively forms the category's semantic content.

Mathematically speaking, Web directories are simple rooted graphs [8]. In this formal respect, categories represent vertices and connections represent edges. The path between two vertices is called the arc, edge or link, and when there is an edge connecting the two vertices, we say that the vertices are adjacent to one another and that the edge is incident on both vertices. The degree of a vertex is equivalent to the number of edges incident on it.

Using the described formalisms, the schema of a simple Web directory with 6 categories distributed in 4 levels, with parent-child associations and two specific links $c_6 \rightarrow c_5$ and $c_3 \rightarrow c_2$ could be depicted with Fig. 2.

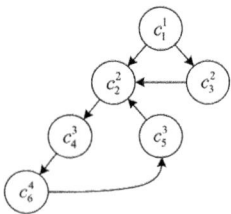

Fig. 2. Schematic representation of Web directory as a simple rooted graph

However, the structure of a realistic Web category (Fig. 3) cannot be described just as a simple graph because of the cross-links which can define additional connections between categories. Apart from paths which connect categories with parent-child relationships, cross-links can associate any two categories.

Cross-links are added *ad hoc* by the Web directory's administrator staff to closely bind together two categories with similar semantic content. The nature of the category semantics and how they relate to one another has to be evaluated by the human administrator. Cross-links are very useful in facilitation of directory's browsing and information retrieval. They will allow users to find the needed Web resource faster in less steps and click-throughs. However, cross-links can, and most often do, form closed category loops. Excessive or unsystematic use of cross-links will make browsing more difficult and the process of information retrieval confusing for a user. In such circumstances users often will not follow the shortest browsing path through directory's categories, but rather will be sidetracked or deflected from their goal category. The semantic quality measures proposed in this paper address this very problem. They serve as objective criteria for the evaluation of Web directories structure in terms of its browsing convenience and overall usability.

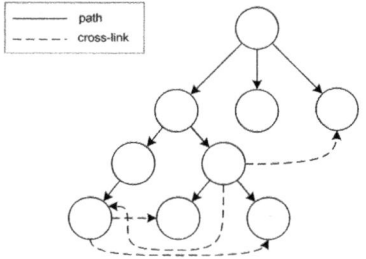

Fig. 3. Realistic Web directory with cross-links which allow loops and multiple paths between any two categories

But if, for the sake of discussion, all categories of a Web directory except the root had paths only to its children, such structure would constitute a rooted tree as in Fig. 4.

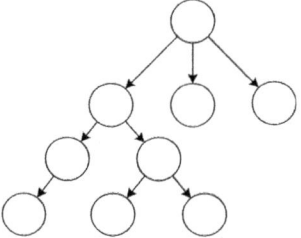

Fig. 4. Idealistic Web directory with only one path between any two categories

In some cases the order of categories appearance may be relevant, e.g. the position of links within a category's Web page is prioritized, and in that case a Web directory can be formally modeled as an ordered and rooted simple graph.

Although the categorization of a Web directory should be defined by a standard and unchanging policy, this is frequently not the case. Web directories often allow site owners to directly submit their site for inclusion, even suggest an appropriate category for the site, and have administrators review the submissions. The directory's administrators must approve the submission and decide in which category to put the link in.

However, rules that influence the editors' decision are not completely objective and are thus difficult to implement unambiguously. Sometimes a site will fall in two or even more categories, or require a new category.

Defining a new category is a very delicate task because it has to adequately represent a number of sites, avoid interfering with domains of other categories, and at the same time the width and depth of the entire directory's structure has to be balanced. A Web directory with elaborate structure at one end and sparse and shallow at the other is confusing for users and difficult to find quality information in.

Furthermore, after several sites have been added to a directory it may become apparent that an entirely new categorization could better represent the directory's content. In this case a part of directory's structure or even all of its levels have to be rearranged which is time consuming and labor intensive task. Reshuffling of the whole directory's structure may be warranted in the test phase, before the directory has entered the full production. But after users have grown accustomed to a certain structure, however suboptimal it may be, it would be unwise to profoundly alter the directory's shape. This would lead to renewed learning phase for all existing users and eventually may put them off in using the directory. Therefore, during exploitation the directory's structure should be altered only be adding and deleting cross-links, not the proper paths between parent-child categories. Alteration of cross-paths will not have such antagonistic effect towards the directory's users as the complete reassembly of directory's paths. But this only emphasizes the importance of creating the near-optimal structure during directory's construction which will have to be changed as little as possible later during the directory's lifetime.

3   The Semantic Web and Web Directories

At the moment, resources available on the WWW are designed primarily for human and not machine use [9]. In order words, knowledge, declarative and procedural, offered by various Web sources is shaped in a way that better suites humans and not machines. The vision of the Semantic Web is directly aimed at solving this dichotomy by introducing self-describing documents that carry data and the accompanying metadata together, and thus organize and interconnect available information so it also becomes processable by computer applications [10].

The structure of a Web directory is basically a subjective construction. It depends on human comprehension and the policy taken by the Web directory's administrator, or even on the users that submit sites to the directory. It is important to note that not all Web directories, or even all segments of a Web directory, have the same editorial policy. Clearly, for the sake of a Web directory's informative clarity and usability, the semantic distance between any two categories should be approximately constant, and not dramatically vary from one category to the next. Whilst, the key for the selection of concepts that represent categories should remain uniform throughout the directory's structure. The only parameters that should be used to judge the quality of a directory are its informative value and usability, to humans and machines equally. In the fifth chapter we will propose several numerical parameters that objectively measure the worth of a directory.

3.1 A Formal Model of Web Directories Semantic Content

In defining a formal model of Web directories semantic content it is necessary to assume that we have at a disposition function *sem* that takes a resource $r_i \in R$ and from its semantic content builds an ontology $o_i \in O$ where R and O are sets of all resources and ontologies, respectively.

$$sem : R \to O \qquad (2)$$

The function *sem* builds an ontology from a resource. In slightly different terms, it creates a solid representation of an abstract property. This property can be described as informal and explicit on the semantic continuum scale [11] and its technical realization is strictly formal. Operations of the function *sem* can be performed by a computer system or a domain expert, in which case we talk about automatic or manual ontology construction, respectively. The necessary mathematical assumption on *sem* is it has well-defined addition and subtraction operators in R and O

$$\oplus : R \times R \to R$$
$$\mathrm{e} \ : R \times R \to R$$
$$\hat{+} : O \times O \to O$$
$$\hat{-} : O \times O \to O \qquad (3)$$

This allows application of union operator across these two sets and concatenation of individual resources and ontologies, as well as determining their respective differences

$$sem(r_1 \oplus r_2) = sem(r_1) \hat{+} sem(r_2)$$
$$sem(r_1 \ \mathrm{e} \ r_2) = sem(r_1) \hat{-} sem(r_2) \qquad (4)$$

We also define a modulo operator $| \bullet |$ on O as

$$| \bullet | : O \times O \to O. \qquad (5)$$

The *semantic content of a category* can be defined in three different ways:

1)   by its Web resources
2)   from subsumed categories
3)   as a constant.

By the first definition, semantic content of a category c_i within a Web directory *wd* derives from the semantic content of all its Web resources r_{ij} where $r_{ij} \in R_i \in c_i$ as

$$sem(c_i) = \hat{+}_{r_{ij} \in R_i} sem(r_{ij}) \qquad (6)$$

According to the second definition, the semantic content of c_i can also equal the aggregation of the semantic content of its children categories $c_j \in C_i^{+1} \in c_i$

$$sem(c_i) = \hat{+}_{c_j \in C_i^{-1}} sem(c_j) \tag{7}$$

Finally, if c_i has no resources $(R_i = \varnothing)$ and subcategories $(C_i = \varnothing)$ it is assumed that the semantic content of c_i is defined by a constant $const_i$ as

$$sem(c_i) = const_i : R_i = \varnothing, C_i = \varnothing \tag{8}$$

The reasoning behind such threefold definition is that the meaning of categories is conformed to the directory's editorial policy. If a category is empty and no resources have been added, it will still have some member semantics attached by the Web directory administrator.

The structure of directory *wd* is *ideal* if for non-empty **R** and **C**

$$\left| \hat{+}_{r_{ij} \in R_i} sem(r_{ij}) \triangleq \hat{+}_{c_j \in C_i} sem(c_j) \right| = \varnothing \tag{9}$$
$$\forall c_i \in wd, R_i \in c_i, C_i \in c_i$$

That is, the structure of directory *wd* can be considered perfect if and only if for each category $c_i \in wd$ the semantic content of its Web resources $R_i \in c_i$ and subsumed categories $C_i \in c_i$ are equal.

Pragmatically, we can define a neighborhood ε within O and say that the structure of directory *wd* is *realistically ideal* if

$$\left| \hat{+}_{r_{ij} \in R_i} sem(r_{ij}) \triangleq \hat{+}_{c_j \in C_i} sem(c_j) \right| \leq \varepsilon \tag{10}$$
$$\forall c_i \in wd, R_i \in c_i, C_i \in c_i$$

The existence of the function *sem*, with the described properties, is fundamental and indivertible in the ontology-based construction of Web directories.

4   Construction Scenarios

The process of building Web directories has three actors [12]:

1. Web directory system (System)
2. Web directory administrator (Admin)
3. Administrator of a Web site listed in the Web directory (Site)

Ontology-based building process involves the same three actors and represents a subset of the general building process. This process includes three main tasks, or actions, that have to be performed by actors in order to construct a Web directory:

1. Semantics identification task (ID)
2. Semantics assignment task (ASSIGN)
3. Web directory addition task (ADD)

Semantics identification task is a process that recommends which ontology class, or classes, should be instantiated and assigned to a given Web resource. Semantics assignment task is a process that follows semantics identification, and actually assigns a set of ontology classes to a resource. Classes that are recommended and assigned do not necessarily have to be identical. If an actor has made an error and recommended the wrong class, the actor performing assignment can overrule his/her recommendation. Finally, when a set of classes has been assigned to a Web resource, it has to be added to a directory. Web directory addition task decides exactly where in a directory's structure the new resource will be placed. This is a complicated task because it can involve creation of an entirely new category, reshuffling and updating existing categories (both horizontally and vertically within the directory's structure), or simply adding the resource to an existing category. The order of these tasks and their mutual interaction is described in the following UML activity diagram (Fig. 3).

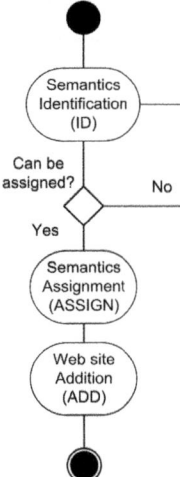

Fig. 5. Main tasks in ontology-based construction of Web directories

Construction process scenarios can be divided in two groups:

1. Prevalently automated scenario (AUTO)
2. Mostly manual scenario (MANUAL)

Each scenario has several possible variations or sub-scenarios. Scenarios are distinguished by the level of human participation. Sub-scenarios describe the roles of the actors involved.

Utilization of human intelligence in majority of tasks is presumed in MANUAL scenario, while in AUTO scenario the Web directory computer system performs more tasks than human actors. In an ideal AUTO scenario the computer executes all tasks independently. Table 1 depicts all scenarios and their variations with respective grades of favorability. By following the highest grades in each scenario it is possible to determine the best actor for each task. Sequences of the best choices for each task

are shown in UML diagrams in Fig. 6 and Fig. 7. Data in the table, temporally structured in the diagrams, reflects the "Best Practice" experience gathered during 15 years
of administrating the Croatian Web directory [13].

Table 1. Favorability of actors and task allocation in ontology-based construction of a Web
directory[1]

Tasks	Roles		
MANUAL scenario	Site	Admin	System
ID	++	+	n/a
ASSIGN	+	+++	++
ADD	-	+++	+++
AUTO scenario	Site	Admin	System
ID	+	+	++
ASSIGN	-	+++	++
ADD	-	+	+++

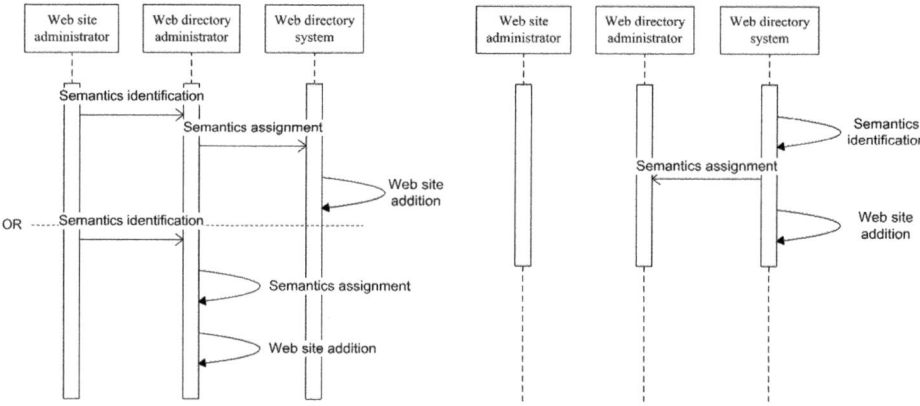

Fig. 6. UML sequence diagram with the
selection of best actors in the MANUAL
scenario

Fig. 7. UML sequence diagram with the
selection of best actors in the AUTO scenario

As can be seen in MANUAL scenario, Site is the best actor to perform ID, and
Admin for ASSIGN. In this scenario ID is intentionally performed only by a human
actor. ADD can be executed equally good by Admin or System, but it would be
wrong to leave this task to Site. The reasoning behind allocation of actors in this scenario is that Site is the least dependable actor and its contribution is the most likely to
be subjective and erroneous. The task will be most successfully performed by Admin,
but it would be inefficient and wrong to give all tasks only to Admin. After all, one of
the principal goals of the proposed system is to alleviate the burden of Web directory
administration from the amenable personnel, and not to leave them with an equally

---

[1] Sub-scenario grades: +++: the most acceptable, ++ favorable, + positive, –negative/unfavorable
scenario, n/a not applicable.

difficult job. The best option is to allocate ID to Site and to leave the final decision about semantics to Admin who is the most knowledgeable and dependable actor of the three.

Much the same reasoning is reflected in the AUTO scenario; however the importance of System in this scenario is emphasized. Thus, System is the optimal choice for executing ID and ADD. Again, Admin will perform the final assignment of ontologies to resources (i.e. ASSIGN) to reduce possible errors to a minimum. In this scenario it was determined that it would be negative to let Site to execute ASSIGN and ADD since Admin or System can perform a better job at this tasks. In this scenario Site and Admin are equally suitable to execute ID. If ASSIGN is also given to System then the Web directory building system is fully automated.

5   Ontologically Based Construction

If it is possible to assign ontology to a Web resource and execute semantics identification and semantics assignment tasks as outlined in the previous chapter, it is also possible to define an ontology-based algorithm for automated construction of a Web directory structure. Such algorithm performs all tasks outlined in Fig. 2. The algorithm's input are links to Web resources that are being added to the Web directory, and output is schema of the directory. Schema can be represented in a number of ways, e.g. as a markup language, or additionally the algorithm can use the schema to automatically build the directory by writing and storing necessary static and dynamic Web files like HTML, JavaScript, PHP, etc.

In order to be able to define the described algorithm we will assume that we have at a disposition function *sem* as explained in 2.1 .

The basis for the algorithm construction process is the definition of category c_i and its set of ontologies O_i as a unified pair (c_i, O_i). In acquiring O_i the algorithm uses the function *sem* and treats c_i as a Web resource. The input is a set of Web resources R and the algorithm picks one resource r_i at the time, translates in into an ontology o_{NEW} and calculates the distance between o_{NEW} and every ontology in the Web directory O looking for the closest. Categories are compared using their member ontologies. At each moment *wd* has n categories and a new category has index $n+1$.

Pseudocode for ontology-based construction of Web directories

```
// add the root category in web directory
add category (c₁, ∅);
// iterate through all web resources
for each rᵢ in R
{
  create new ontology instance O_NEW from resource rᵢ;
  if (K(C) = 1)
  {
  // if web directory contains only the root...
  create category (c_NEW, O_NEW);
  add rᵢ in c_NEW;
  add c_NEW in wd as c_{n+1}^{1+1};
  }
```

```
else
{
  // if web directory contains more categories...
  find the closest category ( cₙ¹ , Oₙ ) to O_NEW;
  d = dist(O_NEW, Oₙ);
  if (d > mindistᵥ)
  {
    create category (c_NEW, O_NEW);
    add rᵢ in c_NEW;
    add c_NEW in wd as  cₙ₊₁ˡ⁺¹ ;
  }
  else if (d > mindist_H)
  {
    create category (c_NEW, O_NEW);
    add rᵢ in c_NEW;
    add c_NEW in wd as  cₙ₊₁ˡ ;
  }
  else
  {
    add rᵢ in  cₙˡ ;
  }
}
}
```

The most significant aspect of the algorithm is reliance on ontologies and ontology aligning methods in order to measure similarity between ontologies and determine their mutual distance. The similarity measure $sim : C^2 \to [0,1]$ between the two categories $c_1, c_2 \in C$ and the distance function $dist(c_1, c_2) = 1 / sim(c_1, c_2)$ is defined in [14][15][16]. The algorithm uses two constants in a predefined metric; *minimal horizontal semantic distance* ($mindist_H$) and *minimal vertical semantic distance* ($mindist_V$) as thresholds in the category addition process. When a new category c_j is being added and category c_i already exists in *wd* if $dist(c_i, c_j) > mindist_H$ then the algorithm will add c_j as a new category of *wd*. Likewise, if $dist(c_i, c_j) > mindist_V$ then c_j will be added in a new level of the directory *wd*, below c_i. If $dist(c_i, c_j) <= mindist_H$ AND $dist(c_i, c_j) <= mindist_V$ the algorithm will merge semantics of c_j and c_i incrementing initial ontology of c_i. Therefore, the thresholds are used in deciding whether it is necessary to add a new category in the directory's structure or to use an existing category. Also, the thresholds indicate where to add a new category: in the same level next to an existing category or below it.

The algorithm has two main branches. The first branch recognizes one special case when cardinal number K of all categories C in *wd* is 1, and the second branch processes three cases with cardinality of categories greater than 1. If $K(C) = 1$ then $l = 1$ and only the root category has been added to *wd*. In this case it is not necessary to calculate the distance between ontologies and a new category can be immediately constructed. If $K(C) > 1$ there are more categories, not just the root, and links to Web resources are assigned to the semantically closest categories. New categories are created if needed.

The single root node does not have a set of links to Web resources ($R_1 = \emptyset$) and it is assigned to an empty ontology ($c_1, \emptyset$), however the algorithm can be modified so it allows predefinition of main topics in a Web portal or Web directory according to the desired administrating policies.

The proposed algorithm is simple because it represents the direct and the most obvious implementation of an ontological principle in Web directory construction. Categories cannot be mutually prioritized, and the end structure is completely dependent on the order of links to Web resources which are the algorithm's input. Furthermore, there is no back-tracking or iterative optimization. For these reasons the algorithm may also be called basic or elementary, since all other ontology-based algorithms should provide better results. It could be used as an etalon for comparison of different algorithms for the construction of Web directories.

Execution of this algorithm can be assigned to different roles in MANUAL and AUTO scenarios (see Table 1). For example, a part of the algorithm, like ASSIGN can be given to human experts (System or Admin) and other tasks – ID and especially ADD – can be executed by an intelligent agent (System). Different assignment will yield diverse results and this presents an interesting topic for further study and experiments.

6 Semantic Quality Measures

During or after Web directory's construction it is highly desirable to establish some measures of value of the accomplished process. The criterion functions that will provide these measurements should be objective and universal. Benefits of such measures would be twofold: *i*) they could provide a matching framework between Web directories, and *ii*) they could be used to assess the semantic structure quality of individual Web directories. In other words, by using them, structures of any two Web directories could be objectively compared and the criteria could point to potential semantic deficiencies in a directory. Information retrieval in Web directories can be executed either through searching or browsing scenarios.

Because of the sheer size of data available on the Web, searching is the dominant information retrieval scenario today. Several performance measures for evaluation of searching scenarios have already been proposed, such as precision, recall, fall-out and F-measure. However, information seeking by browsing scenarios is interesting in reduced information collections like blogs, RSS feeds, social networks [17], but also in individual directory categories. Since information in Web directories may be browsed by intelligent agents as well as human users, the establishment of parameters for objective measurement of Web directory's structure and content is of a significant importance for determining its usability, semantic quality and subsequently other intrinsic characteristics.

We have identified at least three parameters that can be used to objectively assess the semantic quality of a Web directory:

1. Path ratio
2. Maximum revisit
3. Distance decrease progression

All parameters require observation of the browsing pattern of a person or an intelligent agent using the directory. We will assume that the browsing scenario starts at the root category although this is not strictly necessary (nor is often the case in real-world use). The parameters are calculated based on observation of a single Web directory user. Each observation represents one browsing session for a specific resource contained within the directory. After the parameters of individual observations are collected they may be statistically processed and aggregated. This data can then cumulatively represent relevant trends and features in the actions of any number of directory's users.

6.1   Path Ratio Parameter

Path ratio (PR) is calculated as a proportion between the minimum number of categories between the root and the category with the required Web resource, and the number of categories the user traverses while browsing. Therefore, when browsing for a resource r in a Web directory wd the browse $b(r, wd)$ with the length $\left| b(r, wd) \right|$ parameter PR is defined as

$$PR(b) = 1 - \frac{\min \left| b(r, wd) \right|}{\left| b(r, wd) \right|}, PR(b) \in \left[0,1 \right\rangle \tag{11}$$

The rationale behind this parameter is that in the case of the optimal, or direct, browse $b*$ the user will achieve the shortest path between the root and the category with the resource browsed for. Therefore path ratio for the optimal search is $PR(b^*){=}0$. In a suboptimal, or indirect, browse b' user will traverse at least one category more then $b*$ and $PR(b'){>}0$. This is explained in the next figure that illustrates a browsing pattern staring at category c_1^1 and ending at c_9^4.

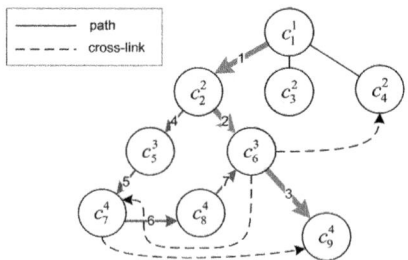

Fig. 8. Optimal (direct) and suboptimal (indirect) browse paths in calculating parameter PR

Browse b_1 with the path $1{\to}2{\to}3$ is optimal because it traces the shortest and the most direct path between the start and the end category so that $PR(b_1){=}0$. While the browse $1{\to}4{\to}5{\to}6{\to}7{\to}3$ will also lead to the end resource, it is suboptimal since its length is greater than that of the optimal browse $(6 > 3)$, thus $PR(b_2) = 1/2$.

6.2 Maximum Revisit Parameter

Maximum revisit (MR) or maximum category revisit is a parameter that describes the maximum number of repeated visits to any category while browsing for one resource. Because Web directories are simple rooted graphs with at least one path between any two nodes, there is never a need to visit the same category twice while browsing for a resource. Therefore, MR specifies the level of wandering or loitering in a Web directory's structure while browsing (Fig. 9).

The best possible browse b for a resource r in a Web directory wd has

$$\mathrm{MR}\big(b(r, wd)\big) = 0 \tag{12}$$

indicating no category revisit, where $MR(b)$ can be any natural whole number including zero $MR(b) = 0, 1, 2, ..., n, n+1 \in N \cup \{0\}$.

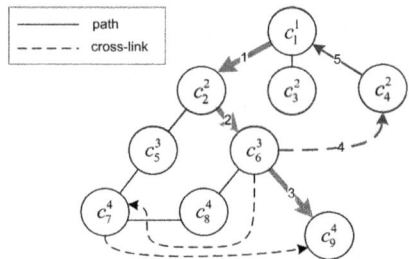

Fig. 9. Optimal and suboptimal browsing paths with revisits in calculating parameter MR

In the Fig 6., browse b_1 with the path $1 \rightarrow 2 \rightarrow 3$ starting in c_1^1 and finishing with c_9^4 has $MR(b_1) = 0$. However, due to the configuration of the directory it is possible to needlessly revisit some or even all categories. This is illustrated in the browse b_2 with the path $1 \rightarrow 2 \rightarrow 4 \rightarrow 5 \rightarrow 1 \rightarrow 2 \rightarrow 3$ which gives $MR(b_2) = 1$. Since $MR(b_1) < MR(b_2)$ browse b_1 is better then b_2.

6.3 Distance Decrease Progression Parameter

Distance decrease progression (DDP) is an ontology-based parameter. It describes the gradient of semantic convergence toward the resource during one browse. As the user browses categories looking for a particular resource, each category s/he visits should be progressively ontologically closer to the resource. If this is not the case, than either s/he is loitering or the directory does not have the optimal structure. Parameter $DPP(s)$ can be defined as a series

$$\mathrm{DPP}(b) = \sum_{i=1}^{n-1} dist(c_i, c_T) - dist(c_{i+1}, c_T) \tag{13}$$

where c_T is the target category containing the resource the user is looking for, c_i is any category being browsed and n is the length, i.e. number of steps, of the browse b. It is also necessary to apply a similarity measure $sim : C^2 \to [0,1]$ between the two categories $c_1, c_2 \in C$ and a distance function $dist(c_1, c_2) = 1 / sim(c_1, c_2)$ in [14][15][16]. If the sequence of partial sums $\{s_1, s_2, ..., s_n, s_{n+1}, ...\}$ converges, than the series is also convergent, where

$$s_n = \sum_{k=1}^{m} dist(c_k, c_T) - dist(c_{k+1}, c_T)$$ (14)

The search b' is optimal if $DPP(b')$ converges to 0.

All three parameters described here should be used in conjunction with each other in order to cumulatively describe this important design feature of Web directories.

6.4 Additional Parameters

Except the three parameters explained previously, it is indeed possible to define additional criteria which measure browsing adequacy of a Web directory's structure.

As for an additional parameter, one can measure semantic distance between different pairs of nodes along the browsing path. Instead of only monitoring the distance between the current node and the goal node, it may be prudent to observe change in the semantic distance among the root and the current node. If a directory's structure is truly optimized for browsing, this distance should monotonously grow as the user progressively gets closer to his target resource. Semantic difference between other significant nodes could also be measured and indicate the advance in browsing. These pivotal nodes could be contextually important directory's categories such as the top nodes of individual categories and subcategories, or nodes which have a multitude of cross-links and represent nexuses to other categories. They can also be or structurally important as the right or the left most categories at a certain directory level. Any node that is semantically or structurally unique can be a good point for determining distances to the user's current node and his target node. One can even triangulate between these three points and thus, using geometry, gain further insight in the browsing progress.

Also, it is possible to construct multiple statistical features using any or all previously described parameters and use them as indicators to track the user's resource browsing pattern. The number of features can be increased further by monitoring distances among the current node, the target node, the root and, perhaps, some pivotal node. The idea would be to establish a network within the directory's structure connecting all semantically significant nodes and the user's current node. This would make it possible to dynamically follow the user's actions and how they semantically relate to the goal node.

Finally, with smaller and simpler directories it is entirely possible that they do not have cross-links between categories but only parent-child connections. It would be interesting to compare the efficiency of goal-directed browsing in such structure versus the same structure with additional category cross-links. Intuitively, the idea would be to find the optimum balance between the cross-links and customary parent-child edges. Higher number of cross-links would certainly increase the interconnectivity of the directory's graph facilitating the transits between various categories, but would also make it harder to select the optimum (i.e. shortest) path to the goal category.

6.5 Applying the Parameters

Node distribution in some Web directories, at a certain level in their structures, does not necessarily have to follow concept semantics partition or this process can be somehow affected and skewed. Examples of this are content division according to date, contributors' names or alphabet, e.g. having node "A" for subnodes with "Apples" content, "B" for "Bananas", "C" for "Citrus", etc. These nodes would have more in common with a concept "Fruit" that with "Alphabet Letter". Subsequently, mutual semantic distance of such nodes would be great and incompatible with the directory's partition. In order to overcome this problem in calculation of the semantic quality parameters one has to simply ignore semantic value of these nodes at a level l and directly link nodes in levels $l-1$ and $l+1$, i.e. immediately above and below the level l. With this monotone semantic difference between nodes can be restored.

Every Web directory should have an easily understandable semantic schema that is reflected in a directory's structure so it becomes self-explanatory which category to browse in order to iteratively and progressively approach the required resource. This issue is closely correlated to the Web usability of directories. However, due to diverse quality of data sources available on the Web it is not easy to construct a directory with an ideal path ratio, maximum revisit and distance decrease progression values. Further planned experiments should provide more information on the everyday applicability of the parameters proposed here.

7 Related Work

All previous work regarding coupling of Web directories with ontologies and the Semantic Web paradigms has been directed at using Web directories, their data and structure, to extract information from WWW with the goal of document classification and ontology learning. In this paper we presented an exactly opposite approach – using available knowledge to construct a Web directory itself.

The paper by Kavalec [4] which described a mechanism for extraction of information on products and services from the source code of public web pages was especially useful in our work. Papers by Mladenić [5], Li [18] and Brin [19] were also helpful.

Open Directory RDF Dump (http://rdf.dmoz.org/) is an interesting effort because it combines the well-known Web directory Open Directory Project (DMOZ) with Resource Description Framework (RDF) ontology language. DMOZ is the largest human-edited directory found on the Web. Its data is shared by a number of different Web sites and often used by researchers when dealing with knowledge representation in taxonomies. However, the RDF data is read-only and available exclusively off-line in large downloadable packages. It would be much better if the data was accessible in smaller chunks and on demand through a dedicated Semantic Web service. Also, any usage of ontologies (even lightweight ones stored in RDF only) presents a new set of problems such as ontology mapping, alignment, discovery, etc. The DMOZ administrators should do more regarding integration of this valuable data with the Semantic Web vision.

We would particularly like to emphasize the work by a research group at University of Zagreb which introduced ontologies in the search mechanism of the Croatian Web directory, and thus successfully resolved problems of low recall, high recall and low precision and vocabulary mismatch [20]. The Croatian Web directory (http://www.hr/) [13] was founded in February 1994 and its purpose has been to promote and maintain the network information services through the "national WWW homepage" and enable easy navigation in Croatian cyberspace using hierarchically and thematically organized directory of WWW services. At the moment of writing the directory contains over 25,000 Web resources listed in more than 750 categories.

8 Conclusion

Web directories are a commonplace method for structuring various semantically heterogeneous resources. The form of simple rooted graphs is well-suited for many uses in information storage, representation and retrieval in Web and desktop environments, such as is-a hierarchies, taxonomies, directory trees, bookmarks, menus, and even emotionally annotated databases [21]. Also, the aspect of social collaboration is very important since networking and the Web enable instant publication and usage of data – ideally within groups of trusted users with shared areas of interest. All this facets emphasize the importance of successful construction, management, information extraction and reuse of information stored within Web directories' structure.

The first goal of this paper was to devise a generic method for automatic construction and maintenance of Web directories content and structure. The second goal was to propose a set of objective criteria that can be used for appraisal of directories structure utility in browsing-based information retrieval. The first two of these parameters (path ratio and maximum revisit) are based on heuristics while the third (distance decrease progression) requires introduction of ontologies in description of knowledge contained in the Web directory, which is possible only if Web directories are placed in the context of the Semantic Web vision.

We recommend caution in using publicly available Web directories to learn new ontologies. Structures of Web directories are often biased and greatly influenced by contributors and the order in which they added resources to directories. Also, the maintenance of a large directory is an overwhelming task prone to errors. Therefore, it may be more advisable to construct ontologies from smaller directories or from directories with rigid administrative policies. Small directories are more numerous than the larger but they will offer less information and in more specialized and segmented areas.

In the future work we would like to expand the initial system and build a hard general ontology which would efficiently encompass smaller ontologies of individual categories and provide a unitary base for ontology matching throughout the Web directory. Furthermore, we would like to test the upgraded system in real-life situations and use it regularly as a decision support system in maintenance of a large Web directory. In the near future we are planning to validate the system and evaluate its features by implementing it within the Croatian Web directory and its domain "Tourism" as a suitable test category. The semantic quality measures would be used as control parameters in an iterative process of constructing and perfecting the Web directory's structure. In the first phase of this experiment we are set to develop a semi-automatic system which only proposes a choice of optimal recommendations without taking explicit action by itself. This would give us an opportunity to fine tune the algorithms and ascertain their practical usefulness.

Also, in the mid-term future we see an opportunity to switch from tag cloud based resource annotation used in many popular Web 2.0 sites such as YouTube, Flickr, IMDB, del.icio.us, Amazon, etc. toward lightweight ontologies. In this case the ontology instances could be browsed in a manner similar to the use of Web directories and the semantic quality measures, as well as the ontology-based directory construction processes, could be used to improve or facilitate the information extraction in such Web sites.

Acknowledgment

This work has been supported by the Croatian Ministry of Science, Education and Sports through research projects "Content Delivery and Mobility of Users and Services in New Generation Networks" and "Adaptive Control of Scenarios in VR Therapy of PTSD", grant numbers 036-0362027-1639 and 036-0000000-2029, respectively. The authors would also like to cordially thank the reviewers for their most helpful suggestions which contributed to the improvement of the paper.

References

1. Berners-Lee, T., Hendler, J., Lassila, O.: The Semantic Web. Scientific American 284(5), 34–43 (2001)
2. Shadbolt, N., Berners-Lee, T., Hall, W.: The Semantic Web revisited. IEEE Intelligent Systems 21(3), 96–101 (2006)
3. Choi, B.: Making Sense of Search Results by Automatic Web-page Classifications. In: Proc. of WebNet 2001 – World Conference on the WWW and Internet, pp. 184–186 (2001)
4. Kavalec, M., Svátek, V.: Information Extraction and Ontology Learning Guided by Web Directory. In: ECAI Workshop on NLP and ML for ontology engineering, Lyon (2002)
5. Mladenić, D.: Turning Yahoo into an Automatic Web Page Classifier. In: Proc. 13th European Conference on Artificial Intelligence, ECAI'98, pp. 473–474 (1998)
6. Cardoso, J.: The Semantic Web Vision: Where Are We? IEEE Intelligent Systems 22(5), 84–88 (2007)
7. Horvat, M., Gledec, G., Bogunović, N.: Assessing Semantic Quality of Web Directory Structure. In: Nguyen, N.T., Kowalczyk, R., Chen, S.-M. (eds.) ICCCI 2009. LNCS (LNAI), vol. 5796, pp. 377–388. Springer, Heidelberg (2009)
8. Sedgewick, R.: Algorithms in C++, 3rd edn. Addison-Wesley, Reading (2001)
9. Horrocks, I.: Ontologies and the Semantic Web. Communications of the ACM 51(12), 58–67 (2008)
10. Antoniou, G., van Harmelen, F.: A Semantic Web Primer. MIT Press, Cambridge (2004)
11. Uschold, M.: Where are the Semantics in the Semantic Web? AI Magazine 24(3), 25–36 (2003)

12. Horvat, M., Gledec, G., Bogunović, N.: Decision Support Systems in Ontology-Based Construction of Web Directories. In: Proc. of the 4th International Conference on Software and Data Technologies, ICSOFT 2009, pp. 281–286 (2009)
13. Gledec, G., Jurić, J., Matijašević, M., Mikuc, M.: WWW.HR - Experiences with Web-server development and maintenance. In: Proc. of the 18th International Conference on Computers in Telecommunications, 22nd International Convention MIPRO'99, pp. 93–96 (1999)
14. Ehrig, M., Sure, Y.: Ontology mapping - an integrated approach. In: Bussler, C.J., Davies, J., Fensel, D., Studer, R. (eds.) ESWS 2004. LNCS, vol. 3053, pp. 76–91. Springer, Heidelberg (2004)
15. Euzenat, J., Shvaiko, P.: Ontology Matching. Springer, Heidelberg (2007)
16. Staab, S., Studer, R.: Handbook on Ontologies. Handbooks in Information Systems. Springer, Heidelberg (2004)
17. Schraefel, M.C.: Building Knowledge: What's Beyond Keyword Search? IEEE Computer Magazine 42(3), 52–59 (2009)
18. Li, J., Zhang, L., Yu, Y.: Learning to Generate Semantic Annotation for Domain, Specific Sentences. In: Delugach, H.S., Stumme, G. (eds.) ICCS 2001. LNCS (LNAI), vol. 2120, p. 44. Springer, Heidelberg (2001)
19. Brin, S.: Extracting patterns and relations from the World Wide Web. In: Atzeni, P., Mendelzon, A.O., Mecca, G. (eds.) WebDB 1998. LNCS, vol. 1590, pp. 172–183. Springer, Heidelberg (1999)
20. Gledec, G., Matijašević, M., Jurić, D.: Improving Search on WWW. HR Web Directory by Introducing Ontologies (2005)
21. Horvat, M., Popović, S., Bogunović, N., Ćosić, K.: Tagging Multimedia Stimuli with Ontologies. In: Proc. of the 32nd International Convention MIPRO 2009: Computers in Technical Systems, Intelligent Systems, pp. 203–208 (2009)

Distributed Deliberative Recommender Systems

Juan A. Recio-García, Belén Díaz-Agudo,
Sergio González-Sanz, and Lara Quijano Sanchez

Department of Software Engineering and Artificial Intelligence,
Universidad Complutense de Madrid, Spain
jareciog@fdi.ucm.es, belend@sip.ucm.es,
sergio.gonzalez@ciemat.es, lara.quijano@fdi.ucm.es

Abstract. Case-Based Reasoning (CBR) is one of most successful applied AI technologies of recent years. Although many CBR systems reason locally on a previous experience base to solve new problems, in this paper we focus on *distributed retrieval* processes working on a network of collaborating CBR systems. In such systems, each node in a network of CBR agents collaborates, arguments and counterarguments its local results with other nodes to improve the performance of the system's global response. We describe D²ISCO: a framework to design and implement deliberative and collaborative CBR systems that is integrated as a part of jCOLIBRI 2 an established framework in the CBR community. We apply D²ISCO to one particular simplified type of CBR systems: recommender systems. We perform a first case study for a collaborative music recommender system and present the results of an experiment of the accuracy of the system results using a fuzzy version of the argumentation system AMAL and a network topology based on a social network. Besides individual recommendation we also discuss how D²ISCO can be used to improve recommendations to *groups* and we present a second case of study based on the movie recommendation domain with heterogeneous groups according to the group personality composition and a group topology based on a social network.

1 Introduction

Case-Based Reasoning (CBR) is based on the intuition that situations tend to recur. It means that new problems are often similar to previously encountered problems and, therefore, that past solutions may be of use in the current situation [1].

Research efforts in the area of *distributed CBR* concentrate on the distribution of resources within CBR architectures and study how it is beneficial in a variety of application contexts. In contrast to single-agent CBR systems, multi-agent systems distribute the case base itself and/or some aspects of the reasoning among several agents. In [2] the research efforts in the area of distributed CBR are categorized using two criteria: (1) how knowledge is organised/managed within the system (i.e. single vs. multiple case bases), and (2) how knowledge is processed by the system (i.e. single vs. multiple processing agents).

N.T. Nguyen and R. Kowalczyk (Eds.): Transactions on CCI I, LNCS 6220, pp. 121–142, 2010.

Much of the work in distributed CBR assumes multi-case base architectures involving multiple processing agents differing in their problem solving experiences [3]. The "ensemble effect" [4] shows that a collection of agents with uncorrelated case bases improves the accuracy of any individual. Multiple sources of experience exist when several CBR agents need to coordinate, collaborate, and communicate. Within this purpose AMAL has been proposed as a case-based approach to groups of agents that coordinate, collaborate, and communicate in order to improve their collective and individual decisions by learning from communication and by argumentation over debated outcomes [4].

Our current work, described in this paper, explains the modification of the AMAL approach to use fuzzy reasoning to combine recommendations that are retrieved from each agent's database using CBR to compute similarity. Recommendations are propagated through a network that is modelled after a social network, while agents model behaviours to exhibit personality traits that feed into a process of group recommendation.

The paper also has important technological contributions. jCOLIBRI 2 [5] is a well established framework in the CBR community that can be used to design different types of CBR systems [6]. However its underlying architecture has taken the conventional so called *single agent, single case base* problem solving approach where one, usually well-maintained, case base functions as the central knowledge resource. In this paper we propose two working extensions, ((S)ALADIN and D2ISCO[18]), to jCOLIBRI 2 to design deliberative and distributed multiagent CBR systems where the case base itself and/or some aspects of the reasoning process are distributed among several agents. Our work focuses on distributed *retrieval* processes working on a network of collaborating CBR systems. We deal with aspects such as the topology of the network, the definition of trust models for the different agents, voting and negotiation techniques between agents to reach a consensus in the final solution. In this paper we consider a simplified type of retrieval-only CBR systems: recommender systems. CBR has played a key role in the development of several classes of recommender systems [7] as it is straightforward to establish a correspondence between retrieval in CBR systems and the process of obtaining goals and preferences of a user in order to rank products, services or information sources in recommender systems.

In the network of agents every agent should be able to define the trustworthiness regarding the connected agents [8,9]. In the recommender systems arena, in order to provide meaningful results, trust, or reputation, must reflect user similarity to some extent; recommendations only make sense when obtained from like-minded people exhibiting similar taste. Our model is based on the social connections of the collaborative agents, including the level of trust of the agent they collaborate with. We use social trust as the basis for recommender systems [10] [11][12]. Social networks offer an opportunity to get information about the social environment of a given user and associate trustworthiness values to it. If a node receives a query and it cannot give a good answer to it, then it will ask for collaborations with other nodes it has relations or links with. The trust models evolve in time according to the real accuracy of the answers provided by a certain node.

We perform a case study for a collaborative music recommender system for individuals and present the results of an experiment of the accuracy of the system results using a fuzzy version of the argumentation system AMAL and a network topology based on a social network.

Although most of the popular recommender systems are focused on recommending items for individual users, the need of systems capable of performing recommendations for groups of people is getting more interest as there are many activities that are carried out in groups, e.g., going to the cinema with friends, watching TV at home or listening music in the car. Existing works on group recommender systems [13] are typically based on the aggregation of the preferences of the members of the group where every person in the group is considered as equal to the others. A group recommender usually manages several subsets of preferences -one per person- that have to be managed independently and combined to create a global recommendation suitable for everyone in the group. According to this, it is natural to think about a distributed architecture where the preferences of every user are managed independently by an autonomous agent. This agent represents the user inside the global recommender system and is in charge of promoting his preferences when making a recommendation process for the whole group. We present a case study of movie recommendation for groups.

The paper runs as follow. Section 2 describes our approach to design distributed CBR systems with deliberation capabilities, and the software support we provide for our approach. We focus on the modification of the AMAL protocol to use fuzzy reasoning to combine recommendations that are retrieved from each agent's database using CBR to compute similarity. A first case study in the music recommendation domain for individual users is presented in 3. In Section 4 we describe how to extend these deliberation capabilities for group recommendations and present a preliminary case study on the movie recommendation domain. Section 5 summarizes the main results and concludes the paper.

2   Distributed Reasoning for Collective Experiences

The development of distributed CBR systems with deliberation capabilities is not a simple task from the software engineering point of view. To alleviate this design cost we have identified a set of different features that characterize different architectures of distributed deliberative systems, namely:

- Number of agents. Distributed systems could range from a few agents to thousands of them, so the platform must be scalable.
- Size of the case base. From small to large sizes, it has a direct impact in the retrieval time.
- Overlapping of the case base of different agents. Some distributed systems contain agents with independent case bases where cases cannot be owned by several agents. On the other hand, some architectures allow the overlapping of individual case bases.

- Type of cases. Case bases can be homogeneous if cases have the same attributes or heterogeneous if their structure changes among agents. This feature has a repercussion in the deliberation protocol and the reasoning technique.
- Network topology. There are different ways to organize and link agents: all-with-all, ring, star, hierarchical, etc.
- Trust model. Depending on the nature of the distributed system, there are several options for building a trust model that will affect the deliberation process.
- Composition of the final result. Every agent can have a different impact in the final result depending on the number or quality of cases provided to the deliberation.
- Deliberation protocol. There are several deliberation protocols that are can be applied only depending on the nature of the agents.
- CBR reasoning. In this kind of systems every agent executes its own CBR reasoning process. This process could be different for every agent or they can execute just the same reasoning method.
- Query propagation. Queries can be propagated in different ways through the agents network.

We also provide software support and we have extended jCOLIBRI 2 [5], a general platform for the implementation of different kinds of CBR systems, to support designing different types of distributed deliberative systems characterized according to these features. The basic extension to support distributed CBR applications in jCOLIBRI 2 is called ALADIN (Abstract Layer for Distributed Infrastructures). This layer defines the main components of every distributed CBR system: agents, directory, messages, etc. and could be implemented using different alternatives: JADE [1], sockets, shared memory, ... It was defined after reviewing the existing literature on distributed CBR and tries to fit the IEEE FIPA standards for multiagent systems. Because ALADIN is only composed of interfaces that define the behavior of the system, we have developed an implementation of this abstract layer using standard network sockets. This extension is called SALADIN (Sockets implementation of ALADIN) and provides a fully functional multi-agent environment for building distributed CBR systems that could be particularized in many ways. In this paper we detail one of these particularizations.

D²ISCO[2] is built on top of SALADIN and it provides one particular choice of the deliberation functionality [14]. D²ISCO deliberation capabilities are rooted in the AMAL argumentation process proposed in [4,15]. These extensions and D²ISCO are available in the jCOLIBRI 2 contributions web page [3]. Next we will detail the deliberation protocol of D²ISCO.

---

[1] JADE is a framework for building multi-agent systems following the FIPA specifications. It is available at: http://jade.tilab.com/

[2] D²ISCO: **D**eliberative, **DIS**tributed & **CO**llaborative extension for jCOLIBRI

[3] jCOLIBRI contributions:
http://gaia.fdi.ucm.es/projects/jcolibri/jcolibri2/contributions.html

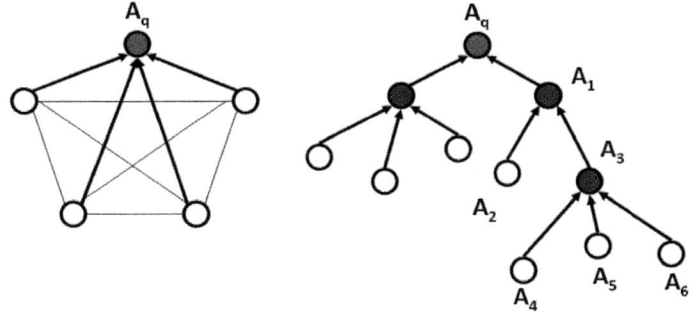

Fig. 1. Comparison between AMAL (left) and D²ISCO (right) topologies

2.1 D²ISCO **Deliberation Protocol**

D²ISCO deliberation capabilities are rooted in the AMAL argumentation process proposed in [4,15]. AMAL follows the same mechanism as human committees, first each individual member of a committee exposes his arguments and discuses those of the other members (joint deliberation), and if no consensus is reached, then a voting mechanism is required.

The interaction protocol of AMAL allows a group of agents $A_1, \ldots, A_n$ to deliberate about the correct solution of a problem Q by means of an argumentation process. Each of these agents uses a CBR system to find a solution for Q using their own case base and then they start a deliberation process to order the local solutions and find the best of them. If the argumentation process arrives to a consensual solution, the joint deliberation ends; otherwise a weighted vote is used to determine the joint solution [15]. Moreover, AMAL also allows the agents to learn from the counterexamples received from other agents. The reasoning protocol begins with an agent (A_q) issuing a query to the agents that is linked to $(A_1, A_2, ..., A_n)$. Each one of these agents retrieves k items from their own case base. Then, an argumentation process consisting of k cycles is performed to defend and discard the proposed items by means of counterexamples. When the process finishes A_q receives at most k trusted items.

The AMAL protocol consists on a series of rounds. In the initial round, each agent states which is its individual local solution for the problem Q. Then, at each round an agent can try to rebut the solution or prediction made by any of the other agents giving a counterexample. When an agent receives a counterargument or counterexample, it informs the other agents if it accepts the counterargument (and changes its solution) or not. Moreover, agents have also the opportunity to answer to counterarguments by trying to generate a counterargument to the counterargument.

Although the original AMAL design does not satisfy requirements for our application it is readily adaptable. Next we summarize some of the requirements we need to adjust from the original AMAL approach:

- Regarding the topology, AMAL proposes to link every agent with all the agents in the system. This N to N topology has repercussions in the efficiency of the argumentation process and it is not scalable to real size systems.
- In real scenarios, users –or agents– are organized and linked by means of topologies that are analogous to social networks. Therefore, the N to N topology does not reflect faithfully the relations among users.
- AMAL is based on Description Logic (DLs) case representation and reasoning what implies an additional knowledge representation effort.
- AMAL does not take into account the trust between agents in the argumentation process.

Our D²ISCO approach for building distributed and deliberative systems solves the requirements mismatch with the original AMAL protocol. Namely, the features of our framework are:

- The topology of the systems follows the structure of a social network. This enables to increase easily the number of agents in the system and to incorporate trust factors in the argumentation process that are obtained from this social network.
- Social networks offer an opportunity to get information about the social environment of a given user and associate trustworthiness values to it. If the social network connects users with similar tastes, that means that it reflects the preferences of the users and make it possible to add this information to the argumentation process. This way, social networks have two possible uses: 1) to obtain the trust among users, and 2) to compute the similarity between users according to its preferences.
- The argumentation process is directed by a lead node/agent A_q that issues the query and organizes the deliberation of its children nodes (A_c). This agent is in charge of accepting or rejecting the counterexamples presented by those children agents.
- Our argumentation and case retrieval process is hierarchical. When solving a problem Q, the agent that issues the query A_q becomes the root of the whole hierarchy of agents –defined by the structure of the social network. Then, the query is sent to the leaves of the tree and the retrieval follows an inverse direction. The leafs of the tree deliberate with their immediate parent A_p node that organizes the reasoning. When this intermediate deliberation finishes, A_p participates in the deliberation organized by its parent node but this time it takes the role of a children node A_c. This behavior is repeated until reaching the root A_q. It is important to note that in every intermediate deliberation A_p receives the cases retrieved by its children nodes A_c and incorporates them in its own case base. Figure 1 illustrate the difference between AMAL and D²ISCO topologies. The direction of the arrows represent the forwarding of cases. The left graph shows a typical AMAL net where every agent is linked with every agent. On the right we find the hierarchical topology of D²ISCO. Here we can note how the argumentation process begins with A_3 being the organizing agent (A_c) and $\{A_4, A_5, A_6\}$ its corresponding children (A_c). Afterward, A_3 takes part of the deliberation

conducted by A_1 where $A_c = \{A_2, A_3\}$. Finally, A_1 contributes in the final deliberation leaded by A_q.

- D²ISCO reasons with the case ratings and it does not requires expressive case representations based on DLs. To substitute the reasoning capabilities of DLs, our approach uses a fuzzy decision system. Moreover this fuzzy system takes into account the trust and similarity between users –obtained from the social network– and the similarity between cases.

- Because we are not using logical formulas to define the counterarguments, our deliberative process applies the concept of *defenses*. Defenses are complete cases that are highly rated by the agent involved in the deliberation and are offered to trust the arguments presented by the agent.

Once we have described the behavior of our approach, we can focus on its main improvement: the fuzzy decision system. Next section summarizes its main features and illustrates it by means of an example.

2.2 Fuzzy Decision System

A key feature of the distributed reasoning protocol described in the previous section is the decision system that accepts or rejects counterexamples and defenses. In the original AMAL protocol these arguments are generated using a description logic. Our proposal relies in a fuzzy reasoner [16] that allows extending the protocol to cases which attributes are not expressed using a description logic, and thus, it is not possible to generate arguments using logic induction. For instance, in the CBR recommender systems, most of the items' attributes are numeric values referring customers' opinions and it is not possible to generate a logic induction using these numeric values. However, these attributes contain important pieces of information that must be used in order to improve the results of the recommender system. The developed fuzzy reasoner allows using these numeric attributes to generate arguments for the reasoning protocol.

It is important to note that the agent that leads the argumentation (A_p) does not retrieve cases from its own case base, but plays an important role in the argumentation because defines the trust in the agents involved in the argumentation process. Trust is an important input for the fuzzy subsystems explained below. It is a numeric value between the leader of the argumentation process A_p an a agent taking part in the argumentation A_r. The value of the trust between agent A_p and agent A_r may vary in time according to the quality of the solutions given by A_r to the queries started by A_p. The value of trust from A_p to A_r can be different to the value of trust from A_r to A_p because the quality of the solutions of A_r can be higher or lower than the solutions given by A_p. A set of membership functions must be defined in order to allow the system using this value.

According to the terminology of recommender systems we define the measure of *goodness* as the *rating* of the item given by the corresponding agent/user. In our case, goodness is a numeric value which minimum and maximum values may vary according to the concrete problem solved by the distributed CBR system (for instance, in the following example the maximum value of goodness is 10 and the minimum is 0). A set of membership functions must be defined in order to allow the system using the goodness value. As the maximum and the minimum values, the membership functions must be fitted to the concrete problem that is being solved. In the following example, five different membership functions have been defined.

The fuzzy decision system is divided into five subsystems implemented using large fuzzy rule bases. Each one of these five subsystems is involved in one step of the argumentation process. The designed subsystems are:

1. **Case evaluation subsystem:** it generates a value V_t measuring the degree of trust for a certain case C_i solving a query Q. It uses as inputs: 1) the value of goodness of C_i in its local case base, 2) the similarity between C_i and the current query Q, and 3) the compatibility between agent A_i that returns C_i and the agent that initiates the query A_q.

   The value V_t is maximum when the value of goodness of C_i is maximum, C_i is equal to the query Q and A_i is similar to the agent that starts the query A_q. V_t will decreased if the value of goodness of C_i falls, C_i is not complete similar to the query Q or A_i is not complete similar to the agent A_q. The minimum value of V_t is reached when the value of goodness of C_i is minimum, C_i has nothing in common to the query Q and A_i and A_q are not compatible at all. It means that a case is a good solution to a query Q if the user's rating (goodness) is high, the case is similar to the query Q and the user is compatible to the user that makes the query.

2. **Counterexample evaluation subsystem:** a counterexample against the case C_i is a case C_e that is rather similar to C_i but it has a low value of goodness. The subsystem measures the trust of a counterexample (V_c). If an agent A_i presents a counterexample, it includes the value V_c that indicates its confidence on its argumentation. To obtain this value, the fuzzy subsystem uses: 1) the goodness of C_e in its local case base, 2) the similarity between C_e and Q, and 3) the compatibility between agent A_i and A_q.

   The value V_c is maximum if the value of goodness of C_e is minimum and the similarity between C_e and Q and between A_i and A_q is maximum. If the value of goodness of C_e rises, or the similarity between C_e and Q or between A_i and A_q falls, the value V_c will fall. The minimum value of V_c is reached when the value of goodness of C_e is maximum, and the similarity between C_e and Q and between A_i and A_q are minimum. It means that a case is a good counterexample if the user's rating (goodness) is low, the case is similar to the case being rebutted and the user is compatible with the user that makes the query.

3. **Counterexample acceptance subsystem:** it decides if a counterexample is accepted. A value (V_a) is computed when an agent A_i proposes a counterexample C_e to the conducting agent A_p. It is based on: 1) the confidence of the counterexample V_c, 2) A_p trust in A_i, and 3) A_p trust in the agent being rebutted. Finally, the counterexample is accepted if the *defuzzifyed* value of V_a is higher than a certain threshold α defined in the system $(V_a > \alpha)$. The

α value is a numeric value that should be tuned for the different problems to be solve by the CBR system.

If there is a large value of V_c, a large value of trust in A_i and a low value of the trust in the agent being rebutted, then the value V_a will be large. If the confidence in the counterexample V_c or the trust in A_i falls, the value V_c will fall. V_c also will fall if the trust in the agent being rebutted rises. It means that is easier to accept a counterexample of an agent if its trust is high and the trust in the agent being rebutted is low. If the trust in of both agents is high, the decision will rely on the value V_c.

4. **Defense evaluation subsystem:** A defense against a counterexample C_e is a case C_d that is rather similar to C_e and it has a high value of goodness. The subsystem measures the trust of a defense (V_d). If an agent A_j presents a defense for one of its solutions to a query, it includes the value V_d that indicates its confidence on its argumentation. This subsystem is analogous to V_c and is based on: 1) the similarity between a case C_d and the counterexample that is being rebutted C_e and 2) the goodness of C_d in its local case base.

The value V_d is high when there is a high value of goodness of C_d and a high similarity between C_d and C_e. The value V_d will fall if any of these values fall. It means that a case is a good defense if it is similar to the counterexample being rebutted and it has a good user's rating.

5. **Defense acceptance subsystem:** it is analogous to the counterexample acceptance subsystem and decides if a defense is accepted by the conducting agent A_p. A value (V_n) is generated when an agent A_j proposes a defense V_d for one of its solutions to a query and against a counterexample with trust V_c of an agent A_i. The subsystem bases its decisions on: 1) the trust of A_p in A_i, 2) the trust of A_p in A_j, 3) the trust value of the counterexample V_c and, 4) the trust value of the defense V_d. Finally, the defense is accepted if the defuzzifyed value of V_n is higher than a certain threshold β defined in the system $(V_n > \beta)$. The β value is a numeric value that should be tuned for the different problems to be solve by the CBR system.

The value V_n will be high if the trust in A_i is low, the trust in A_p is high, the trust is the counterexample V_c is low and the trust in the defense V_d is high. It means that a defense is easier accepted if the trust of the rebutting agent and its counterexample are low and the trust in the defending agent and its defense are high.

Since the fuzzy decision system needs to compare cases and agents, two fuzzy *similarity functions* has been implemented. They obtain a similarity value between cases or agents comparing their attributes one by one. It is also possible to compare a case to query because a query is expressed as a case with missing attributes.

Example. To illustrate the behavior of our deliberative recommender, let's use a real example described in Table 1. Here we will not use intermediate nodes for clarity reasons. Also every agent returns only one case. In the example A_q

Table 1. Argumentation Example

	Rating	Artist	Title	Year	Price	Style
Query (Q)	10	Mike Oldfield	*	*	*	*
Case-A_2 (C_2)	5,58	Mike Oldfield	The Millennium Bell	1999	11	House
Case-A_3 (C_3)	3,77	Mike Oldfield	Hergest Ridge	1974	26	Rock
Case-A_1 (C_1)	1,82	Mike Oldfield	Crises	1983	22	Rock
Round 1 - A_2 has the token						
A_2 counterexample for C_1	0,5	Mike Oldfield	Incantations	1978	27	Rock
Accepted because A_1 cannot generate a defense						
Round result:						
C_2	5,58	Mike Oldfield	The Millennium Bell	1999	11	House
C_3	3,77	Mike Oldfield	Hergest Ridge	1974	26	Rock
Round 2 - A_3 has the token						
A_3 counterexample for C_2	1,36	Deep Dish	George is on	2005	19	House
A_2 defense (C_e)	5,3	Deep Dish	George is on	2005	19	House
A_2 defense is accepted						
Round result:						
C_2	5,58	Mike Oldfield	The Millennium Bell	1999	11	House
C_3	3,77	Mike Oldfield	Hergest Ridge	1974	26	Rock
Round 3 - A_1 has the token						
A_1 counterExample for C_2	1,67	Mike Oldfield	Earth Moving	1989	23	Pop
Accepted because A_2 cannot generate a defense						
Round result:						
C_3	3,77	Mike Oldfield	Hergest Ridge	1974	26	Rock

sends the query to A_1, A_2 and A_3, and they answer returning a case in the order shown in the table (A_2,A_3,A_1). This order is used to decide how to propose the examples and counterexamples.

In the first round, A_2 begins presenting a counterexample to the case C_1 retrieved by A_1. A_q decides to accept the counterexample because A_1 cannot generate any defense by retrieving another counterexample from its case base. This way, C_1 is removed from the initial retrieved set. The following round begins with A_3 having the token. Here it presents a counterexample to the case C_2 retrieved by A_2, but this agent manages to find a defense D_2 that is accepted by A_q. Therefore, the round finishes without changes in the retrieved set. In the third round, A_1 has the token and presents a counterexample for C_2 that is accepted. As this case is removed, the only remaining case is C_3 that is the solution that A_q obtains for its query.

During each round of the argumentation, the fuzzy system participates several times. To illustrate its behavior let's detail the reasoning process of the first round. It begins when A_2 presents a counterexample C_e for C_1. The behavior of this subsystem is shown in the first row of Figure 2. On the left we find the inputs and outputs of the system and on the right we have included a representation of the fuzzy formula with $(rat(C_e) = 0.5)$. The output value is $V_c = 9$ and it is the trust measure sent by A_2 to A_q. Then, A_q decides if the counterexample is accepted taking into account its trust in A_1 –the case being rebutted–, A_2 and V_c. This subsystem is shown in the second row of Figure 2 with V_c set to

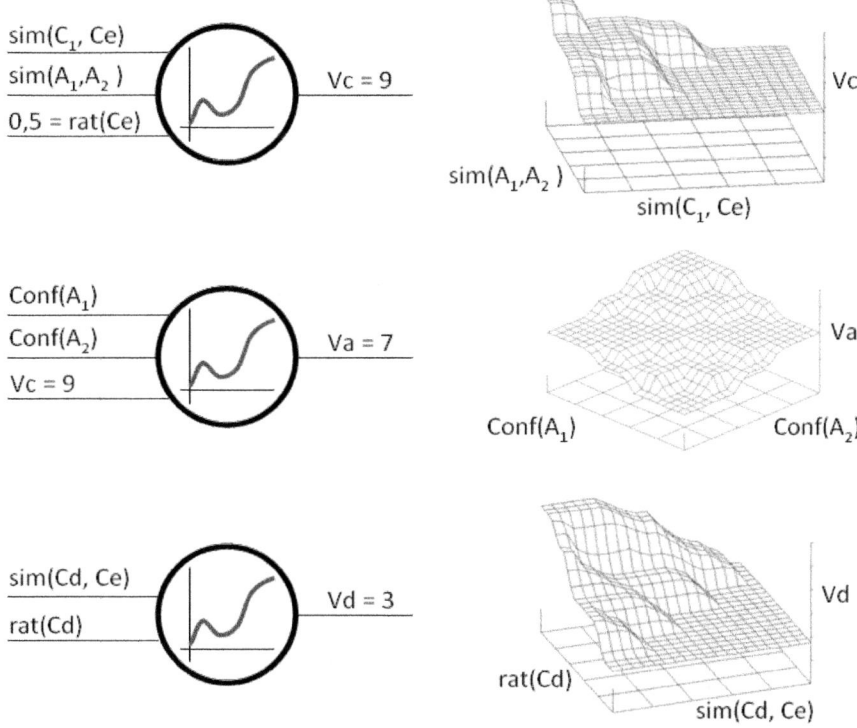

Fig. 2. Example of the behavior of the second, third and fourth fuzzy subsystem

9. Here, the result is $V_a = 7$ and it exceeds the threshold $\alpha > 6.5$ configured in the system. It means that the counterexample is accepted and sent to A_1. Next A_1 has the opportunity of presenting a defense. It looks in its case base but it cannot find any case which $V_d > \beta$ that has been set to $\beta = 5$. This step is represented in the third row of Figure 2. Therefore the first round finishes by removing C_1 from the retrieval set. If A_1 could find a defense, it will be sent –together with V_d– to A_q and a reasoning process similar to the one shown in the second row of Figure 2 would happen.

3   Case Study: Distributed and Collaborative Music Recommender System

In this section we describe a case study in the domain of music recommendation. Music is a classical example where several successful recommender applications have been proposed. The reason is that there are many users interested in finding and discovering new music that would fulfill their preferences. Moreover, the users of this kind of applications tend to interchange recommendations with other users that have similar preferences.

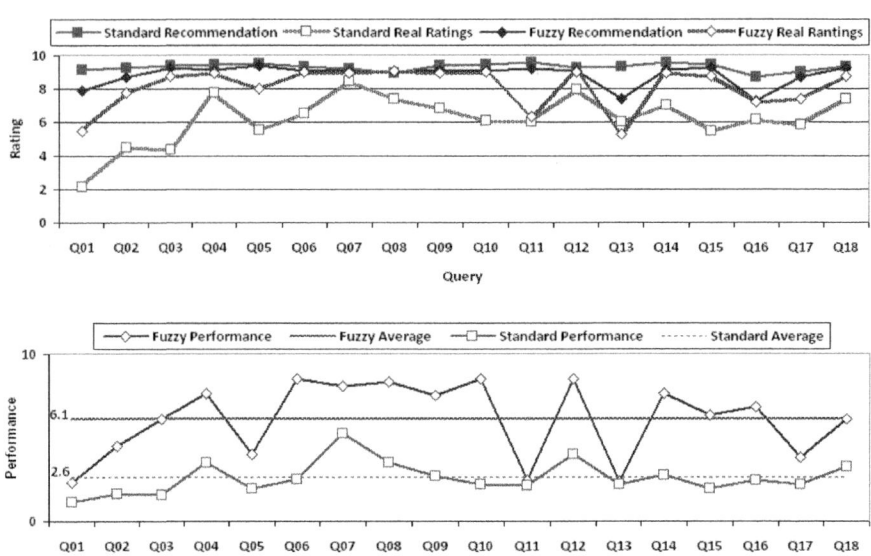

Fig. 3. Results using a social network built with Pearson's coefficients

Relationships between users that make up social networks, reflect the similarity in the preferences of the users and allow them to discover new interesting items. We measure the trust value between two users depending on their corresponding distance in the social network.

The experiments were designed to simulate a real scenario with the highest possible fidelity. As the case base has a catalog of songs, and each user may have a part of this catalog in its internal list of rated items. Every user interacts with its corresponding recommender agent. When a recommender agent receives a query from the user, it forwards the query to the other agents in the system. These agents will use their rated items to recommender songs that fulfill the preferences of the query. Agents are organized according to a social network that ideally reflects the similarity and confidence between users. Our premise is that a real social network will relate users with similar preferences, but this initial intuition was also tested in our experiments by simulating two different networks: a network that relates users with similar preferences and a random social network. To measure the benefits of the architecture of our recommender we used cross-validation over the rated items of a user, by comparing the recommendations performed by a single agent that manages the whole catalog –this is, the real ratings of the user– and the recommendations of our collaborative approach. We have simulated a real social network where we have randomly generated the ratings of the users to control the different factors involved in the experiment. The catalog of songs contains 300 real items. Then we used two numbers of users for every experiment: 10 and 20 users. A local product base of 50 songs was assigned to every user in a random way. It means that these local catalogs may overlap. The ratings of the songs were simulated by assigning preference profiles to the users. Then, ratings were generated using probabilistic distributions associated with every preference of the profile. For example, a user that prefers pop songs will rate higher this kind of items according to certain probability.

The most important component of the experiment is the social network that relates users according to their similarity and mutual confidence. Our initial premise was that a real network will reflect this feature, so we decided to generate the network by linking users with similar preferences. To perform this, we have used the Pearson's coefficient. This metric is a common way for measuring the similarity between users in recommender systems. So, we decided to compute this coefficient between every pair of users in the system and create a network link if a pair has a similarity above certain threshold. However, to test the influence of the topology of the network in the recommendation process we also generated another network with random links. Finally, we used these coefficients to define the confidence level between each pair of users/agents. Figure 3 shows some representative results of our case study. These graphs summarize the ratings obtained with our fuzzy approach compared to the standard AMAL protocol. Here we are raising 18 random queries into a network with 50 users linked by means of the Pearson's coefficients. To measure the performance of the system we used a cross-validation process and compared the ratings for the k best recommended items with the real ratings given by the user to these same items. Ideally, a perfect recommender system will return high rated items according to the preferences of the user. To illustrate this measure, the upper graph of Figure 3 shows the ratings of the recommended items together with the real ratings of the user for these items. Note, that the songs retrieved by both systems (fuzzy and standard) can be different for the same query and it implies that the lines showing the average of the real ratings given by the user for these retrieved sets are different too.

As the graph shows, the original AMAL protocol tends to offer high ratings because it simply chooses the best-rated items from every agent. However, this does not reflect the real ratings given to these items by the user, and therefore the two lines *Standard Recommendation* and *Standard Real Ratings* are quite distant. On the other hand, our fuzzy decision system approximates better the preferences of the user, and the differences with the real ratings are lower meanwhile returning high rated items. This is due to the improvement in the negotiation and decision system thanks to the fuzzy reasoning.

It is important to note that during the experiments we obtained no significant differences when modifying the k value. Moreover we found another noticeable feature: the similarity between the recommended items to the query and the similarity of the corresponding real user-rated items to the query was very close. This result allowed us to leave the similarity aside and concentrate our performance measures on the ratings of the items.

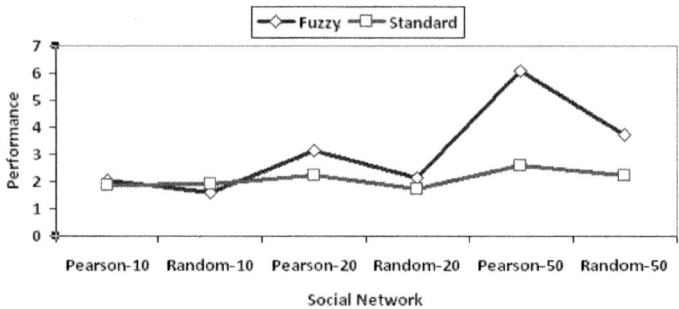

Fig. 4. Global results using different social networks

Because we are trying to maximize the ratings but minimizing their difference with the real ones, we have defined the following performance measure to test our architecture of recommender systems:

$$performance = \frac{rat_{rec}(r)}{1 + |rat_{rec}(r) - rat_{real}(r)|}$$

where r is the set of k items returned by the system, $rat_{rec}(r)$ is the average of the ratings returned by the recommender for r, and rat_{rec} is the average of the real ratings given to r by the user. Figure 3-bottom shows graphically this performance measure for both approaches (fuzzy and original AMAL). Here, a higher value means better performance, and as we can note, the fuzzy approach is always on top. We also include the average of both lines to measure the global performance of the recommendation. These results provide supporting evidence that the fuzzy approach (section 2.2) is significantly better than the original AMAL protocol. Moreover, we have included the performance of the system without any argumentation protocol by issuing the queries to every agent and selecting the top-rated item. Although these ratings are very high, they do not reflect the preferences of the user and the performance of this simple strategy is worse. This fact proves the "ensemble effect" described in [4]: a collection of agents with uncorrelated case bases improves the accuracy of any individual[4].

Finally, we have generated several social networks with different topologies to test the behavior of the architecture of our recommender. Results are shown in Figure 4, where we measure the performance for random and Pearson-based networks with 10, 20 and 50 nodes. Our reasoning process always reports better results with the networks generated using Pearson's coefficients. This fact confirms our premise that social networks will improve the recommendation process. Regarding the fuzzy improvement for the standard AMAL protocol, the Figure shows that the fuzzy approach is better for the networks with 20 and 50 nodes. In the case of the 10-node networks, the fuzzy system is not able to find the minimum similarity relationships between users to perform the decision process

---

[4] Under some restrictions like the aggregation function (e.g. majority voting) or the retrieval strategy (e.g. content-based k-NN).

correctly. However, this is a coherent and meaningless consequence due to the low number of users in the network.

4   From Individual to Group Recommendations

Although many popular recommender systems are focused on recommending items for individual users, the need of systems capable of performing recommendations for groups of people is getting more interest as there are many activities that are carried out in groups, e.g., going to the cinema with friends, watching TV at home or listening music in the car.

There has recently been a body of work about recommenders that extend their recommendations to groups of users [13]. When moving from individuals to groups many new issues arises. For example, acquiring the preferences of the group, helping the group to decide the more convenient option, or explaining the recommendation to the group. Depending on the size and homogeneity of the group the recommender system has to choose the option that satisfies the biggest number of people taking into account the individual user preferences. As stated in [13] the main approaches to generate a preference aggregation based on the individual user preferences are (a) merging the recommendations made for individuals, (b) aggregation of ratings for individuals and (c) constructing a group preference model.

A group recommender usually manages several subsets of preferences -one per person- that have to be managed independently and combined to create a global recommendation suitable for everyone in the group. According to this, it is natural to think in a distributed architecture like D^2ISCO where the preferences of every user are managed independently by an autonomous agent. This agent represents the user inside the global recommender system and is in charge of promoting his preferences when making a recommendation process for the whole group.

Although existing works on group recommender systems are typically based on the aggregation of the preferences of the members of the group where every person in the group is considered as equal to the others, our recent work [17] involves the improvement of current group recommendation techniques by introducing a novel factor: the personality of every individual. Intuitively, when a group of 2 or more friends choose a movie there are some members that are only happy if they impose their opinion, whereas other individuals don't care letting other people decide. Therefore, we have used a personality test to obtain different profiles that interact in different ways when joining a decision making process.

Besides personality, there is another important factor to consider: the structure of the group. We propose a distributed CBR architecture using D^2ISCO where each person in the group is represented by an agent and the final recommendation is influenced by the personality of each member of the group and the way they are interconnected through their social relations, basically friendship, defined in the social network. Therefore our method proposes making recommendations to groups using existing techniques of collaborative filtering [18], taking into account the group personality composition and the social connections between the individuals of the group.

Groups of people can have very different characteristics like size and can be made of people with similar or antagonistic personal preferences. It is a fact that when we face a situation in which the concerns of people appear to be incompatible conflict arises. The existing recommender systems for groups typically solve the conflict trying to maximize the preferences of the biggest number of group members. However, the general satisfaction of the group is not always the aggregation of the satisfaction of its members as different people have different expectations and behaviour in conflict situations that should be taken into account. In our approach we distinguish between different types of individuals in a group. This research characterizes people using the Thomas-Kilmann Conflict Mode Instrument (TKI) [19]. The TKI is a test designed to measure the behavior of people in such situations. It is a leader instrument in conflict resolution assessment that is used often by Human Resources and Organizational Development consultants to facilitate learning about how conflict handling styles affect personal and group dynamics. TKI builds a user's profile by means of 30 single choice questions. The test provides scores for the previous five modes (competing, collaborating, etc), representing the preferences of that person when she has to face conflicts. These scores are normalized to obtain percentiles from a 8000 people sample.

TKI characterizes a person behavior in conflict situations along two basic dimensions: assertiveness and cooperativeness. These two dimensions of behavior can be used to define five personality modes of dealing with conflicts: competing, collaborating, avoiding, accommodating and compromising. Our method takes into account these five personality modes. We have performed a first simulation to determine if the group personality composition influences the recommendation accuracy for the group. In fact, we have preliminary concluded that recommendation accuracy is improved for certain types of groups compared with different simple group recommendation algorithms. We have experimentally evaluated the behavior of this method in the Movie recommendation domain using the Movie-Lens data set with groups of users of different sizes and degrees of homogeneity. The novelty of our approach lies in the use of the member personalities to choose the most interesting movie that would better satisfy the whole group, using the type of personality trait of dealing with conflicts of each member to weight the influence of his/her ratings during the recommendation process.

We have included in the deliberative processes of D^2ISCO the use of real social networks topologies to reflect the real interactions of the users. Our proposal relates also with other works that have employed more social issues in order to include the group member interactions to perform the recommendations. For example, the work described in [20] uses individual satisfaction and the transmission of emotions in order to recommend a sequence of video clips for a group. They consider that a member changes the selection of her best clip according to the clip selected during the previous selection step. This change can be reflected in the recommendation algorithm as an individual satisfaction function that computes the individual affective state. This state influences on the affective state of the other members, getting carried by others emotional state should be taken into account during the group recommendation. Other interesting results from this work are that the most common strategies employed by individuals in real group recommendation are non-dominant strategies such as the average, least misery and average without misery. Additionally, they point out the existence of a tendency where the social status influences on the selection.

4.1 Using the D²ISCO Deliberation Capabilities for Group Recommendations

The development of recommender systems for groups including deliberative capabilities is not a simple task from the software engineering point of view. Such a system involves the management of several users with different preferences that interact remotely to agree on a common decision. This way, we require the infrastructure to build a distributed system where, usually, every user is represented by an agent that manages their preferences. Each agent will be in charge of deliberate with other agents an find a satisfactory solution for the user is representing.

D²ISCO allows including deliberative capabilities in the distributed CBR systems to reach a consensus between the members of the group. Moreover, we have included two novel factors that enables us to improve the recommendation process for groups of users: The personality of every individual and their interconnections.

To include the personality and topology factors in the D²ISCO framework we must split the users into different groups according to their social relationships. Then every group will begin a deliberation process through the reasoning capabilities detailed in Section 2. When every subgroup has found a local solution suitable for its members, a new deliberation process begins where each subgroup is an entity represented by an agent. These new agents will find a global solution that tries to satisfy the preferences of every subgroup.

The reason why this new organization of the structure of the group will affect and improve the result of the recommendation is mainly because with the social network topology we give a more realistic structure and organization of the agents, which is closer to how the argumentations would take place in a real group when they argue on which movie to watch. For a given a group of friends, we draw a network where each node represents a person, and each connection represents that a particular person has a relation with the one he is connected to. Each node discusses his/her opinions with all her neighbors in the network. When two nodes are not connected, it means that the people they are representing don't know each other or that they're not close, this structure is reflecting a face to face discussion where they would have never argue or have to come to a solution between each other. For example if someone brings along his/her boy/girlfriend and the rest of the group doesn't know him, this new member will never start arguing or try convincing someone he has never met before, therefore when we represent this relations we only connect him with the ones that do know him. On the other hand in the all connected network topology every agent will debate with all the rest, no matter if the person he represents knows the other one or not.

Next we summarize our approach:

1. Given: a set of users $U = \{u_1, u_2, \ldots, u_i, \ldots, u_n\}$ (where u_q is the user that launches the query), the set of relationships of an user $rel(u_i)$, and the personality weight $per(u_i)$.

2. Split U into several subsets $S = \{S_1, S_2, \ldots, S_j, \ldots, S_m\}$ where $S_j \subseteq U$.

3. For every $S_j \in S$ compute
$I_j = obtainSubRecommendation(S_j, rel(u_i \in S_j), per(u_i \in S_j))$

4. Being $I = \{I_1, I_2, \ldots, I_j, \ldots, I_m\}$ the set of items recommended by each subset,
For every $I_j \in I$
$w_j = \sum rel(u_i \in S_j).r + \sum per(u_i \in Sj).p$

5. Return the item I_j with the maximum weight w_j

Note that this algorithm implies several processes that must be carefully addressed. Firstly we found the process of splitting the users according to the topology of the social network. In our preliminary experiments we are identifying the k users with more relationships as the "group leaders" and then assigning every remaining user to one of these leaders. Moreover, there is a second way to organize the users: some social networks allow to group users according to the different groups they have joined or by common interests. For example, Figure 5 shows the representation of a real social network in Facebook[5]. This social network allows to classify the users into groups (represented using different areas in the figure, that we have intentionally highlighted). This feature enables us to split the U set into subsets S_j that reflect the relationships of the users in a very realistic manner. Furthermore, Figure 5 serves to confirm our premise that real interactions between users do not follow an all-with-all topology as was illustrated in Figure 1.

After splitting the users, our algorithm applies the method in charge of obtaining the recommendation from every subset S_j. This method is based in the D²ISCO argumentation protocol (detailed in Section 2) that uses arguments and counterarguments in the deliberation process. Finally the global process that combines the partial results (step 4), takes into account the number of relationships inside every subset S_j ($rel(u_i \in S_j)$) and their accumulated personality weight $per(u_i \in S_j)$. The number of relationships is directly obtained from the social network just by counting if two users are friends or not. However, the personality weight is much more difficult to measure. To obtain it, we are using the TKI tests detailed previously. We are summarizing the 5 different modes in just one value. This value is high if the person has a competing and collaborative profile and is low if the person has an avoiding or accommodating

---

[5] This figure has been obtained using the touch graph application in Facebook.
`http://apps.facebook.com/touchgraph/`

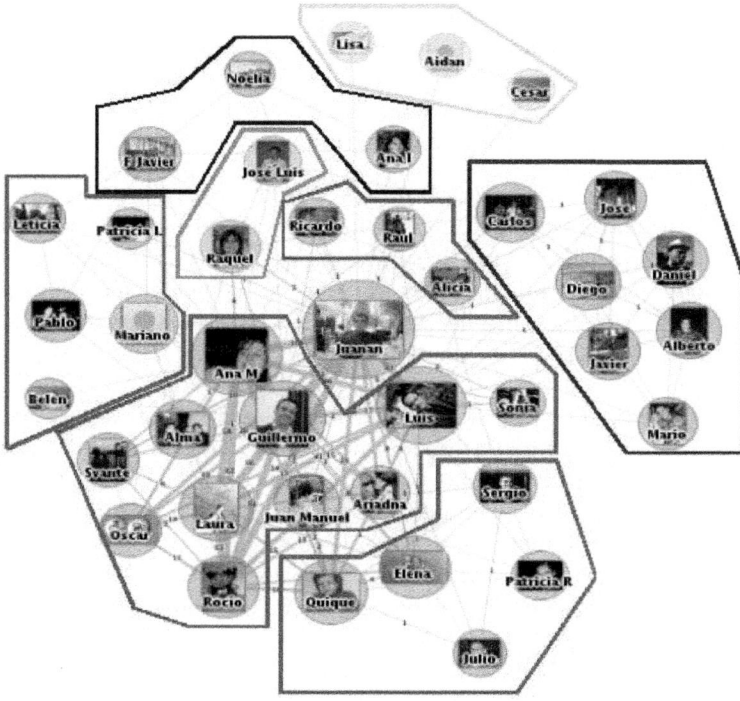

Fig. 5. Users organization in a real social network

personality. Informally, we are giving more importance to the subset that contains more related users and has the highest personality. Parameters r and p are weights for both factors (related users and personality). Parameter r defines how the number of relations of every subset determines the final recommendation. In addition, parameter p weights the impact of the accumulated personality in the recommendation. This accumulated personality is the addition of the personality factor of every user in a subgroup S_j.

4.2 Case Study: Recommender for Groups

To illustrate the advantages of our approach for group recommendations we have ran an preliminary experiment that aids groups of users to choose a movie. A movie recommender system is typically based on rating movies the user has seen and recommending other movies user might like. MovieLens[6] is a good recommendation engine based on collaborative filtering that evaluates user tastes based on ratings to movies seen before. MovieLens is traditionally cited in research works because their developers provide the collected user ratings as a complete anonymous dataset.

---

[6] http://movielens.umn.edu/

Our experiment is based on MovieLens dataset but complemented with a set of 70 students from a AI course at the Universidad Complutense de Madrid. They have filled in some surveys with their personal and group preferences about movies and we used them to develop and test our approach. Our experiment requires the following sources of information:

- $User_i$ ratings for a large set of movies. To obtain a proper rating set we mix a set of ratings extracted from the Movielens Database with ratings obtained from our users . To obtain these ratings we propose our users to rate a list of 50 heterogeneous movies selected from the Movielens data set. In average, users rated 33 movies. Finally we obtain our dataset with a total of 400 users (70 students and the rest anonymous from movielens database) and ≈300k ratings.
- Conflict personality values obtained using the TKI test described.
- Affinity between students to organize groups to run our simulations. We used a test to measure the people affinity to go to the cinema together. This feature represents the social network topology, i.e., if they are friends or not, and then run our simulations using these groups.
- A set of 15 movies that represents the Movie Listings of a cinema. This set was again chosen heterogeneously from the most recent movies in the Movielens Database.
- "Group goes to the cinema" simulation to test our proposal. Our students are joined in groups according to their affinity and they talk for a while to decide which 3 movies they would watch together from the Movie Listings. We also ask these users individually to choose his/her favorite movie from the listings .

With these users and data we have performed an preliminary experiment to test that recommender systems for groups improve accuracy when using the *conflict personality values* and the *social organization* into groups. Further details of this experiment can be found in [17]. Preliminary results indicate that our recommender algorithm obtains better results for groups with people having heterogeneous personalities and having at least a leader in the group. Further systematic experiments need to be done in this area.

5   Conclusions

This paper describes D²ISCO: a framework to design and implement deliberative and collaborative CBR systems. We have performed a case study for a collaborative music recommender system from a catalog of 300 items and networks of up to 50 nodes where the local catalogs overlap. We have presented the results of an experiment of the accuracy of the system results using a fuzzy version of the argumentation system AMAL and a network topology based on a simulated social network. We have generated several social networks using Pearson's relation between ratings. We measure the performance for random and Pearson-based networks with different number of nodes. Our reasoning process and architecture of recommender always reports better results with the networks generated using Pearson's coefficients. This fact confirms our premise that social networks will improve the recommendation process. Regarding the argumentation process we have shown that the fuzzy improvement of the standard AMAL protocol is better with a bigger number of nodes. Besides, although the original AMAL protocol tends to offer high ratings, the fuzzy decision system approximates better the preferences of the user, and the differences with the real ratings are lower meanwhile returning high rated items. This is due to the improvement in the negotiation and decision system thanks to the fuzzy reasoning.

We also present an approach to apply our techniques to group recommendations but including a novel factor: members personality. The novelty of our approach lies in the use of the member personalities to choose the most interesting movie that would better satisfy the whole group, using the type of personality trait of dealing with conflicts of each member to weight the influence of his/her ratings during the recommendation process. We have included in the deliberative processes of D²ISCO the use of real social networks topologies to reflect the real interactions of groups of users. Our case study in the domain of movie recommendations shows that both the social network topology of the agents plus the personality profile of the users are factors than can improve the accuracy of group recommenders compared to classic approaches based on the aggregation of the individual preferences.

D²ISCO has been integrated as a part of jCOLIBRI 2 [5] an established framework in the CBR community. As an ongoing work we are designing a set of reusable templates for collaborative and distributed systems, we are proposing a declarative characterization of this kind of systems based on its observable characteristics, like the number of nodes, topology of the network, number of cases of the local case bases, overlapping between the case bases,and the type of argumentation and reasoning processes. We are evaluating the templates in the context of recommender systems. The recommender domain is specially appropriate to work with social networks topologies, because the recommendations can be biased towards the social environment of each node.

References

1. Leake, D.B., et al.: Case-based reasoning: Experiences, lessons, and future directions. AAAI Press/MIT Press, Menlo Park (1996)
2. Plaza, E., McGinty, L.: Distributed case-based reasoning. Knowledge Eng. Review 20(3), 261–265 (2005)
3. McGinty, L., Smyth, B.: Collaborative case-based reasoning: Applications in personalised route planning. In: Aha, D.W., Watson, I. (eds.) ICCBR 2001. LNCS (LNAI), vol. 2080, pp. 362–376. Springer, Heidelberg (2001)
4. Ontañón, S., Plaza, E.: Arguments and counterexamples in case-based joint deliberation. In: Maudet, N., Parsons, S., Rahwan, I. (eds.) ArgMAS 2006. LNCS (LNAI), vol. 4766, pp. 36–53. Springer, Heidelberg (2007)
5. Díaz-Agudo, B., González-Calero, P.A., Recio-García, J.A., Sánchez-Ruiz-Granados, A.A.: Building cbr systems with jcolibri. Sci. Comput. Program. 69(1-3), 68–75 (2007)

6. Díaz-Agudo, B., González-Calero, P.A., Recio-García, J.A., Sánchez, A.: Building cbr systems with jcolibri. Special Issue on Experimental Software and Toolkits of the Journal Science of Computer Programming 69(1-3), 68–75 (2007)
7. Bridge, D., Göker, M.H., McGinty, L., Smyth, B.: Case-based recommender systems. Knowledge Engineering Review 20(3), 315–320 (2006)
8. Grandison, T., Sloman, M.: A Survey of Trust in Internet Applications. IEEE Communications Surveys and Tutorials 3(4), 2–16 (2000)
9. Golbeck, J., Hendler, J.A.: Inferring binary trust relationships in web-based social networks. ACM Trans. Internet Techn. 6(4), 497–529 (2006)
10. McDonald, D.W.: Recommending collaboration with social networks: a comparative evaluation. In: CHI '03: Proceedings of the SIGCHI conference on Human factors in computing systems, pp. 593–600. ACM, New York (2003)
11. Golbeck, J.: Generating predictive movie recommendations from trust in social networks. In: Stølen, K., Winsborough, W.H., Martinelli, F., Massacci, F. (eds.) iTrust 2006. LNCS, vol. 3986, pp. 93–104. Springer, Heidelberg (2006)
12. Ziegler, C.N., Golbeck, J.: Investigating interactions of trust and interest similarity. Decision Support Systems 43(2), 460–475 (2007)
13. Jameson, A., Smyth, B.: Recommendation to groups. In: Brusilovsky, P., Kobsa, A., Nejdl, W. (eds.) Adaptive Web 2007. LNCS, vol. 4321, pp. 596–627. Springer, Heidelberg (2007)
14. González-Sanz, S., Recio-García, J.A., Díaz-Agudo, B.: D^2ISCO: Distributed Deliberative CBR Systems with jCOLIBRI. In: Nguyen, N.T., Kowalczyk, R., Chen, S.-M. (eds.) ICCCI 2009. LNCS, vol. 5796, pp. 321–332. Springer, Heidelberg (2009)
15. Ontañón, S., Plaza, E.: An argumentation-based framework for deliberation in multi-agent systems. In: Rahwan, I., Parsons, S., Reed, C. (eds.) Argumentation in Multi-Agent Systems. LNCS (LNAI), vol. 4946, pp. 178–196. Springer, Heidelberg (2008)
16. Zimmermann, H.J.: Fuzzy set theory—and its applications, 3rd edn. Kluwer Academic Publishers, Norwell (1996)
17. Recio-García, J.A., Jimenez-Diaz, G., Sánchez-Ruiz-Granados, A.A., Díaz-Agudo, B.: Personality aware recommendations to groups. In: Proceedings of the 2009 ACM Conference on Recommender Systems, RecSys 2009, pp. 325–328. ACM, New York (2009)
18. Herlocker, J.L., Konstan, J.A., Terveen, L.G., Riedl, J.T.: Evaluating collaborative filtering recommender systems. ACM Trans. Inf. Syst. 22(1), 5–53 (2004)
19. Thomas, K., Kilmann, R.: Thomas-Kilmann Conflict Mode Instrument, Tuxedo, N.Y. (1974)
20. Masthoff, J., Gatt, A.: In pursuit of satisfaction and the prevention of embarrassment: affective state in group recommender systems. User Modeling and User-Adapted Interaction 16(3-4), 281–319 (2006)

Fuzzy Cognitive and Social Negotiation Agent Strategy for Computational Collective Intelligence

Amine Chohra, Kurosh Madani, and Dalel Kanzari

Images, Signals, and Intelligent Systems Laboratory (LISSI / EA 3956), Paris-East University
(UPEC), Senart Institute of Technology, Avenue Pierre Point, 77127 Lieusaint, France
{chohra,madani,kanzari}u-pec.fr

Abstract. Finding the adequate (*win-win* solutions for both parties) negotiation
strategy with *incomplete* information for autonomous agents, even in one-to-
one negotiation, is a complex problem. Elsewhere, negotiation behaviors, in
which the characters such as conciliatory or aggressive define a '*psychological*'
aspect of the negotiator personality, play an important role. The aim of this paper is to develop a fuzzy cognitive and social negotiation strategy for autonomous agents with incomplete information, where the characters conciliatory,
neutral, or aggressive, are suggested to be integrated in negotiation behaviors
(inspired from research works aiming to analyze human behavior and those on
social negotiation psychology). For this purpose, first, one-to-one bargaining
process, in which a buyer agent and a seller agent negotiate over single issue
(price), is developed for a time-dependent strategy (based on time-dependent
behaviors of Faratin *et al.*) and for a fuzzy cognitive and social strategy. Second, experimental environments and measures, allowing a set of experiments,
carried out for different negotiation deadlines of buyer and seller agents, are detailed. Third, experimental results for both time-dependent and fuzzy cognitive
and social strategies are presented, analyzed, and compared for different deadlines of agents. The suggested fuzzy cognitive and social strategy allows agents
to improve the negotiation process, with regard to the time-dependent one, in
terms of agent utilities, round number to reach an agreement, and percentage of
agreements.

Keywords: Social and cognitive systems, negotiation, incomplete information,
behaviors, strategies, adaptation.

1 Introduction

Negotiations have received wide attention from the distributed Artificial Intelligence
(AI) community as a pervasive mechanism for distributed conflict resolution between
intelligent computational agents [1]. In fact, the ability to successfully negotiate and
to collaboratively solve problems and seize opportunities is increasingly a necessity of
effective management, and rests on a combination of analytical and interpersonal
skills. In the case of negotiation, analysis is important because collective problem
solvers cannot develop promising strategies without a deep understanding of the
structure and context of the situation, the interests of other parties, the opportunities

N.T. Nguyen and R. Kowalczyk (Eds.): Transactions on CCI I, LNCS 6220, pp. 143–159, 2010.

and barriers to creating and claiming value (twin forces of cooperation and competition) on a sustainable basis, and the range of possible moves and countermoves both at and away from the "bargaining table". Beyond analysis, interpersonal skills are important because negotiation and other forms of collective problem-solving are essentially processes of communication, relationship and trust building (or breaking) and mutual persuasion. "*Interpersonal skills*" refers to mental and communicative algorithms applied during social communications and interaction to reach certain effects or results. The term "interpersonal skills" is used often in business contexts to refer to the measure of a person's ability to operate within business organizations through social communication and interactions. Interpersonal skills are how people relate to one another.

In a context where agents must reach agreements (deals) on matters of mutual interest, *negotiation* techniques for reaching agreements (deals) are required. In general, any negotiation settings will have four different components [2]:

- 1) a negotiation set, the space of possible proposals that agents can make ;
- 2) a protocol, the legal proposals that agents can make ;
- 3) a collection of strategies, one for each agent, which determine what proposals agents will make ;
- 4) an agreement rule that determines the reach agreements (deals) stopping the negotiation.

Negotiation usually proceeds in a series of rounds, with every agent making a proposal at every round. The proposals that agents make are defined by their strategy (a way to use the protocol), must be drawn from the negotiation set, and must be legal, as defined by the protocol (which defines possible proposals at different rounds). If agreement is reached, as defined by the agreement rule, then negotiation terminates with agreement deal. These four parameters lead to an extremely rich and complex environment for analysis. Another source of complexity in negotiation is number of agents involved in process, and the way in which these agents interact [2]. First possibility is one-to-one negotiation, second possibility is many-to-one negotiation (which can be treated as a number of concurrent one-to-one negotiations), and third possibility is many-to-many negotiation (hard to handle).

An interesting survey on negotiation models in the AI field is given in [3], [4], [5]. Elsewhere, Lomuscio *et al.* [6] identified the main parameters on which any automated negotiation depends and provided a classification scheme for negotiation models. The environment that a negotiator is situated in greatly impacts the course of negotiation actions. Instead of focusing on analyzing the strategy equilibrium as a function of (the distribution of) valuations and historical information as in game theory, AI researchers are interested in designing flexible and sophisticated negotiation agents in complex environments with incomplete information. Agents have incomplete and uncertain information about each other, and each agent's information (e.g., deadline, utility function, strategy, ...) is its private knowledge.

An important research work has been developed by Faratin *et al.* [7] which devised a negotiation model that defines a range of strategies and behaviors for generating proposals based on time, resource, and behaviors of negotiators. By another way, in the research works developed aiming to analyze and describe the human behavior in [8], twelve categories representing three major parts of the behavior have been defined: the positive socio-emotional part, a neutral task part, and the negative socio-emotional part. In another side, in research works on the social psychology of the negotiation of Rubin and Brown developed in [9], the interpersonal orientation of a person has an influence on his negotiating behavior. It is predominantly concerned with the degree of a person's responsiveness. If he is not responsive, he stands to gain much in negotiating situation due to deliberateness of his behavior. Responsive people are more co-operative and therefore expect positive results. Personality type should therefore be determined first to obtain the best results in negotiation. Thus, negotiation behaviors, in which characters such as conciliatory, neutral, or aggressive define a 'psychological' personality aspect of a negotiator, play an important role.

Personality is one of major problems (architectures of the brain, mechanisms of the natural intelligence, cognitive processes, mental phenomena, and personality) yet to be addressed in cognitive informatics which is an emerging transdisciplinary research area that encompasses informatics, computer science, software engineering, mathematics, cognition science, neurobiology, psychology, and philosophy [10]. Almost all of the hard problems yet to be solved in these areas can be deduced onto the common root for understanding the mechanisms of natural intelligence and cognitive processes of the brain [11]. Moreover, to achieve human level machine intelligence is a challenge that is hard to meet, because humans have many remarkable capabilities, there are two that stand out in importance. First, the capability to reason, converse, and make rational decisions in an environment of imprecision, uncertainty, incompleteness of information, and partiality of truth and possibility. And second, the capability to perform a wide variety of physical and mental tasks without any measurements and any computations (L. A. Zadeh in [11]).

The aim of this paper is to develop a fuzzy cognitive and social negotiation strategy for autonomous agents with incomplete information, where the characters conciliatory, neutral, or aggressive, are suggested to be integrated in negotiation behaviors (inspired from research works aiming to analyze human behavior and those on social negotiation psychology). For this purpose, first, one-to-one bargaining process, in which a buyer agent and a seller agent negotiate over single issue (price), is developed in Sect. 2 for a time dependent strategy (based on time dependent behaviors of Faratin *et al.* [7]) and for a fuzzy cognitive and social strategy. Second, experimental environments and measures, allowing a set of experiments carried out for different negotiation deadlines of buyer and seller agents, are detailed in Sect. 3. Third, experimental results for both time-dependent and fuzzy cognitive and social strategies are presented, analyzed, and compared for different deadlines of agents in Sect. 4.

2 One to One Negotiation Agent Strategy

In this Section, one-to-one bargaining process, in which a buyer agent and a seller agent negotiate, over single issue (price), is developed for the two strategies.

2.1 Negotiation Set

A negotiation set is the space of possible proposals that agents can make. The negotiation set (objects): the range of issues over which an agreement must be reached. Let i represents the negotiating agents, in bargaining bilateral negotiation i ∈ {buyer(b), seller(s)}, and j the issues under negotiation, in single issue negotiation j = *price*. The value for issue *price* acceptable by each agent i is $x^i \in [min^i, max^i]$.

2.2 Negotiation Protocol

A protocol is the legal proposals that agents can make. The process of negotiation can be represented by rounds, where each round consists of an offer from agent b (buyer) at time t_1 and a counter-offer from an agent s (seller) at time t_2. Then, a negotiation consists in a sequence of rounds: round1 (t_1, t_2), round2 (t_3, t_4), ... Thus, for a negotiation between agents b and s, and if agent b starts first, then it should offer in times (t_1, $t_3, t_5, ..., t^b_{max}$), and agent s provides counter-offers in ($t_2, t_4, t_6, ..., t^s_{max}$), where t^b_{max} and t^s_{max} denote negotiation deadline for agents b and s, respectively. Note that the three different deadline cases are allowed: 1) $t^b_{max} > t^s_{max}$, where considered deadline is $T_{max} = t^s_{max}$; 2) $t^b_{max} = t^s_{max}$, where considered deadline is $T_{max} = t^b_{max} = t^s_{max}$; 3) $t^b_{max} < t^s_{max}$, where considered deadline is $T_{max} = t^b_{max}$.

For agent b, the proposal to offer or accept is within interval $[min^b, max^b]$, where max^b is the buyer reservation price in negotiation thread, and min^b is the lower bound of a valid offer. Similarly, for agent s, the proposal to offer or accept is within interval $[min^s, max^s]$, where min^s is the seller reservation price and max^s is the upper bound of a valid offer. Initially a negotiator offers most favorable value for himself: agent b starts with min^b and agent s starts with max^s. If proposal is not accepted, a negotiator concedes with time proceeding and moves toward other end of the interval.

2.3 Negotiation Behaviors

The paces of concession depend on the negotiation behaviors of agent b and agent s which are characterized by negotiation decision functions. For negotiation strategies, time t is one of predominant factors used to decide which value to offer next.

Time-Dependent Agent Behaviors: Time-dependent functions are used as negotiation decision functions varying the acceptance value (price) for the offer depending on the remaining negotiation time (an important requirement in negotiation), i.e., depending on t and t^b_{max} for agent b and depending on t and t^s_{max} for agent s. Thus, proposal $x^b[t]$ to be offered by agent b and the one $x^s[t]$ to be offered by agent s at time t, with $0 <= t <= t^i_{max}$ belonging to [0, T - 1], are as follows. The proposal $x^s[t]$ to be offered by agent s at time t, with $0 <= t <= t^s_{max}$ belonging to [0, T - 1], is defined by Eq. (1).

$$x^s[t] = min^s + (1 - \alpha^s(t)) (max^s - min^s),$$

where $\alpha^s(t)$ are time-dependent functions ensuring that: $0 <= \alpha^s(t) <= 1$,   (1)
$\alpha^s(0) = K^s$ (positive constant) and $\alpha^s(t^s_{max}) = 1$.

Such $\alpha^s(t)$ functions can be defined in a wide range according to the way in which $\alpha^s(t)$ is computed (the way they model the concession), e.g., polynomial in Eq.(2).

$$\alpha^s(t) = K^s + (1 - K^s)(\frac{min(\,t,t^s_{max}\,)}{t^s_{max}})^{\frac{1}{\beta}}.$$

(2)

Indeed, the constant $\beta > 0$ determines the concession pace along time, or convexity degree of the offer curve as a function of the time. By varying β a wide range of negotiation behaviors can be characterized: Boulware (B) with $\beta < 1$ and Conceder (C) with $\beta > 1$ [5], and the particular case of Linear (L) with $\beta = 1$.

Fuzzy Cognitive and Social Agent Behaviors: The proposal $x^b[t]$ to be offered by agent b at time t, with $0 <= t <= t^b_{max}$ belonging to [0, T - 1], is defined using fuzzy cognitive and social strategy detailed in Sect. 2. 4.

2.4   Negotiation Strategies

A collection of strategies, one for each agent, which the role is to determine what proposals agents will make (which behavior should be used at any one instant).

Time-Dependent Agent Strategy: During a negotiation *thread* (the sequence of rounds with offers and counter-offers in a two-party negotiation), a negotiation strategy based on time-dependent behaviors defined in [7] consists to define the way in which such behaviors are used. In this paper, each strategy uses individually the behaviors Boulware (B), Linear (L), or Conceder (C) during a negotiation thread.

Fuzzy Cognitive and Social Agent Strategy: Suggested fuzzy cognitive and social agent strategy, illustrated by synopsis in Fig. 1, is built of a similarity degree (from the previous buyer offer and the current seller offer), a Fuzzy System 1 (FS1), an updating of the internal agent behaviors, a difference, a Fuzzy System 2 (FS2), a Fuzzy System 3 (FS3), and an updating of the proposal (giving the next buyer offer).

Similarity Degree. Similarity degree S[t], see [12], is computed using the Eq. (3):

$$S[t] = 1 - \frac{\left|x^b[t-1] - x^s[t]\right|}{max\{x^b[t-1], x^s[t]\}} = \frac{min\{x^b[t-1], x^s[t]\}}{max\{x^b[t-1], x^s[t]\}}.$$

(3)

Fuzzy System 1 (FS1). For FS1, time deadline t ---> Tmax = [0, 100] is normalized in [0, 1] and character variations is given from t and similarity degree.

Fuzzy Rule Base 1: from 2 input variables S[t] and t, 2 output variables giving the character variations $\Delta Agg[t]$ and $\Delta Con[t]$, and 3 fuzzy membership functions for each variable as defined in Fig. 2, $3^2 = 9$ fuzzy rules are deduced as in Table 1.

The fuzzy linguistic variables, for each fuzzy membership function, are defined as:

- S[t]: Desirable (D), Acceptable (A), and Undesirable (Und),
- t: Favorable (F), Critical (C), and Unfavorable (Unf),
- $\Delta Agg[t]$ and $\Delta Con[t]$: Very Negative (VN), Negative (N), Positive (P), and Very Positive (VP).

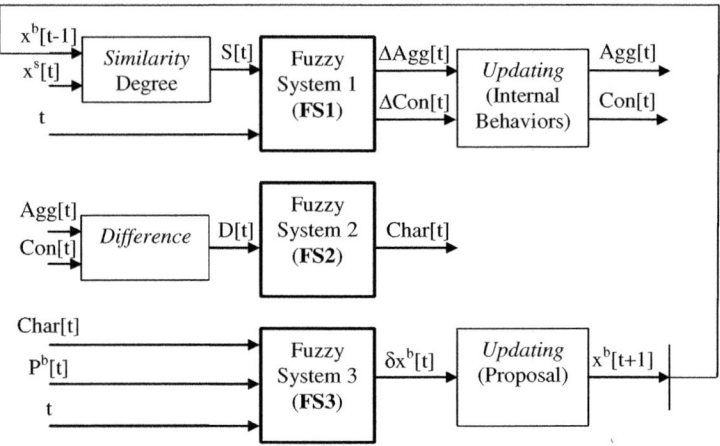

Fig. 1. Fuzzy cognitive and social strategy synopsis

Table 1. Fuzzy rule base 1

If (S^t is D and t is F) Then ($\Delta Agg[t]$ is N and $\Delta Con[t]$ is P),
If (S^t is D and t is C) Then ($\Delta Agg[t]$ is N and $\Delta Con[t]$ is VP),
If (S^t is D and t is Unf) Then ($\Delta Agg[t]$ is VP and $\Delta Con[t]$ is VN),
If (S^t is A and t is F) Then ($\Delta Agg[t]$ is N and $\Delta Con[t]$ is P),
If (S^t is A and t is C) Then ($\Delta Agg[t]$ is N and $\Delta Con[t]$ is P),
If (S^t is A and t is Unf) Then ($\Delta Agg[t]$ is VP and $\Delta Con[t]$ is VN),
If (S^t is Und and t is F) Then ($\Delta Agg[t]$ is P and $\Delta Con[t]$ is N),
If (S^t is Und and t is C) Then ($\Delta Agg[t]$ is P and $\Delta Con[t]$ is VN),
If (S^t is Und and t is Unf) Then ($\Delta Agg[t]$ is VP and $\Delta Con[t]$ is VN).

Updating (Internal Behaviors). Internal behavior updating is achieved by Eq. (4).

$$Agg[t] = Agg[t\text{-}1] + \Delta Agg[t] \text{ and } Con[t] = Con[t\text{-}1] + \Delta Con[t]. \tag{4}$$

Difference. The difference is achieved using Eq. (5).

$$D[t] = Con[t] - Agg[t]. \tag{5}$$

Fuzzy System 2 (FS2). This system gives new agent character from the difference of internal behavior characters.

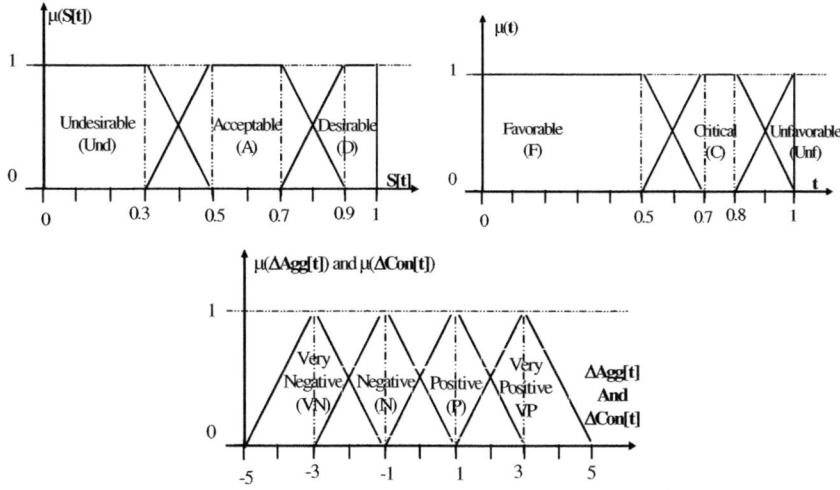

Fig. 2. Fuzzy membership functions of S[t], t, and ΔAgg[t] and ΔCon[t]

Fuzzy Rule Base 2: from 1 input variable D[t], 1 output variable Char[t], and 4 fuzzy membership functions, for each variable as defined in Fig. 3, $4^1 = 4$ fuzzy rules are deduced as in Table 2. Fuzzy linguistic variables, for each fuzzy membership function, are defined:

- D[t]: Very Negative (VN), Negative (N), Positive (P), and Very Positive (VP),
- Char[t]: Very Aggressive (VAgg), Aggressive (Agg), Conciliatory (Con), and Very Conciliatory (VCon).

Table 2. Fuzzy rule base 2

If (D[t] is VN) Then (Char[t] is VAgg),
If (D[t] is N) Then (Char[t] is Agg),
If (D[t] is P) Then (Char[t] is Con),
If (D[t] is VP) Then (Char[t] is VCon).

Fuzzy System 3 (FS3). For FS3, profit of agent b is $P^b[t]$ such as defined in Eq. (6) and variation of the proposal is given from new agent character, agent profit, and t.

$$P^b[t] = max^b - x^s[t]. \qquad (6)$$

where max^b is the reservation price of agent b and $x^s[t]$ the proposal of agent s.

Fuzzy Rule Base 3: from 3 input variables Char[t], $P^b[t]$, t, 1 output variable $\delta x^b[t]$, and 4 fuzzy membership functions for Char[t] defined in Fig. 3, 3 fuzzy membership functions for $P^b[t]$ defined in Fig. 4, 3 fuzzy membership functions for t defined in Fig. 2, and 4 fuzzy membership functions for $\delta x^b[t]$ defined in Fig. 4, $3^2 * 4^1 = 36$ fuzzy rules are deduced in Table 3.

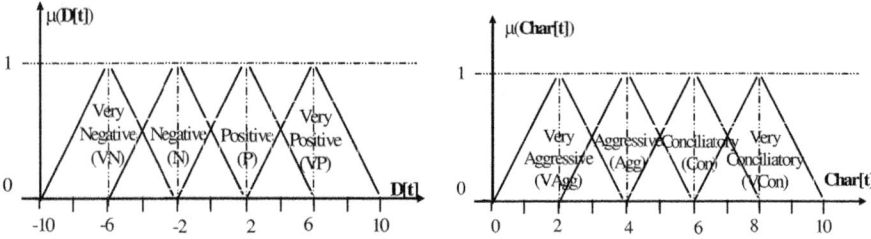

Fig. 3. Fuzzy membership functions of D[t] and Char[t]

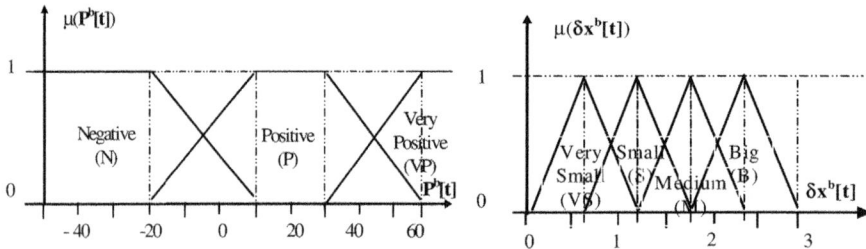

Fig. 4. Fuzzy membership functions of $P^b[t]$ and $\delta x^b[t]$.

The fuzzy linguistic variables, for each fuzzy membership function, are defined as:

- Char[t]: Very Aggressive (VAgg), Aggressive (Agg), Conciliatory (Con), and Very Conciliatory (VCon),
- $P^b[t]$: Negative (N), Positive (P), and Very Positive (VP),
- t: Favorable (F), Critical (C), and Unfavorable (Unf),
- $\delta x^b[t]$: Very Small (VS), Small (S), Medium (M), Big (B), and null.

Table 3. Fuzzy rule base 3

If (Char[t] is VAgg and $P^b[t]$ is N and t is F) Then ($\delta x^b[t]$ is VS),
If (Char[t] is VAgg and $P^b[t]$ is P and t is F) Then ($\delta x^b[t]$ is null),
If (Char[t] is VAgg and $P^b[t]$ is VP and t is F) Then ($\delta x^b[t]$ is null),
If (Char[t] is VAgg and $P^b[t]$ is N and t is C) Then ($\delta x^b[t]$ is VS),
If (Char[t] is VAgg and $P^b[t]$ is P and t is C) Then ($\delta x^b[t]$ is null),
If (Char[t] is VAgg and $P^b[t]$ is VP and t is C) Then ($\delta x^b[t]$ is null),
If (Char[t] is VAgg and $P^b[t]$ is N and t is Unf) Then ($\delta x^b[t]$ is null),
If (Char[t] is VAgg and $P^b[t]$ is P and t is Unf) Then ($\delta x^b[t]$ is null),
If (Char[t] is VAgg and $P^b[t]$ is VP and t is Unf) Then ($\delta x^b[t]$ is null),
If (Char[t] is Agg and $P^b[t]$ is N and t is F) Then ($\delta x^b[t]$ is S),
If (Char[t] is Agg and $P^b[t]$ is P and t is F) Then ($\delta x^b[t]$ is VS),
If (Char[t] is Agg and $P^b[t]$ is VP and t is F) Then ($\delta x^b[t]$ is null),
If (Char[t] is Agg and $P^b[t]$ is N and t is C) Then ($\delta x^b[t]$ is VS),

Table 3. *(continued)*

If (Char[t] is Agg and $P^b[t]$ is P and t is C) Then ($\delta x^b[t]$ is null),
If (Char[t] is Agg and $P^b[t]$ is VP and t is C) Then ($\delta x^b[t]$ is null),
If (Char[t] is Agg and $P^b[t]$ is N and t is Unf) Then ($\delta x^b[t]$ is null),
If (Char[t] is Agg and $P^b[t]$ is P and t is Unf) Then ($\delta x^b[t]$ is null),
If (Char[t] is Agg and $P^b[t]$ is VP and t is Unf) Then ($\delta x^b[t]$ is null),
If (Char[t] is Con and $P^b[t]$ is N and t is F) Then ($\delta x^b[t]$ is M),
If (Char[t] is Con and $P^b[t]$ is P and t is F) Then ($\delta x^b[t]$ is S),
If (Char[t] is Con and $P^b[t]$ is VP and t is F) Then ($\delta x^b[t]$ is null),
If (Char[t] is Con and $P^b[t]$ is N and t is C) Then ($\delta x^b[t]$ is VS),
If (Char[t] is Con and $P^b[t]$ is P and t is C) Then ($\delta x^b[t]$ is VS),
If (Char[t] is Con and $P^b[t]$ is VP and t is C) Then ($\delta x^b[t]$ is null),
If (Char[t] is Con and $P^b[t]$ is N and t is Unf) Then ($\delta x^b[t]$ is null),
If (Char[t] is Con and $P^b[t]$ is P and t is Unf) Then ($\delta x^b[t]$ is null),
If (Char[t] is Con and $P^b[t]$ is VP and t is Unf) Then ($\delta x^b[t]$ is null),
If (Char[t] is VCon and $P^b[t]$ is N and t is F) Then ($\delta x^b[t]$ is B),
If (Char[t] is VCon and $P^b[t]$ is P and t is F) Then ($\delta x^b[t]$ is S),
If (Char[t] is VCon and $P^b[t]$ is VP and t is F) Then ($\delta x^b[t]$ is null),
If (Char[t] is VCon and $P^b[t]$ is N and t is C) Then ($\delta x^b[t]$ is S),
If (Char[t] is VCon and $P^b[t]$ is P and t is C) Then ($\delta x^b[t]$ is VS),
If (Char[t] is VCon and $P^b[t]$ is VP and t is C) Then ($\delta x^b[t]$ is null),
If (Char[t] is VCon and $P^b[t]$ is N and t is Unf) Then ($\delta x^b[t]$ is null),
If (Char[t] is VCon and $P^b[t]$ is P and t is Unf) Then ($\delta x^b[t]$ is null),
If (Char[t] is VCon and $P^b[t]$ is VP and t is Unf) Then ($\delta x^b[t]$ is null).

Updating (Proposal). The new proposal is finally obtained using Eq. (7).

$$x^b[t+1] = x^b[t-1] + \delta x^b[t]. \tag{7}$$

2.5 Agreement Rule

An agreement rule is a rule which determines the reach agreements stopping negotiation. Agent b accepts an offer (or a deal) $x^s[t]$ from agent s at time t if it is not worse than the offer he would submit in the next step, i.e., only if the relation given in Eq. (8) is satisfied. Similarly, agent s accepts an offer (or a deal) $x_b[t]$ from agent b at time t only if the relation given in Eq. (8) is satisfied.

$$\begin{cases} x^b(t+1) >= x^s(t) \\ t <= T_{max} \end{cases}, \begin{cases} x^s(t+1) <= x^b(t) \\ t <= T_{max} \end{cases}. \tag{8}$$

3 Experiments: Environments and Measures

In this Section, experimental environments and measures are presented and a set of experiments, carried out for different deadlines of agents b and s, are detailed.

3.1 Experimental Environments

Environments are defined in bargaining bilateral negotiation between buyer(b) and seller(s), in single issue negotiation j = *price*. The experimental environment is defined by the following variables [t_{max}^b , t_{max}^s , T_{max}, K^b, K^s, min^b, max^b, min^s, max^s].

The negotiation interval (the difference between the minimum and maximum values of agents) for price is defined using two variables: θ^i (the length of the reservation interval for an agent i) and Φ (the degree of intersection between the reservation intervals of the two agents, ranging between 0 for full overlap and 0.99 for virtually no overlap). In the experimental environment: θ^i are randomly selected between the ranges [10, 30] for both agents, and Φ = 0. The negotiation intervals are then computed, setting min^b = 10, by Eq. (9):

$$min^b = 10, \ max^b = min^b + \theta^b, \ min^s = \theta^b \Phi + min^b, \text{ and } max^s = min^s + \theta^s. \qquad (9)$$

The analysis and evaluation of negotiation behaviors and strategies developed in [13], indicated that negotiation deadlines significantly influences the performance of the negotiation. From this, the experimental environment is defined from random selection of the round number within [10, 50] which corresponds to a random selection of T_{max} within [20, 100]. The initiator of an offer is randomly chosen because the agent which opens the negotiation fairs better, irrespective of whether agent is a buyer (b) or a seller (s).

Time-Dependent Agent Behaviors: Parameter β ranges [14], [15], are defined as:

- β ∈ [0.01, 0.20] for Boulware (B) or *Aggressive (Agg)*,
- β = 1.00 for Linear (L) or *Neutral (Neu)*,
- β ∈ [20.00, 40.00] for Conceder (C) or *Conciliatory (Con)*.

Then, the constants K^i are chosen as small positive K^i = 0.1, for seller agent, in order to not constrain the true behavior of each time-dependent (decision) functions.

Fuzzy Cognitive and Social Agent Behaviors: Conciliatory (FCon) and Aggressive (FAgg), where FCon ∈ [0, 10] and FAgg ∈ [0, 10]. Thus, fuzzy cognitive conciliatory, neutral, or aggressive characters are defined as:

- FCon ∈ [0.0, 4.0] and FAgg ∈ [6.0, 10.0] for *Fuzzy Aggressive (FAgg)*,
- FNeu = FCon = FAgg = 5.0 for *Fuzzy Neutral (FNeu)*,
- FCon ∈ [6.0, 10.0] and FAgg ∈ [0.0, 4.0] for *Fuzzy Conciliatory (FCon)*.

3.2 Experimental Measures

To produce statistically meaningful results, for each experiment, precise set of environments is sampled from parameters specified in Sect. 3.1 and number of environments used is N = 200, in each experiment. This ensures that probability of sampled mean deviating by more than 0.01 from true mean is less than 0.05. To evaluate effectiveness of negotiation behaviors, three measures are considered:

- *Average Intrinsic Utility*, the intrinsic benefit is modeled as the agent's utility for the negotiation's final outcome, in a given environment, independently of the time taken and the resources consumed [7]. This utility, U^i, can be calculated for each agent for a *price x* using a linear scoring function, i.e., for a buyer agent b when there is a deal (an agreement) for a *price x* as shown in Eq. (10). If there is no deal in an environment (a particular negotiation), then $U^b = U^s = 0$. Then, the average intrinsic utility for each agent is given by AU^i in Eq. (10), where N is the total number of environments in each experiment, U^i the utility of each agent, for each environment with deal, and N_D is the number of environments with deals.

$$U^b = max^b - x, \text{ and } U^s = x - max^s, \text{ and } AU^i = \frac{\sum_{n=1}^{N} U^i[n]}{N_D}. \tag{10}$$

- *Average Round Number*, rounds to reach an agreement (a deal), a lengthy negotiation incurs penalties for resource consumption, thus shrinking the utilities obtained by the negotiators indirectly [16]. The average round number AR is given in Eq. (11), where R_D is the number of rounds, for each environment with deal, and N_D is the number of environments with deals.

- *Percentage of Deals*, the percentage of deals D(%) is obtained from the *Average Deal* AD given in Eq. (11), where N_D is the number of environments with deals. Then, Percentage of Deals D(%) is given in Eq. (11).

$$AR = \frac{\sum_{n=1}^{N} R_D[n]}{N_D}, \text{ and } AD = \frac{N_D}{N}, \ D(\%) = AD \cdot 100\%. \tag{11}$$

In order to analyze the performance of strategies, two measures are obtained [17], once an agreement is achieved: 1) *utility product*, UP, product, $AU^b \cdot AU^s$, of the utilities is computed as shown in Eq. (12), this measure indicates joint outcome ; 2) *utility difference*, UD, difference, $|AU^b - AU^s|$, of utilities is computed as shown in Eq. (12), this measure indicates distance between both utilities.

$$UP = AU^b \cdot AU^s \text{ and } UD = |AU^b - AU^s|. \tag{12}$$

There is an important relation between these product and difference utility measures and a compromise should be taken into account. Even though a high joint outcome is expected (for a relatively *win-win* results), it is also important that the difference between both utilities is low. For this reason, the analysis and evaluation of the obtained results is based not only on the utility product but also on the utility difference (a compromise should then be taken into account).

Also, to analyze performance of strategies, an interesting measure is suggested:

- *average performance*, the Average Performance (AP^i) of each agent is an average evaluation strategy measure implying the average negotiation deadline At^i_{max} and three (03) experimental measures, i.e., the average intrinsic utility AU^i, the average round number AR, and the average deal AD as shown in Eq. (13).

$$AP^i = \frac{AU^i + \left(1 - \dfrac{AR}{At^i_{max}}\right) + AD}{3}, \ with \ At^i_{max} = \frac{\sum_{n=1}^{N} t^i_{max}[n]}{N_D},\qquad(13)$$

where N_D is number of environments with deals, and N is total number of environments in each experiment.

4 Experimental Results of Negotiation Strategies

In this Section, experimental results of time-dependent and fuzzy cognitive and social negotiation strategies are presented, analyzed, and compared for different deadlines.

4.1 TimeDependent(Buyer)-TimeDependent(Seller)

The results presented in the following concern time-dependent strategy for both b and s agents, and they are given for different agent deadlines: $t^b_{max} > t^s_{max}$, $Tmax = t^b_{max} = t^s_{max}$, and $t^b_{max} < t^s_{max}$. These results are obtained, for each deadline, from 9 experiments (Agg-Agg, Agg-Neu, Agg-Con, Neu-Agg, Neu-Neu, Neu-Con, Con-Agg, Con-Neu, and Con-Con). Thus, results shown in Table 4, Table 7, and Table 10 give b and s agent utilities, those in Table 5, Table 8, and Table 11 give average round numbers, percentage of deals, utility products and differences, and those in Table 6, Table 9, and Table 12 give their average performances and absolute difference.

Table 4. Results AU^b and AU^s: case $t^b_{max} > t^s_{max}$

Seller	Buyer(Agg)	Buyer(Neu)	Buyer(Con)
Agg	45.09, 6.27	23.86, 25.06	2.23, 46.54
Neu	34.34, 17.62	36.60, 18.51	6.11, 43.21
Con	50.23, 0.25	49.12, 4.58	24.93, 21.48

Table 5. Results AR, D(%), UP, and UD: case $t^b_{max} > t^s_{max}$

Seller	Buyer(Agg)	Buyer(Neu)	Buyer(Con)
Agg	31.000, 2%, 282.71, 38.82	22.466, 30%, 597.93, 1.20	17.944, 36%, 103.78, 44.31
Neu	31.200, 17%, 605.07, 16.72	15.200, 35%, 677.46, 18.09	3.769, 39%, 264.01, 37.10
Con	24.578, 19%, 12.55, 49.98	4.382, 34%, 224.96, 44.54	1.000, 39%, 535.49, 3.45

Table 6. Results AP^b, AP^s, and $\left(\left|AP^b - AP^s\right|\right)$: case $t^b_{max} > t^s_{max}$

Seller	Buyer(Agg)	Buyer(Neu)	Buyer(Con)
Agg	15.240, 2.171 (13.069)	8.293, 8.599 (**0.306**)	1.121, 15.817 (14.696)
Neu	11.706, 6.003 (**5.703**)	12.586, 6.493 (6.093)	2.484, 14.835 (12.351)
Con	17.037, 0.275 (16.762)	16.801, 1.936 (14.865)	8.769, 7.615 (**1.154**)

Table 7. Results AU^b and AU^s: *case Tmax* $= t_{max}^b = t_{max}^s$

Seller	Buyer(Agg)	Buyer(Neu)	Buyer(Con)
Agg	22.25, 22.48	7.49, 38.36	0.93, 47.21
Neu	40.56, 8.16	22.25, 22.26	5.50, 46.13
Con	47.57, 0.94	44.47, 5.33	25.52, 35.32

Table 8. Results AR, D(%), UP, and UD: case *Tmax* $= t_{max}^b = t_{max}^s$

Seller	Buyer(Agg)	Buyer(Neu)	Buyer(Con)
Agg	28.906, 32%, 500.18, 0.23	25.440, 25%, 287.31, 30.87	20.405, 37%, 43.90, 46.28
Neu	27.592, 20%, 330.96, 32.40	16.500, 34%, 495.28, 0.01	4.028, 35%, 253.71, 40.63
Con	21.794, 34%, 44.71, 46.63	4.214, 28%, 237.02, 39.14	1.000, 28%, 901.36, 9.80

Table 9. Results AP^b, AP^s, and ($\left| AP^b - AP^s \right|$): case *Tmax* $= t_{max}^b = t_{max}^s$

Seller	Buyer(Agg)	Buyer(Neu)	Buyer(Con)
Agg	7.696, 7.772 (**0.076**)	2.772, 13.062 (10.290)	0.653, 16.079 (15.426)
Neu	13.766, 2.966 (10.800)	7.771, 7.775 (**0.004**)	2.260, 15.804 (13.544)
Con	16.182, 0.638 (15.544)	15.226, 2.179 (13.047)	8.927, 12.194 (**3.267**)

Table 10. Results AU^b and AU^s: case $t_{max}^b < t_{max}^s$

Seller	Buyer(Agg)	Buyer(Neu)	Buyer(Con)
Agg	5.03, 55.26	2.14, 58.46	0.30, 50.02
Neu	29.93, 22.43	16.25, 32.05	3.88, 43.40
Con	52.25, 2.23	45.00, 6.47	20.11, 34.89

Table 11. Results AR, D(%), UP, and UD: case $t_{max}^b < t_{max}^s$

Seller	Buyer(Agg)	Buyer(Neu)	Buyer(Con)
Agg	30.330, 3%, 277.95, 50.23	28.857, 7%, 125.10, 56.32	25.500, 18%, 15.00, 49.72
Neu	13.047, 12%, 671.32, 7.50	14.806, 31%, 520.81, 15.80	4.269, 26%, 168.39, 39.52
Con	19.185, 27%, 116.51, 50.02	3.763, 38%, 291.15, 38.53	1.000, 33%, 701.63, 14.78

Table 12. Results AP^b, AP^s, and ($\left| AP^b - AP^s \right|$): case $t_{max}^b < t_{max}^s$

Seller	Buyer(Agg)	Buyer(Neu)	Buyer(Con)
Agg	1.767, 18.636 (16.869)	0.829, 19.723 (18.894)	0.280, 16.960 (16.680)
Neu	10.241, 7.795 (**2.446**)	5.729, 11.058 (**5.329**)	1.677, 14.868 (13.191)
Con	17.680, 1.086 (16.594)	15.428, 2.600 (12.828)	7.138, 12.069 (**4.931**)

4.2 FuzzyCognitiveandSocial(Buyer)-FuzzyCognitiveandSocial (Seller)

The results presented in the following concern the fuzzy cognitive and social strategy for both buyer(b) and seller(s) agents, and they are given for different deadlines of agents: $t_{max}^b > t_{max}^s$, Tmax $= t_{max}^b = t_{max}^s$, and $t_{max}^b < t_{max}^s$. These results are obtained, for each deadline, from 9 experiments (FAgg-FAgg, FAgg-FNeu, FAgg-FCon,

FNeu-FAgg, FNeu-FNeu, FNeu-FCon, FCon-FAgg, FCon-FNeu, and FCon-FCon). Thus, results shown in Table 13, Table 16, and Table 19 give the b and s agent utilities, those in Table 14, Table 17, and Table 20 give average round numbers, percentage of deals, utility products and differences, and those in Table 15, Table 18, and Table 21 give their average performances and absolute difference.

Table 13. Results AU^b and AU^s: case $t^b_{max} > t^s_{max}$

Seller	Buyer(FAgg)	Buyer(FNeu)	Buyer(FCon)
FAgg	8.91, 10.47	8.59, 16.56	8.19, 20.80
FNeu	14.64, 8.41	12.76, 13.43	13.38, 18.75
FCon	16.68, 6.28	16.47, 12.47	15.59, 16.86

Table 14. Results AR, D(%), UP, and UD: case $t^b_{max} > t^s_{max}$

Seller	Buyer(FAgg)	Buyer(FNeu)	Buyer(FCon)
FAgg	16.000, 9%, 93.28, 1.56	15.666, 12%, 142.25, 7.97	14.642, 14%, 170.35, 12.61
FNeu	14.000, 9%, 123.12, 6.23	13.200, 15%, 171.36, 0.67	14.000, 19%, 250.87, 5.37
FCon	11.266, 15%, 104.75, 10.40	12.750, 16%, 205.38, 4.00	12.833, 6%, 262.84, 1.27

Table 15. Results AP^b, AP^s, and ($\left| AP^b - AP^s \right|$): case $t^b_{max} > t^s_{max}$

Seller	Buyer(FAgg)	Buyer(FNeu)	Buyer(FCon)
FAgg	3.266, 3.720 (**0.454**)	3.171, 5.762 (2.591)	3.048, 7.191 (4.143)
FNeu	5.185, 3.050 (2.135)	4.580, 4.750 (**0.170**)	4.798, 6.530 (1.732)
FCon	5.896, 2.382 (3.514)	5.823, 4.437 (1.386)	5.496, 5.866 (**0.370**)

Table 16. Results AU^b and AU^s: case $Tmax = t^b_{max} = t^s_{max}$

Seller	Buyer(FAgg)	Buyer(FNeu)	Buyer(FCon)
Fagg	8.48, 8.33	9.79, 16.92	8.82, 22.01
Fneu	13.49, 7.64	17.50, 17.18	15.96, 21.54
Fcon	21.25, 7.48	17.58, 12.65	15.44, 15.35

Table 17. Results AR, D(%), UP, and UD: case $Tmax = t^b_{max} = t^s_{max}$

Seller	Buyer(FAgg)	Buyer(FNeu)	Buyer(FCon)
Fagg	12.166, 6%, 70.63, 0.15	16.375, 8%, 165.64, 7.13	15.500, 8%, 194.12, 13.19
Fneu	14.000, 6%, 103.06, 5.85	18.214, 14%, 300.65, 0.32	16.375, 16%, 343.77, 5.58
Fcon	14.750, 16%, 158.95, 13.77	13.384, 13%, 222.387, 4.93	12.381, 21%, 237.004, 0.09

Table 18. Results AP^b, AP^s, and ($\left| AP^b - AP^s \right|$): case $Tmax = t^b_{max} = t^s_{max}$

Seller	Buyer(FAgg)	Buyer(FNeu)	Buyer(FCon)
Fagg	3.112, 3.062 (**0.050**)	3.532, 5.909 (2.377)	3.213, 7.610 (4.397)
Fneu	4.772, 2.822 (1.950)	6.112, 6.005 (**0.107**)	5.615, 7.475 (1.860)
Fcon	7.388, 2.798 (4.590)	6.162, 4.518 (1.644)	5.481, 5.451 (**0.030**)

Table 19. Results AU^b and AU^s: case $t_{max}^b < t_{max}^s$

Seller	Buyer(FAgg)	Buyer(FNeu)	Buyer(FCon)
Fagg	7.06, 7.08	8.68, 14.83	7.91, 18.29
Fneu	22.67, 11.92	14.25, 13.83	15.17, 19.44
Fcon	16.14, 6.13	16.08, 11.57	15.40, 14.51

Table 20. Results AR, D(%), UP, and UD: case $t_{max}^b < t_{max}^s$

Seller	Buyer(FAgg)	Buyer(FNeu)	Buyer(FCon)
Fagg	10.166, 6%, 49.98, 0.02	14.400, 5%, 128.72, 6.15	13.625, 8%, 144.67, 10.38
Fneu	5.000, 1%, 270.22, 10.75	14.166, 6%, 197.07, 0.42	15.500, 10%, 294.90, 4.27
Fcon	11.000, 11%, 98.93, 10.01	11.866, 15%, 186.04, 4.51	11.833, 18%, 223.45, 0.89

Table 21. Results AP^b, AP^s, and ($\left| AP^b - AP^s \right|$): case $t_{max}^b < t_{max}^s$

Seller	Buyer(FAgg)	Buyer(FNeu)	Buyer(FCon)
Fagg	2.621, 2.670 (**0.049**)	3.123, 5.233 (2.110)	2.883, 6.399 (3.516)
Fneu	7.851, 4.289 (3.562)	4.985, 4.904 (**0.081**)	5.294, 6.782 (1.488)
Fcon	5.658, 2.367 (3.291)	5.644, 4.190 (1.454)	5.428, 5.180 (**0.248**)

With regard to the time-dependent strategy, the obtained results demonstrate that the suggested fuzzy cognitive and social strategy allows agents to improve the nego-tiation process in terms of agent utilities, round number to reach an agreement, and percentage of agreements in *almost* all cases:

- $t_{max}^b > t_{max}^s$ with **0.454, 0.170,** and **0.370** for fuzzy congnitive and social see Table 15 (**5.703, 0.306,** and **1.154** for time-dependent see Table 6),

- Tmax = $t_{max}^b = t_{max}^s$ with **0.050, 0.107,** and **0.030** for fuzzy congnitive and social see Table 18 (**0.076, 0.004,** and **3.267** for time-dependent see Table 9),

- $t_{max}^b < t_{max}^s$ with **0.049, 0.081,** and **0.248** for fuzzy congnitive and social see Table 21 (**2.446, 5.329,** and **4.931** for time-dependent see Table 12).

5 Conclusion

In this paper, a *fuzzy cognitive* and *social* strategy has been suggested for autonomous agent systems with *incomplete* information intending to find adequate (*win-win* solu-tions for both parties) strategy, in one-to-one single issue negotiation. With regard to time-dependent strategy, the obtained results demonstrate that suggested fuzzy cogni-tive and social strategy allows agents to improve negotiation process in terms of agent utilities, round number to reach an agreement, and percentage of agreements. Thus, in order to succeed a negotiation, a combination of time, psychological personality as-pect, and fuzziness are necessary for an autonomous agent.

The main advantage of this work is to suggest a combination of the time, a psycho-logical personality aspect, and a fuzzy reasoning. However, of course the resulting negotiation approach, with incomplete information, presented still not yet completed and stated because of several limitations.

Such limitations which need to be investigated concern mainly:

- the simple way the fuzzy reasoning is integrated, in this work the fuzzy rule bases use simple rules to represent the knowledge,
- the simple basic approach of the psychological personality aspect which is a very simplified approach of the real psychological personality aspect of a negotiator.

Another interesting alternative for future research could be the learning from interaction in negotiation which is fundamental, from embodied cognitive science and understanding natural intelligence perspectives [18], [19], for understanding human behaviors and developing new solution concepts [20].

References

1. Rosenschein, J., Zlotkin, G.: Rules of Encounter. MIT Press, Cambridge (1994)
2. Wooldridge, M.: An Introduction to MultiAgent Systems. John Wiley & Sons, England (2002)
3. Jennings, N.R., Faratin, P., Lomuscio, A.R., Parsons, S., Sierra, C., Wooldridge, M.: Automated negotiation: prospects, methods, and challenges. Int. J. of Group Decision and Negotiation 10(2), 199–215 (2001)
4. Gerding, E.H., van Bragt, D., Poutré, J.L.: Scientific Approaches and Techniques for Negotiation: A Game Theoretic and Artificial Intelligence Perspective. CWI, Technical Report, SEN-R0005 (2000)
5. Li, C., Giampapa, J., Sycara, K.: Bilateral negotiation decisions with Uncertain Dynamic outside options. IEEE Trans. on Systems, Man, and Cybernetics, Part C: Special Issue on Game-Theoretic Analysis and Stochastic Simulation of Negotiation Agents 36(1), 1–13 (2006)
6. Lomuscio, A.R., Wooldridge, M., Jennings, N.R.: A classification scheme for negotiation in electronic commerce. Int. J. of Group Decision and Negotiation 12(1), 31–56 (2003)
7. Faratin, P., Sierra, C., Jennings, N.R.: Negotiation decision functions for autonomous agents. International Journal of Robotics and Autonomous Systems 24(3-4), 159–182 (1998)
8. Bales, R.F.: Interaction Process Analysis: A Method for the Study of Small Groups. Addisson-Wesley, Cambridge (1950)
9. Rubin, J.Z., Brown, B.R.: The Social Psychology of Bargaining and Negotiation. Academic Press, New York (1975)
10. Wang, Y.: Cognitive informatics: a new transdisciplinary research field. Brain and Mind 4, 115–127 (2003)
11. Wang, Y., Anderson, J.A., Chan, C., Yao, Y., Kinsner, W., Latombe, J.-C., Patel, D., Pedrycz, W., Sheu, P., Tsai, J., Zadeh, L.A., Zhang, D.: A doctrine of Cognitive Informatics (CI). Fundamental Informaticae 90(3), 203–228 (2009)
12. Faratin, P., Sierra, C., Jennings, N.R.: Using similarity criteria to make issue trade-offs in automated negotiations. Artificial Intelligence 142, 205–237 (2002)
13. Wang, K.-J., Chou, C.-H.: Evaluating NDF-based negotiation mechanism within an agent-based environment. Robotics and Autonomous Systems 43, 1–27 (2003)
14. Pruitt, D.: Negotiation Behavior. Academic Press, London (1981)
15. Raiffa, H.: The Art and Science of Negotiation. Harvard University Press, Cambridge (1982)

16. Lee, C.-F., Chang, P.-L.: Evaluations of tactics for automated negotiations. Group Decision and Negotiation 17(6), 515–539 (2008)
17. Ros, R., Sierra, C.: A negotiation meta strategy combining trade-off and concession moves. Auton. Agent Multi-Agent Sys. 12, 163–181 (2006)
18. Pfeifer, R., Scheier, C.: Understanding Intelligence. MIT Press, Cambridge (1999)
19. Chohra, A.: Embodied cognitive science, intelligent behavior control, machine learning, soft computing, and FPGA integration: towards fast, cooperative and adversarial robot team (RoboCup). Technical GMD Report, No. 136, Germany (June 2001) ISSN 1435-2702
20. Zeng, D., Sycara, K.: Benefits of learning in negotiation. In: Proc. of the 14th National Conference on Artificial Intelligence (AAAI-97), Providence, RI, July 1997, pp. 36–41 (1997)

The Living Cell as a Multi-agent Organisation: A Compositional Organisation Model of Intracellular Dynamics

C.M. Jonker[1], J.L. Snoep[2,4], J. Treur[1], H.V. Westerhoff[3,4], and W.C.A. Wijngaards[1]

[1] Vrije Universiteit Amsterdam, Department of Artificial Intelligence,
De Boelelaan 1081a, NL-1081 HV Amsterdam, The Netherlands, EU
{jonker,treur,wouterw}@cs.vu.nl
[2] University of Stellenbosch, Department of Biochemistry, Private Bag X1,
Matieland 7602, Stellenbosch, South Africa
jls@maties.sun.ac.za
[3] Stellenbosch Institute for Advanced Study, South Africa and [4] BioCentrum Amsterdam
Department of Molecular Cell Physiology, De Boelelaan 1087, NL-1081 HV Amsterdam,
The Netherlands, EU
hw@bio.vu.nl

Abstract. Within the areas of Computational Organisation Theory and Artificial Intelligence, techniques have been developed to simulate and analyse dynamics within organisations in society. Usually these modelling techniques are applied to factories and to the internal organisation of their process flows, thus obtaining models of complex organisations at various levels of aggregation. The dynamics in living cells are often interpreted in terms of well-organised processes, a bacterium being considered a (micro)factory. This suggests that organisation modelling techniques may also benefit their analysis. Using the example of *Escherichia coli* it is shown how indeed agent-based organisational modelling techniques can be used to simulate and analyse *E.coli*'s intracellular dynamics. Exploiting the abstraction levels entailed by this perspective, a concise model is obtained that is readily simulated and analysed at the various levels of aggregation, yet shows the cell's essential dynamic patterns.

Keywords: Organisational modeling, intracellular, dynamics, modular control analysis, regulation and control.

1 Introduction

In the area of modelling intracellular processes, the most widely used approach is based on differential equations, which are integrated numerically (Westerhoff, 2001; Stuart and Humphries, 1996). For some small unicellular organisms, a few isolated chemical pathways are understood in sufficient kinetic detail to obtain a description of their import and primary processing of nutrients; e.g., for *Escherichia coli*, blood cells and yeast (Rohwer et al., 2000, Teusink *et al.*, 2000; Wang *et al.*, 2001, Ben-Jacob *et al.*, 1997; Rizzi et al., 1997; Takahashi, Ishikawa, Sadamoto, Sasamoto, Ohta, Shiozawa, Miyoshi, Naito, Nakayama and Tomita, 2003; Snoep, 2005;

N.T. Nguyen and R. Kowalczyk (Eds.): Transactions on CCI I, LNCS 6220, pp. 160–206, 2010.
© Springer-Verlag Berlin Heidelberg 2010

Jamshidi and Palsson, 2006). However, this approach has difficulties when tackling larger cellular systems. First, hundreds or more reaction parameters are needed, for which reliable values are rarely available (Teusink *et al.*, 2000; Kholodenko *et al.*, 1999). This can seriously compromise the feasibility of the general model. Second, actual behaviour of intracellular pathways may be much less complex than is theoretically possible on the basis of the complexity of the chemical processes (e.g., Rotterdam *et al.*, 2002). At best, and only if all system parameters and internal connections are known and sufficiently tuned, the traditional approach delivers a computer replica of (part of) the living cell. If this replica functions correctly, then it can be seen as a validation of the system parameters and of the knowledge obtained for the different pathways. However, if the replica does not function correctly, the huge number of parameters makes localizing aberrations practically impossible. Furthermore, the replica is almost as remote from human understanding as the target system itself. This is because the modelling approach requires a description that is complete, inherently low-level, detailed and complex. In contrast, the human mind operates by abstraction in order to understand an essence.

Conceptual analysis of the cell's internal functioning from a biological perspective often LEADSTO descriptions where specific processes function together according to some form of organisation. For example, viewed from a global perspective (top-down), sub-processes of the overall process are distinguished such as transcription, translation, and metabolism, and these sub processes interact with each other according to a structured pattern. Viewed from a more local perspective (bottom-up), groups of specific biochemical reactions are 'lumped' together to form functional units. This type of approach recognizes that some conglomerates of biochemical processes act as functional units such as "metabolic pathway", "catabolism", "transcriptome" and "regulon". Some of these concepts have been or are being defined formally (Kahn & Westerhoff, 1991; Rohwer *et al.*, 1996; Schilling *et al.*, 2000), but implementation is still in its infancy. This perspective involves modelling the overall process at different levels of aggregation based on functional units. Crucial challenges are:

(1) how to describe the functionality of such a functional unit,
(2) how to describe the manner in which multiple functional units interact and co-operate to obtain a well-organised overall process, and
(3) how to implement software support for simulation and analysis based on these different aggregation levels

To manage complex dynamics in human societies, organisational structures are also often exploited. Within the area of Computational Organisation Theory and Artificial Intelligence, in particular Agent Systems, organisation modelling techniques have been developed to simulate and analyse dynamics within organisations in society. For example, Pajares et al. (2003) present an agent-based organisation model of industry; representing firms by agents that make strategic decisions on investments, product innovation and whether to stay or leave the industry. The manageability of the dynamics emerging from multiple agents in a society depends on some form of organisational structure. An organisational model for a multi-agent system provides a structuring of the processes in such a manner that an agent involved can function appropriately. The dynamics within a given organisational structure is much more dependable than in an entirely unstructured situation. Usually these organisation modelling techniques are applied to factories and the internal organisation of their process flows, obtaining high-level models of complex organisations at different levels of aggregation.

Dynamics at the different levels of aggregation within an organisation are related to each other. In particular, the dynamics of the whole process depends on dynamics of processes at lower levels of aggregation, i.e. more specific processes. Lomi and Larsen (2001) emphasize the importance of such interlevel relationships. Organisations can be seen as adaptive complex information processing systems of (bounded) rational agents, and as tools for control; central questions are (Lomi and Larsen, 2001):

- from the first view: 'given a set of assumptions about (different forms of) individual behaviour, how can the aggregate properties of a system be determined (or predicted) that are generated by the repeated interaction among those individual units?'
- from the second view: 'given observable regularities in the behaviour of a composite system, which rules and procedures - if adopted by the individual units - induce and sustain these regularities?'.

Both views and problems require means to express relationships between dynamics at different levels of aggregation. In our approach logical relationships between dynamic properties at different aggregation levels provide a manner to express such interlevel relationships (mathematically).

Literature on Organisation Theory is largely informal or semi-formal (see for example Mintzberg, 1979). The idea of using simulation as a formal technique to research organisational dynamics stems already from the 1950s. However, the power of computers then restricted the applicability of the simulations of those times. Although several results based on those simulations were frequently cited in the literature, simulation did not become a popular tool in sociological or biological research.

Recently formal and computational modelling techniques have received more attention within Organisation Theory. Modellers base themselves on recent developments within Organisation Theory, involving concepts like organizational behaviour and adaptation, organizational embeddedness, organizational ecology, and competitive survival. Examples of this formalisation trend can be observed in books such as (Prietula, Gasser, and Carley, 1997; Lomi and Larsen, 2001), and in recently created journals such as Computational and Mathematical Organisation Theory (e.g., Moss et al., 1998). Executable models serve as a basis for simulation experiments. These can be used, for example, in evaluating sample behaviours of (real or simulated) organisations. A language for executable models should be formal, and not too complex, to avoid computational complexity. Software tools to support such a language serve as *simulation environment* (e.g. Moss, Gaylard, Wallis and Edmonds, 1998; Prietula, Gasser, and Carley, 1997).

Within the agent systems area a number of organisation modelling approaches have been developed. One of them is the Agent-Group-Role-approach (AGR) introduced in (Ferber and Gutknecht, 1998), and extended with a dynamic modelling language in (Ferber et al., 2001). Within this approach the organisational structure is the specification of a specific multi-agent organisation based on a definition of groups, roles and their relationships within the organisation. An organisation as a whole is composed of a number of groups (e.g., divisions or departments). A group structure identifies the roles and (intragroup) role interaction within a group, and the transfers between roles needed for such interactions. In addition, intergroup role relations between roles of different groups specify the connectivity of groups within an organisation. In such an organisation model, a number of descriptions are basic for the dynamics: roles fulfilled by agents, groups consisting of a number of roles, and of interactions between roles and between groups. A limitation of the AGR approach is that only three aggregation levels can be modelled. To smoothly model an organisation comprising an arbitrary number of aggregation levels, and as an alternative to the AGR approach, the compositional organisation modelling approach is introduced and exploited to model organisational structures.

An organisation structure model by itself provides no dynamics. In a sense it abstracts from the dynamics. However, to be able to analyse and/or simulate dynamics within an organisation, as part of an organisation model, also some specification of *dynamic properties* is required. Dynamic properties relate states of the organisation over time. Usually one particular dynamic property refers not to the whole state but to a limited set of specific elements or aspects of these states. This set can be viewed as the scope of a dynamic property. Depending on the property at hand, this scope can be broad (or global), or narrow (or local). For example, global properties of an organisation as a whole may refer to a number of different aspects (sometimes such a property is called *integrative*), whereas properties of the interaction between two specific roles within an organisation will refer only to aspects related to these roles (e.g., a role interaction protocol). Thus to obtain an adequate description of the complex interacting processes at different levels of aggregation, descriptions in terms of dynamic properties are used: an *organisation dynamics model*.

In Nature several forms of organisational structure have evolved. Examples include insect organisations such as ant-hills, beehives, wasp-hives, as wells as herds, wolf-packs, the coordinated processes of organs in vertebrates, and last but not least the living cell itself. For some of these, simulations can be found in literature; however, these do not invoke structures developed in Organisation Theory. In this paper it is investigated whether and how organisation modelling techniques can be used to model the complex dynamics in living cells.

First the modelling approach is addressed for organisation structure (Section 2) and for dynamics within an organisation (Section 3). Section 4 introduces a model for the organisation of the main processes within an *E. coli* cell and their dynamics: metabolism, transcription and translation. In Section 5 the dynamics of the organisation of more specific subprocesses is described. Section 6 presents some of the simulation results. Section 7 is a discussion. In Appendix A to D more details of the organisation model of *E. coli* are shown.

2 Modelling Approach: Organisation Structure

Within the Agent-Group-Role or AGR organisation modelling approach (Ferber and Gutknecht, 1998), an organisation structure is described at three aggregation levels: the *organisation* consists of a set of *groups*, and each group consists of the *roles* in that group. Furthermore, *connections* between roles and between groups are possible;

see Figure 1. Here the smaller ovals indicate roles and bigger ovals groups. Connections are indicated by the two types of arrows (dashed indicates an intergroup interaction, not dashed indicates a transfer). To indicate which role belongs to which group is depicted by drawing the smaller role oval within the bigger group oval. Moreover the organisation is *realized* by *agents* fulfilling roles (not depicted). The main concepts are briefly described as follows:

- The *agents*. The model places no constraints on the internal architecture of agents. An agent is only specified as an active communicating entity which plays roles within groups. This agent definition is intentionally general to allow agent designers to adopt the most accurate definition of agent-hood relative to their application.

  - A *group* is defined as an atomic set of agent roles. Each agent takes part by fulfilling roles in one or more groups. In its most basic form, the group is only a way to name a set of roles.
  - A *role* is an abstract representation of an agent function or service within a group. Each agent can handle multiple roles, and each role handled by an agent is local to a group.

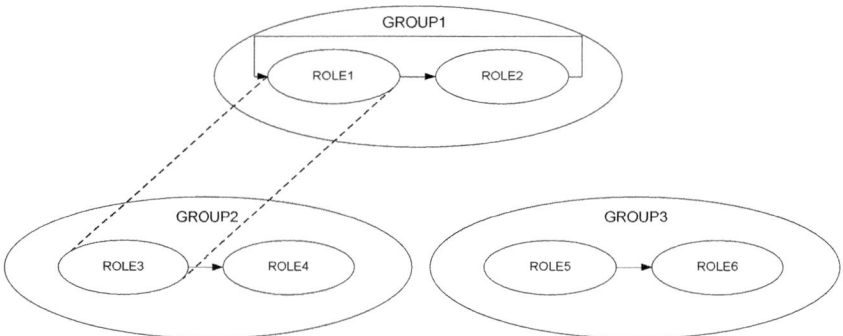

Fig. 1. Example organization modeled within AGR

The use of a compositional modelling strategy is common in Computer Science, Artificial Intelligence and Organisation Theory. It has been instantiated in different forms, as functional design, modularized design, task analysis or decomposition, object oriented design, component-based design and agent oriented design, among others (cf. Tanenbaum, 1976; Knuth, 1981; Booch, 1991; Brazier, Jonker and Treur, 2002; Ferber and Gutknecht, 1998). The main point is that the system is too complex to be understood when presented in a direct, flat manner, thus some elements of the model have to be grouped together, and these groups can then be further grouped. The differences between the approaches mentioned are in the choice of grouping and possible combinations of these groups and elements. A key design issue then of compositional modelling is the criterion of grouping processes together. Where, and when can a (process) component be separated from another component, and what interactions the components can have is determined. Note that in this paper the word *component* indicates a *process component*.

Compositionality provides means for *information hiding*. When a component contains several elements that are not visible to the components interacting with the component as a whole, these elements are said to be hidden; some information in the model is not visible to the other components. This is important, as it allows the amount of information at higher levels in the component structure that is visible, to be less than the total amount of information of all the parts and thus give a more manageable view of what is happening. Of course, an item can only be hidden if it does not affect anything it is hidden from, except through its non-hidden encompassing component (cf. Rohwer et al, 1996).

Compositional modelling proves most effective when building the model. Both in directing effort in breadth - as the abstract overviews give a means to see if everything is covered - and in depth, when at a specific point more detail is needed, the compositional model allows (at a certain aggregation level) the composition of a role (*parent role*) out of several sub-roles (*child roles*) to effectuate the detailing. Parts of the system may be modelled in increasing detail, in a so-called *refinement*. In the example above, first the factory role can be modelled according to its division roles, a division role can be refined according to its department roles and a department role can be further refined to unit roles within the department.

The organisation of the cell as a whole consists of the environment and the cell. The cell is in interaction with the environment. In Figure 2 the hierarchical structure behind the highest aggregation levels of the organisation model is depicted. In this picture the right hand side nodes connected to a node are called the children of the latter node, which itself is called a parent node for those children. For example, the node Cell is the parent node of the nodes Transcription, Translation, and Metabolism. The latter nodes are children of Cell.

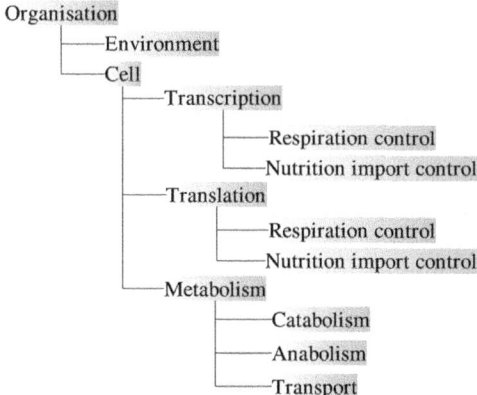

Fig. 2. Overview of the hierarchy behind the highest aggregation levels of the organisation model

In Figure 3 the organisation structure of the highest aggregation levels of the model is depicted. 'Roles' within a group are depicted by small ovals within a bigger oval (cf. Fig. 1). In particular, the cell's functioning is based on three roles: Transcription, Translation, and Metabolism. Within Biochemistry, what is indicated by the modelling concept 'role' is commonly called a 'process'. This distinction will be made in the remainder of the paper: for the modelling entity the word 'role' is used, for the entity in the context of the biological domain the word 'process'.

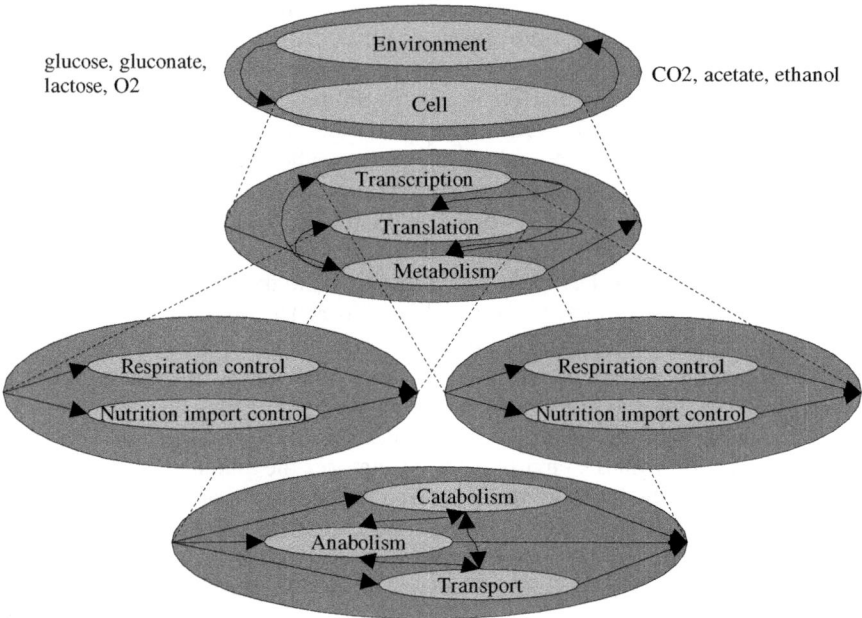

Fig. 3. The highest aggregation levels of the organisation structure

Each of these roles can again be viewed as a group, as indicated by the dotted lines connecting to a large oval below. Arrows between small ovals within a bigger oval indicate information transfer between roles. An arrow between a small oval and the encompassing larger oval indicates (interlevel) interaction between the role indicated by the small oval (the child role) and the group indicated by the bigger oval (relating to the parent role of the latter). Given the dotted lines, this entails (interlevel) interaction between the child role and the parent role.

Both the Transcription group and the Translation group include the roles Respiration Control and Nutrition Import Control. The Metabolism group includes the roles Catabolism, Anabolism and Transport.

3 Modelling Approach: Organisation Dynamics

To be able to simulate or analyse dynamics within an organisation, in addition to the static organisation structure specification discussed above, as part of an organisation model also a specification of the dynamics within the organisation is needed. To this end, in the specification of an organisation model different types of specifications of *dynamic properties* are distinguished. These properties serve as constraints on the dynamics of the respective roles and interactions. In (Jonker, Treur, and Wijngaards,

2002) an executable temporal language was introduced to specify the different types of dynamic properties. After a more general introduction, this temporal language to specify dynamic properties is introduced.

Within a compositional organisation model dynamic properties can be specified for each of the *roles* at the different aggregation levels. Furthermore, dynamic properties can be specified for *transfer* between roles at a given aggregation level. Moreover, *interlevel interaction dynamics* can be specified in the form of dynamic properties relating output of a child role to output of its parent role, or relating input of the parent role to input of a child role.

If specified appropriately, the dynamic properties of a role at a higher aggregation level are related to the dynamic properties of its child roles. The general pattern is the following logical implication:

dynamic properties for children roles &
dynamic properties for transfer between children roles &
dynamic properties for interlevel interaction between parent role and children roles
$\Rightarrow$ dynamic properties for parent role

In more mathematical notation this can be expressed as follows. Here P denotes a parent role with (a conjunction of) dynamic properties DP(P), and with children roles C1, C2, C3, with dynamic properties DP(C1), DP(C2), DP(C3), respectively. Moreover, TRD(R) denotes the dynamic properties for transfer between children roles of role R, and IID(R) the dynamic properties of interlevel interaction between role R and its children roles. Using these notations, the pattern above can be expressed as:

$$DP(C1) \text{ \& } DP(C2) \text{ \& } DP(C3) \text{ \& } TRD(P) \text{ \& } IID(P) \quad \Rightarrow \quad DP(P)$$

as before, & means conjunction, and $\Rightarrow$ implication, i.e., if all dynamic properties on the left hand side hold, then the right hand side holds.

Notice that this can be iterated if each (or some) of the children roles are themselves parent role for other children roles. Given such an implication, if a particular trace of organisation dynamics satisfies the properties of the child roles, and the transfer and interlevel interaction properties, then it will also satisfy the dynamic properties of the parent role. Applied in a recursive manner, this implies that properties of the organisation as a whole can be obtained from (or realised by) properties at lower aggregation levels.

In Biology also specific forms of organisation have been developed and exploited. In particular, for the processes in the cell the following main categories or functional units are distinguished: metabolism, translation and transcription (cf. Wijker et al., 1995). These are the main parts of the regulation and control cycle of a cell. The metabolism expands to catabolism, anabolism and transport. The catabolism is the category of processes that decompose substances and extract free energy from them. In the anabolism the processes reside that utilize this free energy to create more and more complex substances reside. The transport processes move substances across the cell membrane.

Section 4 shows in more detail how a compositional organisation modelling approach helps to manage the complexity of intracellular processes. The reasons for grouping certain processes together will be in accordance with biological knowledge. The executable temporal language used is a temporal language extending the paradigm of Executable Temporal Logic (Barringer et al., 1996; Fisher, 1994, 2005) with real-valued time. Roughly spoken, in this executable language it can only be expressed that if a certain state property holds for a certain time interval, then after some delay another state property should hold for at least a certain time interval; see also (Bosse, Jonker, Mey, and Treur, 2007). The *LEADSTO* language enables one to model direct temporal dependencies between two state properties in successive states. A specification of dynamic properties in LEADSTO format has as advantages that it is executable and that it can often easily be depicted graphically. For the approach described in this paper, the choice has been made to consider time as continuous, described by real values, but for state properties, both quantitative and qualitative variants can be used. The approach subsumes approaches based on simulation of differential or difference equations, and discrete qualitative modelling approaches, but also combines them. For example, it is possible to model the exact (real-valued) time interval for which some qualitative property holds. Moreover, the relationships between states over time are described by either logical or mathematical means, or a combination thereof. This will be explained below in more detail.

Dynamics is considered as evolution of states over time. The notion of state as used here is characterised on the basis of an ontology defining a set of properties that do or do not hold at a certain point in time. Ontologies are specified as signatures in order-sorted predicate logic, i.e., sets of sorts and subsort relations, constants in sorts, functions and predicates over sorts.

Definition (State Properties)

Let Ont be a given ontology Ont.
a)   The set of *state atoms* (or *atomic state properties*) based on Ont is denoted by APROP(Ont), and the set of *state ground atoms* by GAPROP(Ont).
b)   The set of *state properties* STATPROP(Ont) based on Ont consists of the propositions that can be made (using conjunction, negation, disjunction, implication) from the atoms. Moreover, GSTATPROP(Ont) is the subset of *ground state properties*, based on ground atoms. A subset of the set of state properties is the set CONLIT(Ont) of *conjunctions of literals (atoms or negations of atoms)*.

The textual LEADSTO format is defined as follows.

Definition (LEADSTO format)

Let a state ontology Ont be given.
Any expression for Ont of the form

$$\forall x_1, ..., x_n \quad \alpha \rightarrowtail_{e, f, g, h} \beta$$

where α (the *antecedent*) and β (the *consequent*) are state properties in CONLIT(Ont), with variables among $x_1, .., x_n$, and e, f, g, h non-negative real numbers, is a LEADSTO *expression*. When no variables or quantifiers occur in this expression, it is called a LEADSTO *ground expression*.

Informally, for the case without variables, a LEADSTO expression $\alpha \rightarrow\!\!\!\rightarrow_{e,\,f,\,g,\,h} \beta$ means (also see Figure 4):

> *If state property α holds for a certain time interval with duration g, then after some delay (between e and f) state property β will hold for a certain time interval of length h.*

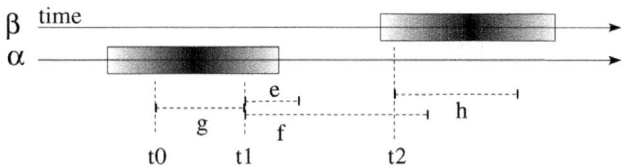

Fig. 4. The timing relationships

Within the LEADSTO language it is possible to use sorts, variables over sorts, real numbers, and mathematical operations, such as in the property (where x is a constant):

$$\forall v\ \text{has\_value}(x, v) \rightarrow\!\!\!\rightarrow_{e,\,f,\,g,\,h} \text{has\_value}(x, v^*0.25)$$

This property expresses the fact that, if has_value(x, v) holds during g time units, then after a delay between e and f time units, has_value(x, v*0.25) will hold during h time units.

The definition of the relationships as given above, will also manage situations where the sources hold for longer than the minimum interval length g. The total duration that the source holds, is also added to the duration that the result will hold, provided $e + h \geq f$. This is because under the given constraint the definition can be applied at each subinterval where α holds, resulting in many overlapping intervals of β. The end result is that the additional duration also extends the duration that the resulting notion β holds. Below we shall use seconds for the unit of time for e, f, g, and h.

The dynamics of each of the roles in the cell model is specified in LEADSTO format. For each of the roles, first it is indicated what are inputs and outputs for the role, and next what characterises its dynamics. The environment for the cell can be used to specify environmental conditions over time. In the model it can be used to specify as output of the environment (to be used by the input of the cell) environmental conditions concerning the presence of glucose, gluconate, lactose, O_2, N, P, S. Moreover, depending on the functioning of the cell, the environment receives as input the presence of some substances produced by the cell, i.e., the presence of CO_2, ethanol and acetate. This view on the environment is that it is a component whose output provides the cell with input, and whose input is fed by the output of the cell. The current model is specified for an experimental setup where a bacterial culture is bubbled through with oxygen and nitrogen, quickly flushing out CO_2. It is also possible to model CO_2 or acetate as staying present in the environment once exported, simply by adding a property specifying that the presence of the substance continues once it has arrived.

Input: present(CO2_outside), present(ethanol_outside), present(acetate_outside)
Output: present(glucose_outside), present(gluconate_outside), present(lactose_outside),
          present(O2_outside), present(N_outside), present(P_outside), present(S_outside)

An example of a 'follows' relation to specify environmental conditions is the following, the property ED1 (for Environmental Dynamics):

ED1

true $\;\longrightarrow\!\!\!\!\!\longrightarrow_{1;5;10;10}\;$ output: present(glucose_outside) & present(O2_outside) &
present(N_outside) & present(P_outside) & present(S_outside)

4   The Cell and Its Three Main Roles

From the top-level perspective the cell can be viewed as a single role that interacts with its environment. Within the cell this role is organised according to three main roles. Dynamic properties in LEADSTO format characterising the dynamics of these roles are specified in more detail below. Note that the chosen model corresponds closely to the way instructors teach their students about the behaviour and functions of the cell. The model is at a high level of abstraction, precisely for this reason. It is easy to talk about the cell in this way. One of the added values of this paper is that the runtime behaviour of the model shows that such a high level of abstraction can be used and still have behaviour that is correct at that level of abstraction. Furthermore, the abstractions are not created on the verbal accounts of the instructors only, but for each abstraction a mapping exists to the underlying concepts in the cell down to the level of mmol/liter of substances. The mapping was made using detailed knowledge in the literature and otherwise based on our own expertise in this area. From a philosophy of science perspective, our approach corresponds to a qualitative model based on causal relations.

4.1   Cell

The cell can use as input from the environment the presence of glucose, gluconate, lactose, O_2, N, P, S. It may produce CO_2, ethanol and acetate (apart from cell growth).

Input: present(glucose_outside), present(gluconate_outside), present(lactose_outside),
            present(O2_outside), present(N_outside), present(P_outside), present(S_outside)
Output: present(CO2_outside), present(acetate_outside), present(ethanol_outside)

Viewed at the highest aggregation level, the cell's dynamics can be described by a number of temporal input-output relations, in LEADSTO language. These dynamic properties specify under which environmental conditions the cell produces what particular output for the environment. For example, properties CD1, CD2, CD3 (here CD stands for Cell Dynamics) specify that if O_2 is available, as well as at least one of the nutrients glucose, lactose, gluconate, and resources, then the cell produces CO_2. The other properties specify the anaerobic case. The conjunction of all of these dynamic properties is denoted by DP(Cell).

CD1

input: present(O2_outside) & present(glucose_outside) & present(N_outside) &
present(P_outside) & present(S_outside) $\longrightarrow\!\!\!\!\!\longrightarrow_{72;216;4;4}$ output: present(CO2_outside)

CD2

input: present(O2_outside) & present(lactose_outside) & present(N_outside) &
present(P_outside) & present(S_outside) & not present(glucose_outside) $\rightarrow\!\!\!\rightarrow_{72;216;4;4}$ output:
present(CO2_outside)

CD3

input: present(O2_outside) & present(gluconate_outside) & present(N_outside) &
present(P_outside) & present(S_outside) $\rightarrow\!\!\!\rightarrow_{72;216;4;4}$ output: present(CO2_outside)

CD4

input: not present(O2_outside) & present(glucose_outside) & present(N_outside) &
present(P_outside) & present(S_outside)
$\rightarrow\!\!\!\rightarrow_{72;216;4;4}$ output: present(acetate_outside) & present(ethanol_outside)

CD5

input: not present(O2_outside) & present(lactose_outside) & present(N_outside) &
present(P_outside) & present(S_outside)
$\rightarrow\!\!\!\rightarrow_{72;216;4;4}$ output: present(acetate_outside) & present(ethanol_outside)

CD6

input: not present(O2_outside) & present(gluconate_outside) & present(N_outside) &
present(P_outside) & present(S_outside)
$\rightarrow\!\!\!\rightarrow_{72;216;4;4}$ output: present(acetate_outside) & present(ethanol_outside)

4.2 Metabolism

The role Metabolism, which includes import and export, can use substances present
outside the cell, but also substances produced by Translation, or Transcription (ADP, P).
The enzymes produced by translation function as catalysts in metabolism. It can produce substances that are exported to the environment, as well as substances used by
the other two roles, e.g., amino acids for Translation, and nucleotides for Transcription.

Input: present(glucose_outside), present(gluconate_outside), present(lactose_outside),
present(O2_outside), present(N_outside), present(P_outside), present(S_outside),
present(fermentation_enzymes), present(respiration_enzymes),
present(lactose_import_enzymes), present(glucose_import_enzymes),
present(gluconate_import_enzymes),
present(ADP), present(P)

Output: present(ATP), present(CO2_outside), present(acetate_outside), present(ethanol_outside),
present(nucleotides), present(aminoacids), present(CRPcAMP), present(allolactose),
present(gluconate6P_observation_amount), present(ArcB_P)

The following dynamic properties specify that under appropriate environmental
conditions the Metabolism will produce ATP, amino acids and nucleotides (apart
from cell growth).

The timing is given as 72;216;4;4 which means that e=72, f=216, g=4 and h=4.
Thus after 4 seconds have passed that the antecedents hold, then a delay between 72
and 216 seconds passes, after which the consequent holds for 4 seconds. Note that
continued holding of the antecedent for more than 4 seconds will lead to continued
holding of the consequent. Also note that after the consequent duration has passed, the
property does not specify whether the consequent will then hold or not, it could be
true or false. If other properties affect the same consequent, this consequent may con-
tinue to hold even though the current property does not affect it any more.

MD1

input:not present(glucose_outside) $\rightarrow\!\!\!\rightarrow_{0;0;0.230;0.230}$ output: present(CRPcAMP).

MD2

input: present(lactose_outside) $\rightarrow\!\!\!\rightarrow_{0;0;0.230;0.230}$ output:present(allolactose).

MD3

input: present(gluconate_outside) $\rightarrow\!\!\!\rightarrow_{0;0;0.230;0.230}$ output
present(gluconate6P_observation_amount).

MD4

input: present(glucose_outside) & present(N_outside) & present(P_outside) & present(S_outside)
& present(ADP) & present(P) & present(O2_outside) & present(glucose_import_enzymes) &
present(respiration_enzymes)
 $\rightarrow\!\!\!\rightarrow_{4;40;4;4}$ output:present(CO2_outside) & present(ATP) & present(nucleotides) &
present(aminoacids).

MD5

input: present(lactose_outside) & present(N_outside) & present(P_outside) & present(S_outside)
& present(ADP) & present(P) & present(O2_outside) & present(lactose_import_enzymes) &
present(respiration_enzymes)
 $\rightarrow\!\!\!\rightarrow_{4;40;4;4}$ output:present(CO2_outside) & present(ATP) & present(nucleotides) &
present(aminoacids).

MD6

input: present(gluconate_outside) & present(N_outside) & present(P_outside) &
present(S_outside) & present(ADP) & present(P) & present(O2_outside) &
present(gluconate_import_enzymes) & present(respiration_enzymes)
 $\rightarrow\!\!\!\rightarrow_{4;40;4;4}$ output:present(CO2_outside) & present(ATP) & present(nucleotides) &
present(aminoacids).

MD7

input: present(glucose_outside) & present(N_outside) & present(P_outside) & present(S_outside)
& present(ADP) & present(P) & not present(O2_outside) & present(glucose_import_enzymes) &
present(fermentation_enzymes)
 $\rightarrow\!\!\!\rightarrow_{4;40;4;4}$ output: present(acetate_outside) & present(ethanol_outside) & present(ATP) &
present(nucleotides) & present(aminoacids).

MD8

input: present(lactose_outside) & present(N_outside) & present(P_outside) & present(S_outside)
& present(ADP) & present(P) & not present(O2_outside) & present(lactose_import_enzymes) &
present(fermentation_enzymes)
 $\rightarrow\!\!\!\rightarrow_{4;40;4;4}$ output: present(acetate_outside) & present(ethanol_outside) & present(ATP) &
present(nucleotides) & present(aminoacids).

MD9

input: present(gluconate_outside) & present(N_outside) & present(P_outside) &
present(S_outside) & present(ADP) & present(P) & not present(O2_outside) &
present(gluconate_import_enzymes) & present(fermentation_enzymes)
 $\rightarrow\!\!\!\rightarrow_{4;40;4;4}$ output: present(acetate_outside) & present(ethanol_outside) & present(ATP) &
present(nucleotides) & present(aminoacids).

MD10

input: present(O2_outside) $\rightarrow\!\!\!\rightarrow_{0;0;0.230;0.230}$ output: present(ArcB_P).

The conjunction of these properties is denoted by DP(Metabolism).

4.3 Translation

Translation involves amino acids, ATP, and particular types of mRNA. It can produce
particular enzymes, ADP, and P.

Input: present(aminoacids), present(ATP), present(respiration_mRNA),
         present(fermentation_mRNA), present(glucose_import_mRNA),
         present(lactose_import_mRNA), present(gluconate_import_mRNA)

Output: present(ADP) present(P), present(respiration_enzymes) present(fermentation_enzymes),
present(lactose_import_enzymes), present(glucose_import_enzymes),
present(gluconate_import_enzymes)

The following dynamic properties specify under which circumstances which particular output will be generated, i.e., the enzyme(s) is (are) produced for which the associated mRNA is present. The conjunction of all of these properties is denoted by DP(Translation).

TaD1
input: present(aminoacids) & present(ATP) & present(respiration_mRNA)
$\twoheadrightarrow_{0;0;60;600}$ output: present(ADP) & present(P) & present(respiration_enzymes)
TaD2
input: present(aminoacids) & present(ATP) & present(fermentation_mRNA)
$\twoheadrightarrow_{0;0;60;600}$ output: present(ADP) & present(P) & present(fermentation_enzymes)
TaD3
input: present(aminoacids) & present(ATP) & present(glucose_import_mRNA)
$\twoheadrightarrow_{0;0;60;600}$ output: present(ADP) & present(P) & present(glucose_import_enzymes)
TaD4
input: present(aminoacids) & present(ATP) & present(lactose_import_mRNA)
$\twoheadrightarrow_{0;0;60;600}$ output: present(ADP) & present(P) & present(lactose_import_enzymes)
TaD5
input: present(aminoacids) & present(ATP) & present(gluconate_import_mRNA)
$\twoheadrightarrow_{0;0;60;600}$ output: present(ADP) & present(P) & present(gluconate_import_enzymes)

4.4 Transcription

Transcription can use nucleotides, ATP, ArcB_P, allolactose, and gluconate6P observation amount; moreover for some functionality it depends on the presence of CRPcAMP. The gluconate6P observation amount refers to an amount of gluconate6P in the cell that signals the presence of gluconate in the environment. This amount is smaller than the amount of gluconate6P that would be present when gluconate is actively imported. The presence of appropriate DNA is not mentioned here as a condition, since it is assumed to be present internally, not as input. Depending on circumstances it can produce particular forms of mRNA, besides ADP and P.

Input: present(nucleotides), present(ATP), present(CRPcAMP), present(allolactose),
present(gluconate6P_observation_amount), present(ArcB_P)
Output: present(respiration_mRNA), present(fermentation_mRNA), present(glucose_import_mRNA),
present(lactose_import_mRNA), present(gluconate_import_mRNA),
present(ADP), present(P)

The following dynamic properties specify under which circumstances which output is generated; i.e., here the decisions are made which mRNA(s) will be generated for given circumstances. For example, always glucose import mRNA is generated (assuming ATP and nucleotides present), respiration and fermentation mRNA, are generated if ArcB_P is present or absent, respectively, and the production of lactose import mRNA and gluconate each depend on specific other conditions (allolactose, CRPcAMP, resp. gluconate6P observation amount, CRPcAMP). The conjunction of all of these properties is denoted by DP(Transcription).

TcD1
    input: present(ArcB_P) & present(nucleotides) & present(ATP)
    $\twoheadrightarrow_{60;60;1;40}$ output: present(ADP) & present(P) & present(respiration_mRNA)
TcD2
    input: not present(ArcB_P) & present(nucleotides) & present(ATP)
    $\twoheadrightarrow_{60;60;1;40}$ output: present(ADP) & present(P) & present(fermentation_mRNA)

TcD3
    input: present(nucleotides) & present(ATP)
    $\twoheadrightarrow_{60;60;1;40}$ output: present(ADP) & present(P) & present(glucose_import_mRNA)
TcD4
    input: present(allolactose) & present(CRPcAMP) & present(nucleotides) & present(ATP)
    $\twoheadrightarrow_{60;60;1;40}$ output: present(ADP) & present(P) & present(lactose_import_mRNA)
TcD5
    input: present(gluconate6P_observation_amount) & present(CRPcAMP) &
    present(nucleotides) & input:present(ATP)
    $\twoheadrightarrow_{60;60;1;40}$ output: present(ADP) & output:present(P) & present(gluconate_import_mRNA)

4.5   Transfer Properties and Interlevel Interaction Properties

In addition to the role properties, also transfer properties and interlevel role interaction properties have been specified. Both have zero time delay. This is achieved by putting the LEADSTO parameters e, f, g, h according to e = f = -g , and g=h, so that the result will occur simultaneously with the antecedent, and also will have the same length. This is instantaneous transfer, without possibility of loss of communication and without delay. The example model uses the settings –.1,-.1,.1,.1. As the roles take place at the same place, it is reasonable to assume that a generated output is immediately available as input. As an example, the following is a property template for transfer between Transcription and Translation, where p is any state property that belongs both to the output of transcription and the input of translation.

$$\text{output(transcription): p} \twoheadrightarrow_{-.1;-.1;.1;.1} \text{input(translation): p}$$

This dynamic property relates output of the role Transcription to input of the role Translation at the same aggregation level in an instantaneous manner, i.e., without any time difference. The other transfer properties are similar. The conjunction of all dynamic properties for transfer between children roles of the (parent) Cell role is denoted by TRD(Cell).

An example of a property template for interlevel interaction between Metabolism and Cell is the following (here p belongs to the output of both metabolism and cell):

$$\text{output(metabolism): p} \twoheadrightarrow_{-.1;-.1;.1;.1} \text{output(cell): p}$$

This dynamic property relates output of a role at a lower level to output of its parent role one aggregation level higher in an instantaneous manner, i.e., without any time difference. Similarly inputs of lower level roles can be related to input of their parent role. The conjunction of all such dynamic properties for interlevel interaction between children roles and the (parent) Cell role is denoted by IID(Cell). Here, the abbreviation IID stands for the Interlevel Interaction Dynamics.

4.6 Logical Interlevel Relations between the Dynamic Properties within Cell

Within a compositional organisation model the dynamic properties of a higher level role are related to the dynamic properties of its child roles. Recall the general pattern from Section 3:

dynamic properties for child roles &
dynamic properties for transfer between child roles &
dynamic properties for interlevel interaction between parent role and children roles
$\Rightarrow$ dynamic properties for parent role

For the Cell as parent role, and Transcription, Translation and Metabolism as children roles this can be made more specific in the following manner:

DP(Transcription) & DP(Translation) & DP(Metabolism) &
TRD(Cell) & IID(Cell) $\Rightarrow$ DP(Cell)

In the above relation, DP stands for Dynamic Properties, TRD stands for the TRansfer Dynamics and IID stands for the Interlevel Interaction Dynamics.

This relation indeed holds. However, it can be made more specific by not involving whole sets of dynamic properties but specific subsets. For example, if the dynamic property CD1 for the cell is considered, this is already entailed by a smaller set of properties, i.e., a subset of the left hand side DP(Transcription) & DP(Translation) & DP(Metabolism) & TRD(Cell) & IID(Cell). Careful investigation of these more specific logical relationships yielded the following ones.

MD0 & MD4 & MD10 &
TcD1 & TcD3 &
TaD1 & TaD3 &
TRD(Cell) & IID(Cell) $\Rightarrow$ CD1

MD0 & MD1 & MD2& MD5 & MD10 &
TcD1 & TcD4 &
TaD1 & TaD4 &
TRD(Cell) & IID(Cell) $\Rightarrow$ CD2

MD0 & MD1 & MD3 & MD6 & MD10 &
TcD1 & TcD5 &
TaD1 & TaD5 &
TRD(Cell) & IID(Cell) $\Rightarrow$ CD3

MD0 & MD7 &
TcD2 & TcD3 &
TaD2 & TaD3 &
TRD(Cell) & IID(Cell) $\Rightarrow$ CD4

MD0 & MD1 & MD2 & MD8 &
TcD2 & TcD4 &
TaD2 & TaD4 &
TRD(Cell) & IID(Cell) $\Rightarrow$ CD5

MD0 & MD1 & MD3 & MD9 &
TcD2 & TcD5 &
TaD2 & TaD5 &
TRD(Cell) & IID(Cell) $\Rightarrow$ CD6

Note that for all of the properties of the Cell, the assumption must be met that at the start ATP, nucleotides and amino acids are available for the transcription and translation. This means that the cell should be alive at the start. This property is an initial condition called MD0, and was not covered in the description of the Metabolism earlier, because it has a different status; it is not in the general LEADSTO format. The property is:

MD0

[0:60] output: present(ATP) & present(nucleotides) & present(aminoacids)

The property MD0 is for the initialisation of the model. Because of the dynamics of the cell the substances mentioned in MD0 will be present if present earlier. This indicates that the cell stays prepared to regulate itself and to adapt to changes in its environment.

5 Dynamic Properties at Lower Aggregation Levels

From the three main roles within the cell, further refinement of Transcription and Translation will be addressed in Sections 5.1, 5.2 and 5.3. The main roles within Metabolism (Catabolism, Anabolism, and Transport) will be addressed in Sections 6, 7, and 8, respectively.

5.1 Translation and Its Two Main Roles

An overview is given of the input, the output and the dynamic properties of the roles within Translation. Note that the delay, here specified as between 0 and 0, only starts after the duration of the antecedent, so only after 60 seconds have passed will the enzymes start to be present.

Translation – Respiration Control
Input: present(aminoacids), present(ATP), present(respiration_mRNA),
    present(fermentation_mRNA)
Output: present(ADP), present(P), present(respiration_enzymes) present(fermentation_enzymes)

TaRD1
    input:present(respiration_mRNA) & present(aminoacids) & present(ATP)
    $\twoheadrightarrow_{0;0;60;600}$ output:present(ADP) & present(P) & present(respiration_enzymes)
TaRD2
    input:present(fermentation_mRNA) & present(aminoacids) & present(ATP)
    $\twoheadrightarrow_{0;0;60;600}$ output:present(ADP) & present(P) & present(fermentation_enzymes)

The conjunction of these properties is denoted by DP(Translation-Respiration-Control).

Translation – Nutrition import control
Input: present(aminoacids), present(ATP), present(glucose_import_mRNA),
     present(lactose_import_mRNA),
          present(gluconate_import_mRNA)
Output: present(ADP), present(P), present(lactose_import_enzymes),
     present(glucose_import_enzymes),
          present(gluconate_import_enzymes)

TaND1
          input:present(glucose_import_mRNA) & present(aminoacids) & input:present(ATP)
          $\twoheadrightarrow_{0;0;60;600}$ output:present(ADP) & present(P) & present(glucose_import_enzymes)
TaND2
          input:present(lactose_import_mRNA) & present(aminoacids) & present(ATP)
          $\twoheadrightarrow_{0;0;60;600}$ output:present(ADP) & present(P) & present(lactose_import_enzymes)
TaND3
          input:present(gluconate_import_mRNA) & present(aminoacids) & present(ATP)
          $\twoheadrightarrow_{0;0;60;600}$ output:present(ADP) & present(P) & present(gluconate_import_enzymes)

The conjunction of these properties is denoted by DP(Translation-Nutrition-Import-Control).

Logical relationships within Translation

Because

  DP(Translation) = DP(Translation-Respiration-Control) & DP(Translation-Nutrition-Import-Control),

it trivially holds that

          DP(Translation-Respiration-Control)
          & DP(Translation-Nutrition-Import-Control)
          & TRD(Translation) & IID(Translation) $\Rightarrow$ DP(Translation)

5.2 Transcription and Its Two Main Roles

An overview is given of the input and output and the dynamic properties of the roles within Transcription.

Transcription – Respiration Control
Input: present(nucleotides), present(ATP), present(ArcB_P)
Output: present(ADP), present(P), present(respiration_mRNA), present(fermentation_mRNA)

  TcRD1
          input:present(ArcB_P) & present(nucleotides) & present(ATP)
          $\twoheadrightarrow_{60;60;1;40}$ output:present(ADP) & present(P) & present(respiration_mRNA)
  TcRD2
          input: not present(ArcB_P) & present(nucleotides) & present(ATP)
          $\twoheadrightarrow_{60;60;1;40}$ output:present(ADP) & present(P) & present(fermentation_mRNA)

The conjunction of these properties is denoted by DP(Transcription-Respiration-Control).

Transcription – Nutrition import control

Input: present(nucleotides), present(ATP), present(CRPcAMP), present(allolactose),
             present(gluconate6P_observation_amount)
Output: present(ADP), present(P), present(glucose_import_mRNA), present(lactose_import_mRNA),
             present(gluconate_import_mRNA)

TcND1
    input:present(nucleotides) & present(ATP)
    $\twoheadrightarrow_{60;60;1;40}$ output:present(ADP) & present(P) & present(glucose_import_mRNA)
TcND2
       input:present(allolactose) & present(CRPcAMP) & present(nucleotides) & present(ATP)
    $\twoheadrightarrow_{60;60;1;40}$ output:present(ADP) & present(P) & present(lactose_import_mRNA)
TcND3
    input:present(gluconate6P_observation_amount) & present(CRPcAMP) &
    present(nucleotides) & input:present(ATP)
    $\twoheadrightarrow_{60;60;1;40}$ output:present(ADP) & output:present(P) & present(gluconate_import_mRNA)

The conjunction of these properties is denoted by DP(Transcription-Nutrition-Import-
Control).

Logical relationships within Transcription

Because,

DP(Transcription) = DP(Transcription-Respiration-Control) & DP(Transcription-Nutrition-Import-Control),

it trivially holds

       DP(Transcription-Respiration-Control)
       & DP(Transcription-Nutrition-Import-Control)
       & TRD(Transcription) & IID(Transcription) $\Rightarrow$ DP(Transcription)

5.3 Metabolism and Its Three Main Roles

An overview is given of the input and output and the dynamic properties of the roles
within Metabolism.

Catabolism

Input: present(glucose6P), present(gluconate6P), present(lactose), present(pyruvate),
            present(ADP), present(P), present(fermentation_enzymes), present(respiration_enzymes),
            present(O2), present(NAD(P))
Output: present(pyruvate), present(glucose6P), present(PEP), present(ATP), present(CO2),
            present(acetate), present(ethanol), present(NAD(P)H).

To keep the conserved moiety of NAD(P) and NAD(P)H in continued existence, the
NAD(P) is kept present always. Thus the energy-poor version is kept available, while
the energy-rich NAD(P)H can fluctuate.

Persistent: input:present(NAD(P)).

CaD1
    (input:present(glucose6P) or present(gluconate6P) or present(lactose)) & present(ADP) &
    present(P) & present(NAD(P)) & present(O2) & present(respiration_enzymes)
    $\twoheadrightarrow_{4;12;4;4}$ output:present(pyruvate) & present(glucose6P) & present(ATP) & present(NAD(P)H)
    & present(PEP) & present(CO2)

CaD2

(input:present(glucose6P) or present(gluconate6P) or present(lactose)) & present(ADP) & present(P) & present(NAD(P)) & present(fermentation_enzymes)
$\twoheadrightarrow_{4;12;4;4}$ output: present(pyruvate) & present(glucose6P) & present(ATP) & present(NAD(P)H) & present(PEP) & present(acetate) & present(ethanol)

Anabolism

Input: present(ATP), present(NAD(P)H), present(glucose6P), present(pyruvate), present(N), present(P), present(S)
Output: present(ADP), present(P), present(NAD(P)), present(aminoacids), present(nucleotides)

AD1

input:present(ATP) & present(NAD(P)H) & present(glucose6P) & present(pyruvate) & present(N) & present(P) & present(S)
$\twoheadrightarrow_{2;6;4;4}$ output:present(ADP) & present(P) & present(NAD(P)) & present(nucleotides) & present(aminoacids)

Transport

Input: present(glucose_outside), present(lactose_outside), present(gluconate_outside), present(O2_outside), present(N_outside), present(P_outside), present(S_outside), present(PEP), present(ATP), present(acetate), present(ethanol), present(CO2), present(lactose_import_enzymes), present(glucose_import_enzymes), present(gluconate_import_enzymes)
Output: present(glucose6P), present(lactose), present(gluconate6P), present(O2), present(CRPcAMP), present(allolactose), present(gluconate6P_observation_amount), present(ArcB_P), present(N), present(P), present(S), present(pyruvate), present(ADP), present(P), present(acetate_outside), present(ethanol_outside), present(CO2_outside)

TrD1

input:present(glucose_outside) & present(PEP) & present(glucose_import_enzymes)
$\twoheadrightarrow_{-4;0;4;4}$ output:present(glucose6P) & present(pyruvate)

TrD2

input:present(gluconate_outside) & present(ATP) & present(gluconate_import_enzymes)
$\twoheadrightarrow_{-4;0;4;4}$ output:present(gluconate6P) & present(ADP) & present(P)

TrD3

input:present(lactose_outside) & present(ATP) & present(lactose_import_enzymes)
$\twoheadrightarrow_{-4;0;4;4}$ output:present(lactose) & present(ADP) & present(P)

TrD4

input:present(O2_outside) $\bullet\twoheadrightarrow_{0;0;4;4}$ output:present(O2) & present(ArcB_P)

TrD5

input:present(N_outside) & present(ATP)
$\twoheadrightarrow_{0;0;4;4}$ output:present(N) & present(ADP) & present(P)

TrD6

input:present(P_outside) & present(ATP)
$\twoheadrightarrow_{0;0;4;4}$ output:present(P) & present(ADP) & present(P)

TrD7

input:present(S_outside) & present(ATP)
$\twoheadrightarrow_{0;0;4;4}$ output:present(S & present(ADP) & present(P)

TrD8

input:present(acetate) $\twoheadrightarrow_{0;0;4;4}$ output:present(acetate_outside)

TrD9

input:present(ethanol) $\twoheadrightarrow_{0;0;4;4}$ output:present(ethanol_outside)

TrD10

    input:present(CO2) $\twoheadrightarrow_{0;0;4;4}$ output:present(CO2_outside)

TrD11

    input: not present(glucose_outside)

    $\twoheadrightarrow_{-4;0;4;4}$ output:present(CRPcAMP)

TrD12

    input:present(lactose_outside)

    $\twoheadrightarrow_{0;0;0.230;0.230}$ output:present(allolactose)

TrD13

    input:present(gluconate_outside)

    $\twoheadrightarrow_{0;0;0.230;0.230}$ output:present(gluconate6P_observation_amount)

Logical relationships within Metabolism

Also in this case the following logical relationship holds:

    DP(Catabolism) & DP(Anabolism) & DP(Transport) &
TRD(Metabolism) & IID(Metabolism) $\Rightarrow$ DP(Metabolism)

The more specific logical relationships are as follows.

    TrD11 & TRD(Metabolism) & IID(Metabolism) $\Rightarrow$ MD1

    TrD12 & TRD(Metabolism) & IID(Metabolism) $\Rightarrow$ MD2

    TrD13 & TRD(Metabolism) & IID(Metabolism) $\Rightarrow$ MD3

    TrD1 & TrD4 & TrD5 & TrD6 & TrD7 & TrD10 &
CaD0 & CaD1 &
AD0 & AD1 &
TRD(Metabolism) & IID(Metabolism) $\Rightarrow$ MD4

    TrD3 & TrD4 & TrD5 & TrD6 & TrD7 & TrD10 &
CaD0 & CaD1 &
AD0 & AD1 &
TRD(Metabolism) & IID(Metabolism) $\Rightarrow$ MD5

    TrD2 & TrD4 & TrD5 & TrD6 & TrD7 & TrD10 &
CaD0 & CaD1 &
AD0 & AD1 &
TRD(Metabolism) & IID(Metabolism) $\Rightarrow$ MD6

    TrD1 & TrD5 & TrD6 & TrD7 & TrD8 & TrD9 &
CaD0 & CaD2 &
AD0 & AD1 &
TRD(Metabolism) & IID(Metabolism) $\Rightarrow$ MD7

    TrD3 & TrD5 & TrD6 & TrD7 & TrD8 & TrD9 &
CaD0 & CaD2 &
AD0 & AD1 &
TRD(Metabolism) & IID(Metabolism) $\Rightarrow$ MD8

    TrD2 & TrD5 & TrD6 & TrD7 & TrD8 & TrD9 &
CaD0 & CaD2 &
AD0 & AD1 &
TRD(Metabolism) & IID(Metabolism) $\Rightarrow$ MD9

    TrD4 & TRD(Metabolism) & IID(Metabolism) $\Rightarrow$ MD10

The initialisation properties here are AD0 and CaD0, given as:

AD0

 [0:60] output: present(NAD(P))

CaD0

 [0:60] output: present(PEP) & present(ATP)

These properties are used to initialise the simulation as well.

6   Simulation and Analysis Results

For a simulation based approach to be acceptable, the simulation has to fulfill the following criteria (Hollendbeck, 2000): replication, prediction, data availability, and validation. Therefore, the simulation has to be described in sufficient detail, along with the details of initial values. The parameters and variables of the simulation have been identified on the basis of the available data on the cell (and in particular ecoli) in literature. The aim of this last section is to show the validity of the model presented.

A software environment has been built to support both simulation and analysis of organisation models. For a compositional organisation model this software allows the user to select which parts of the hierarchy need to be taken into account, and then to run a simulation or analysis, see Figure 5.

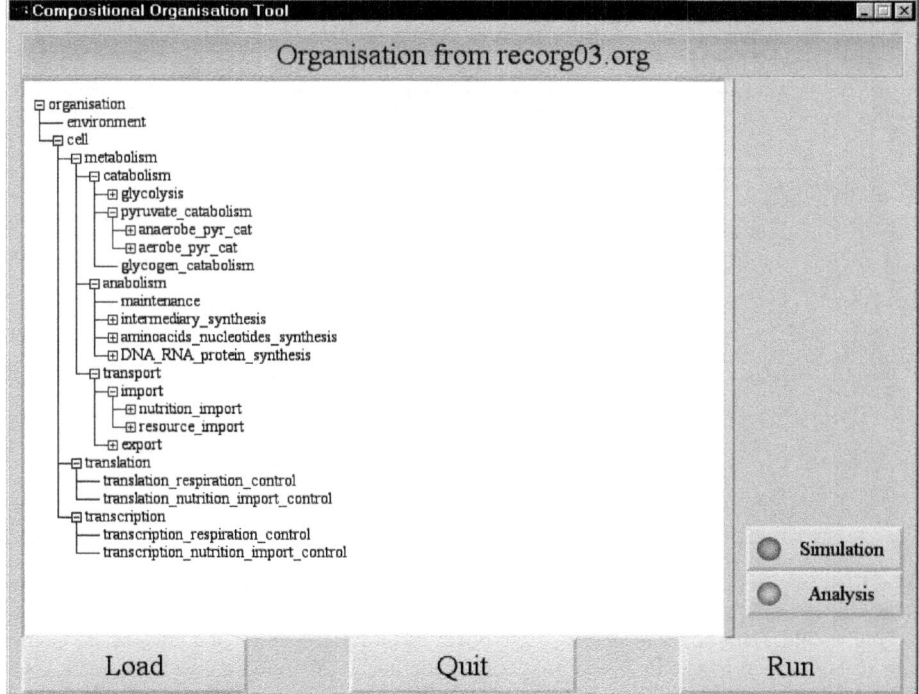

Fig. 5. Screenshot of the compositional organisation modelling tool, selecting which level of aggregation to use for simulation or analysis

6.1 Simulation

Given the available dynamic properties at each aggregation level, a choice can be made to perform simulation at a high level of aggregation, or at a lower level. Simulation at a higher level of aggregation uses the rougher, less detailed dynamical properties of the higher level roles. Simulation at a lower level of aggregation uses the more detailed dynamic properties of the lower level roles. Because of information hiding, the higher level properties are less in number and less detailed, resulting in more efficient simulation due to the lower complexity. The level of aggregation for simulation can be selected per role. If a particular role is selected for detailed, lower level, simulation, one possibility would be to assume that the part around it is constant. Another possibility, used here, is to simulate the parts around it using them at a higher level of aggregation, using the less detailed properties. Thus it is possible to indicate the level of detail to use for simulation for each part of the tree separately (as depicted in Figure 4), by navigating the tree selecting some parts for more or less detail than other parts. Simulation is performed using the dynamic LEADSTO properties associated to

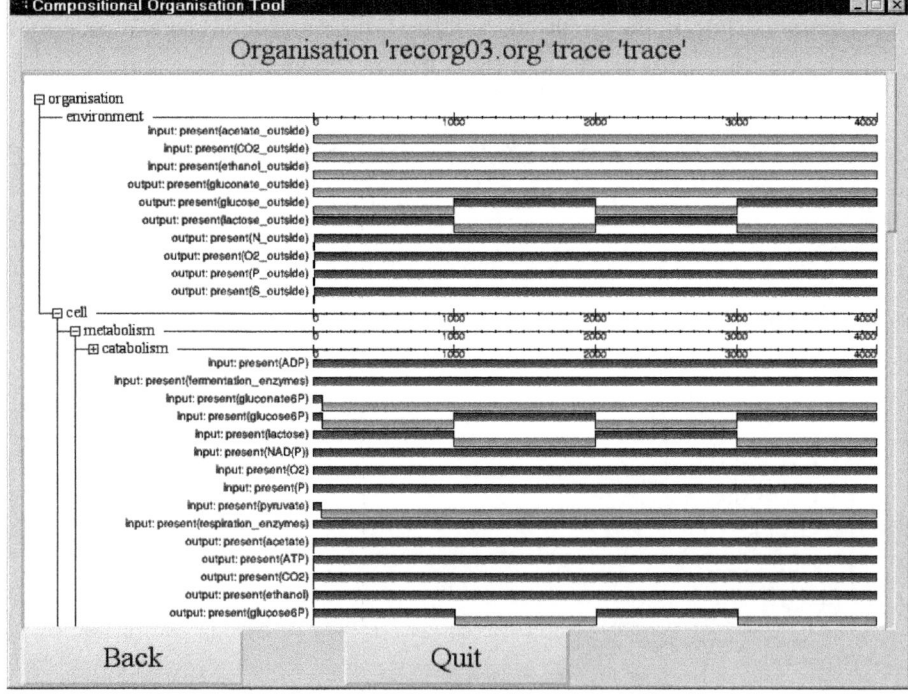

Fig. 6. Screenshot of the compositional organisation tool, browsing the results of a simulation. Time flows to the right, in seconds. The roles environment en catabolism have their input and output visible. Dark boxes mean true, light boxes mean false. Lactose and glucose are alternating in the environment in a way that was predefined. All 'environment 'properties were completely defined by the outside world. All other properties obtained an initial value at the beginning but were further determined by the system. The lactose and glucose6P inside the cell are input to the catabolism.

the leaves of the subtree selected: the end nodes (not indicated by -) in Figure 5. Roughly spoken, the simulation algorithm takes care that if the antecedent of a 'follows' property is true in the trace constructed so far, the trace will be extended by making the consequent true as well. If several rules fire to make the same consequent true, which means some substance has a concentration above a threshold, then the consequent will be true in the conjunction of both intervals. The modeller should make sure that no rules fire to make the same consequent true and false at the same time, as this is an inconsistency. By searching and applicable rules whose consequent has not been added to the trace yet, the trace is extended to further time intervals. The simulations are initialised by setting all inputs to true for a period of time, 0 .. 60 seconds in the examples. If needed, a subset of the input of a component can be specified per component; only that subset will be initiated in that case.

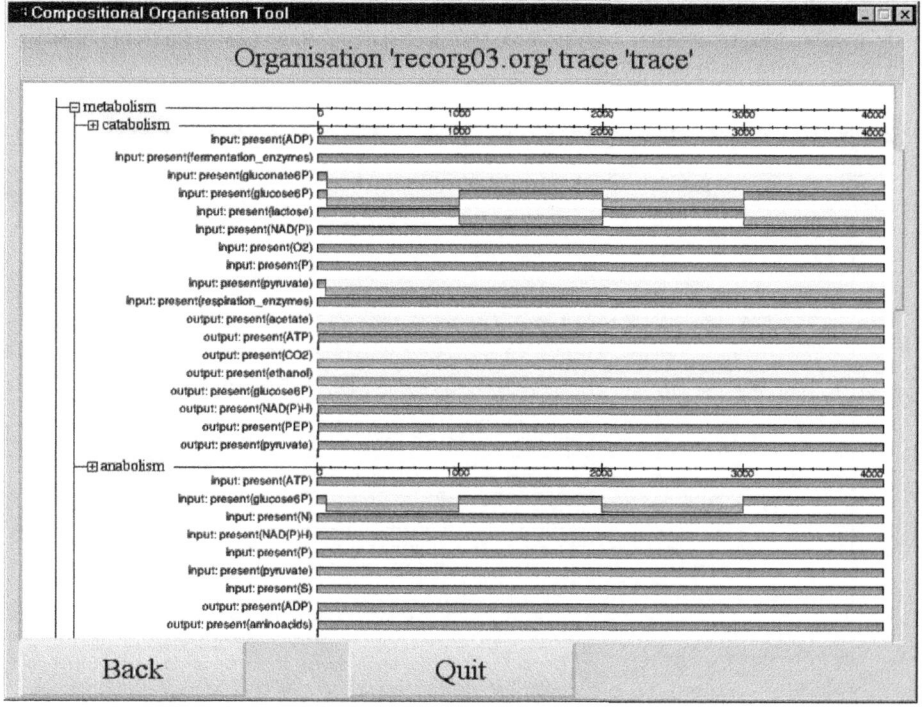

Fig. 7. Screenshot showing the results of an analysis of a trace obtained by simulation

After a simulation the user is presented with the results, where for each part (role with its subroles) the input, internal and output atoms are shown changing over time, see Figure 6. Atoms are the input and output identifiers for the roles. Time flows to the right. When an (atomic) state property is true this is depicted by a dark box above the line, whilst false is depicted by a lighter box below the line. As in the paradigm of Executable Temporal Logic (Barringer et al., 1996), the simulation algorithm achieves that the constructed trace satisfies all the 'follows' properties used for the simulation (assuming that the model does not include inconsistencies). This does not automatically imply that all dynamic properties at higher levels of aggregation will hold for such a constructed trace. This is because during model construction the lower level properties used in simulation might not imply the higher level properties, and analysis would reveal this (validation of the model). However, if the logical relationships between dynamic properties at different levels of aggregation hold as discussed, the higher level dynamic properties will (have to) hold. This is useful for validation of the dynamic properties: For each trace obtained by simulation, it can be checked automatically whether any LEADSTO property holds. If a higher level property does not hold for a given trace, then this indicates incorrectness of some of the lower level properties. This analysis process will be discussed in the next section.

The simulation of Fig. 6, took less than 1.8 hours of computation time, for 533 identifiers and 828 temporal relationships (not all shown in the Figure). In this simulation several changes (imposed by us) on the environment lead to cell dynamics where one steady state after another was encountered, and also states on the way from one steady state to another are derived. Of the 59 components in the actual simulation, for reasons of presentation, only some are shown.

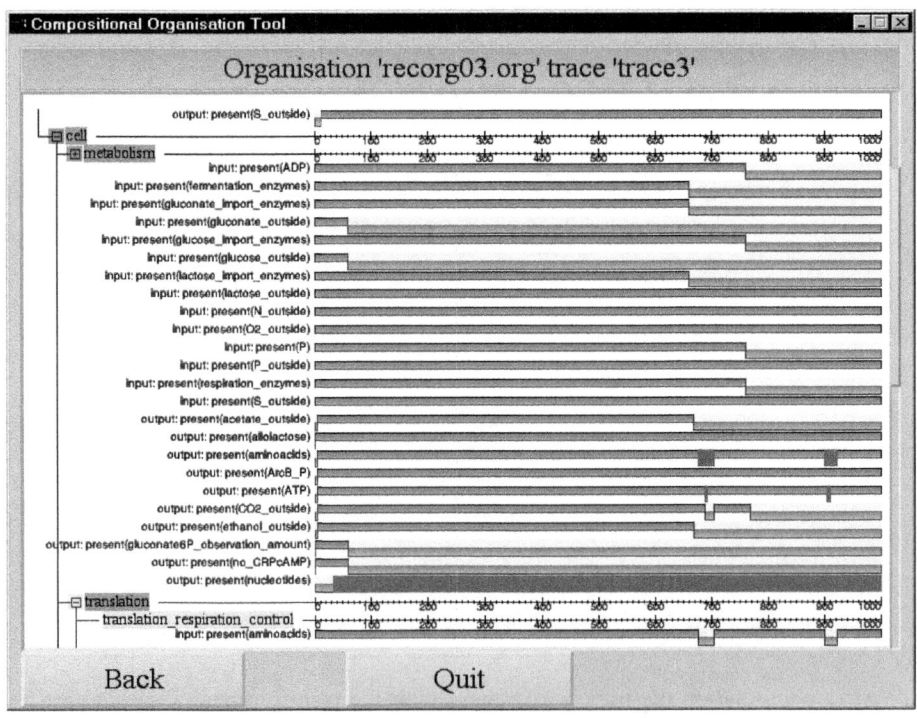

Fig. 8. Results of analysis, viewing the metabolism

6.2 Analysis

The simulations for two slightly different models can be compared. This can be used to localize the differences between the two models. Different models can be obtained by making different choices for the levels of aggregation to use for simulation or analysis. Note that an analysis model contains not only the LEADSTO properties of the leaves of the tree, but also the dynamical properties of higher level roles. Our analysis software focuses on this option. Another option would be to obtain a trace from a laboratory experiment and check this with respect to the dynamic properties of the organisation model. Whether the trace is obtained by another model or by experiment, the differences between a trace and the analysis model are analysed.

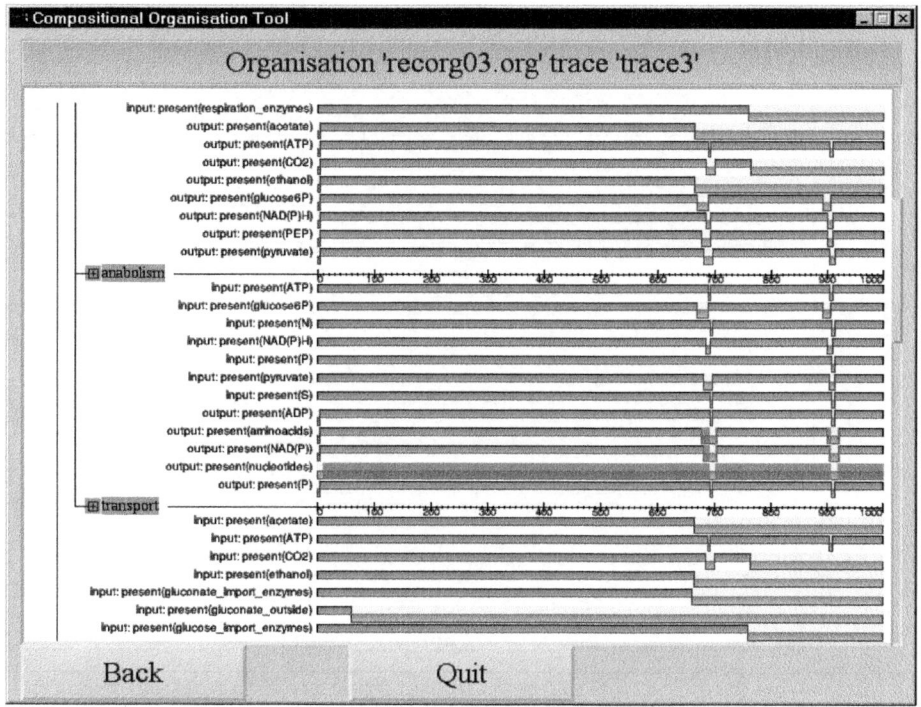

Fig. 9. Results of analysis, viewing the anabolism

The Analysis Software works by checking for each role whether its action and premissae are related correctly in the given trace with respect to the simulation model. The analysis software changes the colours where the trace differs from the prediction of the model. In the trace the blue colour is changed to green in undisputed spots, whilst deviations are flagged yellow (unexpected by the analysis model) or red (expectation unfulfilled for the analysis model). A light yellow colour means that a false interval was not explained, it was not expected. A stronger yellow colour means that a non-false interval was not expected. Yellow means that the LEADSTO properties that are checked do not completely specify the trace. A red colour means that an interval was expected by a LEADSTO property, but did not happen in reality. If this occurs, the LEADSTO property that is checked and the LEADSTO properties used to specify the behaviour do not fit together, since the former predicts something different from what happens in the trace. The analysis results should be interpreted according to circumstances. If the trace has been produced by a simulation, then either the properties used for simulation are wrong or the property checked is wrong. If a "natural", laboratory, trace is analysed, then the property checked has to be wrong. To aid browsing the results, the name of each component is highlighted in yellow or red if any errors have been found in that role's input or output. Also the + and - box next to a component are highlighted if there are any errors in the subtree below a component.

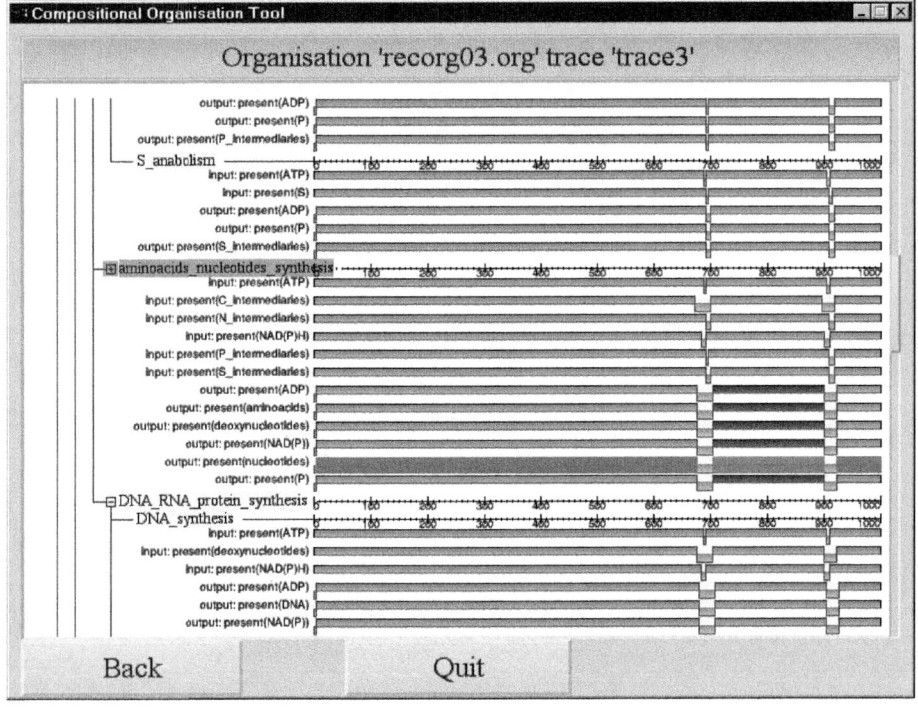

Fig. 10. Results of analysis, viewing the aminoacids nucleotides synthesis

In Figs 8-11 an example top-down analysis of a trace is shown. In the complete model the component nucleotides synthesis was crippled, by having it no longer generate any nucleotides. We shall now show how the analysis mode of our Software facilitated finding where the bug was. A simulation was run both of the crippled and of the uncrippled model. Then both were submitted to the 'Analysis' routine. Then a check was done at the top level. This check was inspected, see Figure 8. As can be seen many errors occurred because of the crippling. One clearly marked is that the metabolism properties expected nucleotides on the output, but they never appeared, amongst others, later on in the trace.

In Figure 9, the metabolism is further inspected to reveal that the anabolism also expected nucleotides, but they are missing.

In Figure 10 the aminoacids nucleotides synthesis component is inspected, showing that nucleotides were again missing.

In Figure 11, the nucleotides synthesis component is shown. It reported no serious errors – since it operated perfectly fine according to the faulty property. Since the nucleotides synthesis role property was sabotaged, and simulation produced a trace conforming to it, during the analysis the property will not show discrepancies with the trace. There are no nucleotides on the output however. This causes the properties of higher level components to show discrepancies with the trace, clearly flagging where to investigate. In this example it can be seen how the properties of the higher level components aid in finding bugs in the specification of the model.

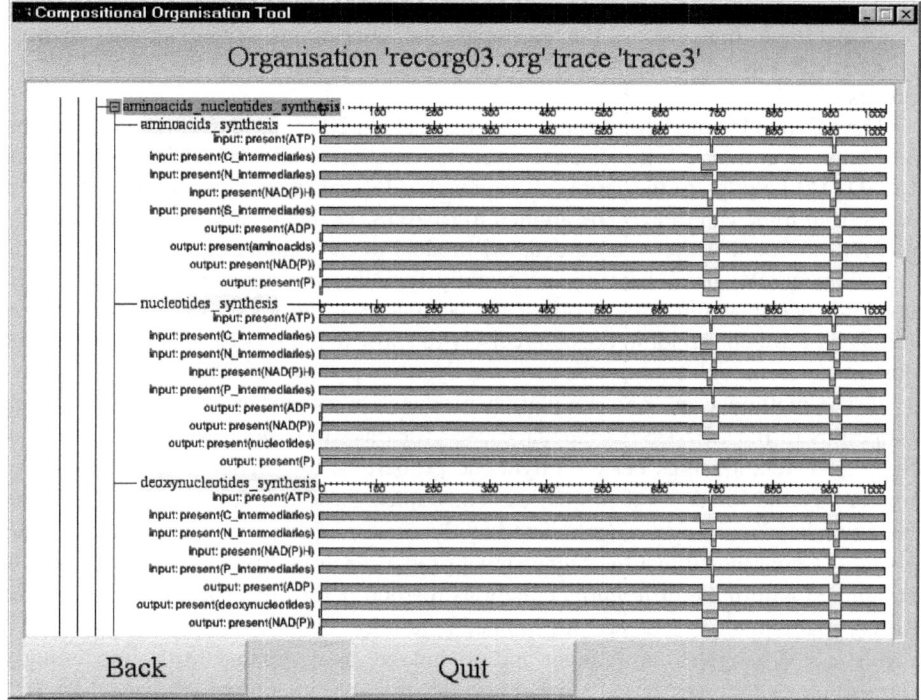

Fig. 11. Results of analysis, viewing the nucleotides synthesis

7 Discussion

In this paper it was shown how organisational modelling techniques can be exploited to manage complexity of intracellular processes. The organisational modelling techniques were adopted from the area of Computational Organisation Theory and Artificial Intelligence, where they are used to describe how complex dynamics in human societies can be managed using multi-agent organisation structures. Usually these organisation modelling techniques are applied to organisations such as factories and the internal organisation of their process flows, obtaining high-level models of complex organisations at different levels of aggregation. From the biological perspective complex intracellular dynamics are often interpreted in terms of well-organised processes; sometimes a cell is considered a (micro)factory. Using the example of *Escherichia coli* it was shown how indeed such organisational modelling techniques can be used to simulate and analyse *E. coli*'s intracellular dynamics. Exploiting the abstraction levels entailed by this organisation modelling perspective, a concise model was obtained that is easy to simulate and analyse at different levels of aggregation.

The abstraction was based on a detailed mapping of the abstract notions to detailed information on the concentration levels of the various substrates involved in the processes of the cell. That way the downward compatibility of our model to the traditional models of the cell (often presented in terms of differential equations) was ensured,. Upward compatibility is maintained, but of course only with respect to the abstractions made in our model. For example, the continuous nature of the chemical processes in the cell is reduced to more characteristic and abstract notions of the cell process.

The LEADSTO modelling approach (Bosse et al., 2007) used as a vehicle, has some elements in common with discrete event simulation methods. A difference is that LEADSTO belongs to the family of executable logical languages, and therefore concepts from logic can directly be applied to LEADSTO specifications. Technically, it is possible to connect these more detailed models to our simulation in the LEADSTO environment. We have done so successfully for other domains. That way the higher level behaviour would emerge out of the behaviour at the lower levels of abstraction. In this case we chose not to do so, precisely to show that a model at the higher level of abstraction is enough to show the essential dynamic patterns of the cell.

In the method used, any simulation produces a *trace* that satisfies the dynamic properties in the LEADSTO language used for the simulation. As a consequence of the logical relationships between dynamic properties, the higher level properties are implied by the lower level properties. Thus, once these interlevel relationships have been validated, for any trace simulated by dynamic properties at a certain aggregation level, it is guaranteed that the higher-level properties hold. Such an approach can also be applied within the differential equations method if for higher levels of aggregation differential equations are used for lumped reactions. The use of different aggregation levels is a distinguishing element and advantage, as compared to the modelling of intracellular processes based on beliefs, desires and intentions (the socalled BDI-model) presented for the steady state and non-steady state case in (Jonker, Snoep, Treur, Westerhoff and Wijngaards, 2002, 2008). The BDI-modelling approach, however, has the advantage of interpretation of intracellular processes in readily understood intentional terms for internal states, whereas in the current paper internal states are described in biochemical terms that are accessible to biochemists only.

The modeling, or rather calculation (Westerhoff, 2001), of living systems is becoming more and more timely, with the vast amount of experimental data surmounting the possibility of evaluation by the unaided human mind. Detailed models have been the answer until now (e.g. Teusink et al., 2000, Wang et al., 2001; Takahashi, et al., 2003; Snoep, 2005; Jamshidi and Palsson, 2006), but they have been limited to smaller parts of the cell, in part because of the complexity of handling larger parts. Existing whole-cell models have been lacking the true kinetic information of the enzymes or have had to rely on oversimplified aspects thereof (Covert et al., 2001). Ways of simplifying this type of modeling without loss in essential information on the dynamic behavior have been sought after. This paper is not the first attempt at simplification by modeling living cells in terms of hierarchical and modular structures.

Heinrich et al. (1976) championed an approach based on the time hierarchy of a system, treating fast relaxing and slowly relaxing subsystems differently. Kahn and Westerhoff (1991) developed a hierarchical approach for metabolic control analysis where they distinguished modules within a cell that do not communicate by material fluxes between them (see also Hofmeyr & Westerhoff, 2001). Westerhoff et al (1983), Schuster et al (1983), Brown et al. (1990) and Rohwer et al. (1996) developed modular approaches to flux-connected biochemical networks. In a way, these approaches mimicked what has been biochemical intuition for qualitative approaches to cell function. All these earlier approaches however missed the possibility to discuss the organization of cell function in much the same way as one discusses the organization of human society.

The high-level of abstraction of the organizational model results in an inherently faster computation compared to a model based on differential equations. This computational advantage mainly stems from the fact that to model dynamic relations between states in a trajectory or trace, in the presented model LEADSTO properties are used instead of differential equations that have to be computed in very small steps. Using LEADSTO properties also flat, unorganised models can be built, but the organisational structure can be used to obtain even more efficiency. An additional computational advantage can be obtained if simulation is performed on the basis of LEADSTO properties at higher aggregation levels, abstracting from processes at lower aggregation levels. However, in that case no information is obtained on the dynamics of these processes at lower levels. It depends on the interest of the simulator whether or not this is a drawback. If only the global dynamics is of interest, a simulation at a higher aggregation level may suffice. We have not engaged in this stategy in the present manuscript but may do so in the future.

There are perhaps a few situations where the present method does differ critically in its quantitative predictions from the method of differential equations. For instance, when delay times are comparable to relaxation times of concentrations, the present method might become less accurate and even produce apparent oscillations where there are none in reality. The oscillations then derive from negative feedback loops over long delays that stem from the modelling method rather than that they are inherent in the system that is being modelled. A second aspect where the method used here, as well as the methods developed by Glass & Kauffman (1973), Jonker et al. (2001) and Jonker & Treur (2002) may be inferior to the method of integrating differential equations, is the tendency to treat concentrations digitally in a binary system. Indeed binary modeling methods such as proposed by Glass and Kauffman (1973) may not be subtle enough for some aspects of cell function (cf. Endy & Brent, 2001). In reality concentrations can assume a wide range of values and reaction rate are quite sensitive to the concentrations. Metabolic control is in fact based on such subtlety (Hofmeyr, 2002). On the other hand, it does take a while before an entire mRNA or protein molecule has been synthesized and this discrete time effect is rarely simulated in differential equation models, whereas it comes naturally in the method developed here. Some other assumptions made are that the model presented in the paper does not model reactions as consuming substrates. Instead, products have a minimum lifetime, which can be extended but will eventually expire. The approach allows the addition of substrate consumption by specifying this in the consequents of the LEADSTO properties.

With respect to the specific model of *E. coli* developed here, a number of *caveats* are appropriate. First, parts of the biochemistry of this bacterium are insufficiently known for the model to become completely detailed and precise. Paradoxically, of some parts of *E. coli* biochemistry much more is known and in much more detail than what has been implemented here. With respect to those parts however, we have engaged in (over) simplification because of the unavoidable lack of precision in the other parts should not make enhanced precision worthwhile. After all, the present study merely served to illustrate the method of organizational modeling for living cells. In order to obtain an optimal model of *E. coli* a separate study will be needed. An amelioration of the model could be achieved by using more valuations for substances than present or not present as done now. For example, a worthwhile addition could be the use of a scale of three values: low, medium and high for ATP and NAD(P)H. The approach allows the use an arbitrary number of levels per substance. Within the model, some state properties (atoms) were assumed persistent. For example, in catabolism input(NAD(P)), and also one in glucose_import2. These state properties (on input, output or internal) will always hold since they start to hold. They are used here to keep the conserved moieties present at all times. The energy-drained versions were kept in existence, whilst the energy-rich versions could fluctuate and possibly disappear. The NAD(P) and IIAglc substances are assumed persistent in the model. The notation NAD(P)H and NAD(P) was used to abstract from NADH, NADPH, NAD and NADP. NADH and NADPH were taken together to avoid the added complexity of transhydrogenase reactions and pathways.

Notwithstanding these *caveats*, the reader may have noted remarkable similarities between the performance of the model and what is known concerning the physiology of *E. coli*. Here and in parallel studies by the same authors, the well known strong regulation of cell physiology by oxygen and glucose in this organism was reproduced. This suggests that organizational modelling may well help to grasp the essence of the physiology of living cells. An added value of this abstraction approach may be that it provides teachers with the justification to explain the overall cell behaviour in such abstract terms. The mappings and the runtime behaviour of the abstract model validate their practice. Their abstractions correspond to the abstraction by the LEADSTO properties based on discretization of states and have the benefits of understandability and efficient simulation. These benefits are enhanced by the introduction of overall properties, again based on biochemical knowledge, that span different levels of aggregation and simplify the analysis of the model. Higher-level properties enable the analysis of traces obtained using simulation of lower level properties and make it easier to find errors in the model. The simulations show the cell's essential dynamic patterns depending on (static or dynamic) environmental conditions, both for reaching a steady state (in case of a static or fast fluctuating environment) and for oscillating dynamics (e.g., in case of a periodically changing environment). As soon as the student is interested in more details of such dynamics, he can zoom in to that level by taking the more standard simulations of the indivual pathways that are based on differential equations.

Interesting further work would be to investigate further the relationship between the approach in this paper and methods based on differential equations. In this paper logical relations between dynamical properties of components and subcomponents are established. Perhaps something similar can be done for differential equations instead of logical formula to specify dynamic properties.

References

Barringer, H., Fisher, M., Gabbay, D., Owens, R., Reynolds, M.: The Imperative Future: Principles of Executable Temporal Logic. Research Studies Press Ltd. and John Wiley & Sons (1996)

Ben-Jacob, E., Cohen, I., Czirók, A., Vicsek, T., Gutnick, D.L.: Chemomodulation of Cellular Movement and Collective Formation of Vortices by Swarming Bacteria. Physica A 238, 181–197 (1997)

Booch, G.: Object oriented design with applications. Benjamins Cummins Publishing Company, Redwood City (1991)

Bosse, T., Jonker, C.M., van der Meij, L., Treur, J.: A Language and Environment for Analysis of Dynamics by Simulation. International Journal of Artificial Intelligence Tools 16, 435–464 (2007)

Brazier, F.M.T., Jonker, C.M., Treur, J.: Principles of Component-Based Design of Intelligent Agents. Data and Knowledge Engineering 41, 1–28 (2002)

Brown, G.C., Hafner, R.P., Brand, M.D.: A 'top-down' approach to the determination of control coefficients in metabolic control theory. Eur. J. Biochem. 188, 321–325 (1990)

Covert, M.W., Schilling, C.H., Famili, I., Edwards, J.S., Goryanin, I.I., Selkov, E., Palsson, B.O.: Metabolic modeling of microbial strains in silico. Trends Biochem. Sci. 26(3), 179–186 (2001)

Dardenne, A., van Lamsweerde, A., Fickas, S.: Goal-directed Requirements Acquisition. Science in Computer Programming 20, 3–50 (1993)

Dubois, E., Du Bois, P., Zeippen, J.M.: A Formal Requirements Engineering Method for Real-Time, Concurrent, and Distributed Systems. In: Proceedings of the Real-Time Systems Conference, RTS'95 (1995)

Endy, D., Brent, R.: Modelling cellular behavior. Nature 409, 391–395 (2001)

Ferber, J., Gutknecht, O., Jonker, C.M., Müller, J.P., Treur, J.: Organization Models and Behavioural Requirements Specification for Multi-Agent Systems. In: Demazeau, Y., Garijo, F. (eds.) Multi-Agent System Organisations, Proceedings of the 10th European Workshop on Modelling Autonomous Agents in a Multi-Agent World, MAAMAW'01 (2001)

Ferber, J., Gutknecht, O.: A meta-model for the analysis and design of organizations in multi-agent systems. In: Third International Conference on Multi-Agent Systems (ICMAS '98) Proceedings. IEEE Computer Society, Los Alamitos (1998)

Fisher, M.: A survey of Concurrent METATEM — the language and its applications. In: Gabbay, D.M., Ohlbach, H.J. (eds.) ICTL 1994. Lecture Notes in AI, vol. 827, pp. 480–505. Springer, Heidelberg (1994)

Fisher, M.: Temporal Development Methods for Agent-Based Systems. Journal of Autonomous Agents and Multi-Agent Systems 10, 41–66 (2005)

Galton, A.: Temporal Logic. Stanford Encyclopedia of Philosophy (2003),
    http://plato.stanford.edu/entries/logic-temporal/#2

Gear, C.W.: Numerical Initial Value Problems in Ordinary Differential Equations. Prentice-Hall, Englewood Cliffs (1971)

Glass, L., Kauffman, S.: The logical analysis of continuous, non-linear biochemical control networks. J. Theor. Biol. 39, 103–129 (1973)

Heinrich, R., Rapoport, S.M., Rapoport, T.A.: Metabolic Regulaiton and Mathematical Models. Progr. Biophys. Mol. Biol. 32, 1–82 (1977)

Hofmeyr, J.H.S.: Metabolic Control Analysis in a nutshell. BioComplexity (2002) (in the press)

Hofmeyr, J.H.S., Westerhoff, H.V.: Building the cellular puzzle: Control in Multi-level reaction networks. J. Theor. Biol. 208, 261–285 (2001)

Jamshidi, N., Palsson, B.O.: Systems biology of the human red blood cell. Blood Cells, Molecules and Diseases 36, 239–247 (2006)

Jonker, C.M., Letia, I.A., Treur, J.: Diagnosis of the Dynamics within an Organisation by Trace Checking of Behavioural Requirements. In: Wooldridge, M., Weiß, G., Ciancarini, P. (eds.) AOSE 2001. LNCS, vol. 2222, pp. 17–32. Springer, Heidelberg (2002)

Jonker, C.M., Treur, J., Wijngaards, W.C.A.: Specification, Analysis and Simulation of the Dynamics within an Organisation. Journal of Applied Intelligence 27, 131–152 (2001)

Jonker, C.M., Snoep, J.L., Treur, J., Westerhoff, H.V., Wijngaards, W.C.A.: Putting Intentions into Cell Biochemistry: An Artificial Intelligence Perspective. Journal of Theoretical Biology 214, 105–134 (2002)

Jonker, C.M., Snoep, J.L., Treur, J., Westerhoff, H.V., Wijngaards, W.C.A.: BDI-Modelling of Complex Intracellular Dynamics. Journal of Theoretical Biology 251, 1–23 (2008)

Jonker, C.M., Treur, J.: Compositional Verification of Multi-Agent Systems: a Formal Analysis of Pro-activeness and Reactiveness. International Journal of Cooperative Information Systems 11, 51–92 (2002)

Kahn, D., Westerhoff, H.V.: Control Theory of Regulatory Cascades. J. Theor. Biol. 153, 255–285 (1991)

Kholodenko, B.N., Demin, O.V., Moehren, G., Hoek, J.B.: Quantification of short term signaling by the epidermal growth factor receptor. J. Biol. Chem. 274(42), 30169–30181 (1999)

Knuth, D.E.: The Art of Computer Programming. Addison-Wesley, Reading (1981)

Lomi, A., Larsen, E.R.: Dynamics of Organizations: Computational Modeling and Organization Theories. AAAI Press, Menlo Park (2001)

Mintzberg, H.: The Structuring of Organisations. Prentice Hall, Englewood Cliffs (1979)

Moss, S., Gaylard, H., Wallis, S., Edmonds, B.: SDML: A Multi-Agent Language for Organizational Modelling. Computational and Mathematical Organization Theory 4(1), 43–70 (1998)

Pajares, J., Lopez, A., Hernandez, C.: Industry as an Organisation of Agents: Innovation and R&D Management. Journal of Artificial Societies and Social Simulation 6(2) (2003), http://jasss.soc.surrey.ac.uk/6/2/7.html

Press, W.H., Teukolsky, S.A., Vetterling, W.T., Flannery, B.P.: Numerical recipes in C: the art of scientific computing, 2nd edn. Cambridge University Press, Cambridge (1992)

Prietula, M., Gasser, L., Carley, K.: Simulating Organizations. MIT Press, Cambridge (1997)

Rizzi, M., Baltes, M., Theobald, U., Reuss, M.: In vivo analysis of metabolic dynamics in Saccharomyces cerevisiae: II. Mathematical model. Biotechnol. Bioeng. 55, 592–608 (1997)

Rohwer, J.M., Schuster, S., Westerhoff, H.V.: How to recognize monofunctional units in a metabolic system. J. theor. Biol. 179, 213–228 (1996)

Rohwer, J.M., Meadow, N.D., Roseman, S., Westerhoff, H.V., Postma, P.W.: Understanding glucose transport by the bacterial phosphoenolpyruvate:glycose phosphotransferase system on the basis of kinetic measurements in vitro. J. Biol. Chem. 275(45), 34909–34921 (2000)

Rotterdam, B.J., van Crielaard, W., van Stokkum, I.H., Hellingwerf, K.J., Westerhoff, H.V.: Simplicity in complexity: the photosynthetic reaction center performs as a simple 0.2 V battery. FEBS Lett. 510(1-2), 105–107 (2002)

Snoep, J.L.: The Silicon Cell initiative: working towards a detailed kinetic description at the cellular level. Curr. Opin. Biotechnol. 16, 336–343 (2005)

Stuart, A.M., Humphries, A.R.: Dynamical Systems and Numerical Analysis. Cambridge University Press, Cambridge (1996)

Takahashi, K., Ishikawa, N., Sadamoto, Y., Sasamoto, H., Ohta, S., Shiozawa, A., Miyoshi, F., Naito, Y., Nakayama, Y., Tomita, M.: E-Cell 2: Multi-platform E-Cell simulation system. Bioinformatics 19, 1727–1729 (2003)

Tanenbaum, A.S.: Structured Computer Organisation. Prentice-Hall, London (1976)

Teusink, B., Passarge, J., Reijenga, C.A., Esgalhado, E., van der Weijden, C.C., Schepper, M., Walsh, M.C., Bakker, B.M., van Dam, K., Westerhoff, H.V., Snoep, J.L.: Can yeast glycolysis be understood in terms of in vitro kinetics of the constituent enzymes? Testing biochemistry. Eur. J. Biochem. 267(17), 5313–5329 (2000)

Wang, J., Gilles, E.D., Lengeler, J.W., Jahreis, K.: Modeling of inducer exclusion and catabolite repression based on a PTS-dependent sucrose and non-PTS-dependent glycerol transport systems in Escherichia Coli K-12 and its experimental verification. J. Biotechnol. 92(2), 133–158 (2001)

Weiss, G. (ed.): Multiagent Systems. MIT Press, Cambridge (1999)

Westerhoff, H.V.: The silicon cell, not dead but live! Metab. Eng. 3(3), 207–210 (2001)

Wijker, J.E., Jensen, P.R., Vaz Gomes, A., De Waal, A., Van Workum, M., Van Heeswijk, W.C., Molenaar, D., Wielinga, P., Diderich, J., Bakker, B.M., Teusink, B., Hemker, M., Rohwer, J., Van der Gugten, A.A., Kholodenko, B.N., Westerhoff, H.V.: Energy, control and DNA structure in the living cell. Biophys. Chem. 55, 153–165 (1995)

Wooldridge, M., Jennings, N.R. (eds.): ECAI 1994 and ATAL 1994. LNCS, vol. 890. Springer, Berlin (1995)

Appendix A *E. coli*'s Internal Dynamics: Catabolism

In this section the dynamics of the children roles of Catabolism are discussed in more detail: Glycolysis, Pyruvate-Catabolism, and glycogen catabolism.

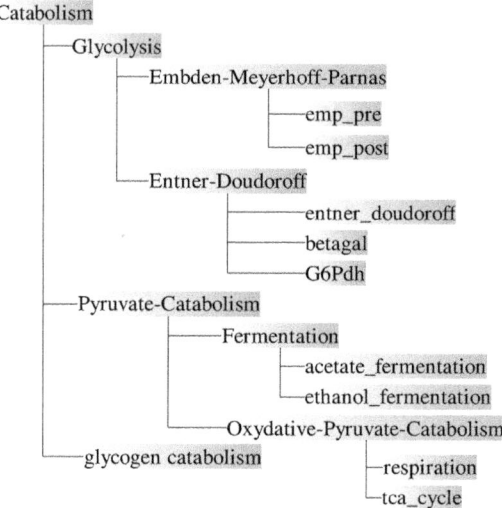

Fig. 12. Catabolism Organisation structure

A.1 Organisation Structure for Catabolism

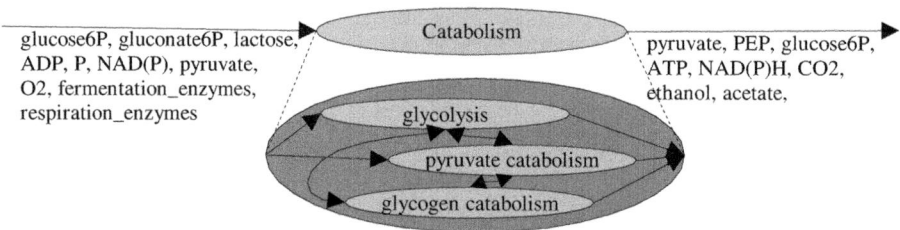

Fig. 13. Catabolism organisation structure

A.2 Organisation Dynamics within Catabolism

Catabolism

Input: present(glucose6P), present(gluconate6P), present(lactose), present(pyruvate), present(ADP), present(P), present(fermentation_enzymes), present(respiration_enzymes), present(O2), present(NAD(P))

Output: present(pyruvate), present(glucose6P), present(PEP), present(ATP), present(CO2), present(acetate), present(ethanol), present(NAD(P)H).

Persistent: input:present(NAD(P)).

CaD1

 (input:present(glucose6P) or present(gluconate6P) or present(lactose)) & present(ADP) &
present(P) & present(NAD(P)) & present(O2) & present(respiration_enzymes)
$\longrightarrow\!\!\!\!\rightarrow_{4;12;4;4}$ output:present(pyruvate) & present(glucose6P) & present(ATP) & present(NAD(P)H)
& present(PEP) & present(CO2)

CaD2

 (input:present(glucose6P) or present(gluconate6P) or present(lactose)) & present(ADP) &
present(P) & present(NAD(P)) & present(fermentation_enzymes)
$\longrightarrow\!\!\!\!\rightarrow_{4;12;4;4}$ output:present(pyruvate) & present(glucose6P) & present(ATP) & present(NAD(P)H)
& present(PEP) & present(acetate) & present(ethanol)

Glycogen catabolism
Input: present(ATP)
Output: present(glucose6P), present(ADP), present(P).

The glucose6P produced when glycogen is catabolised is further processed by the
glycolysis and pyruvate catabolism to release ATP.

SD1

 input: not present(ADP) & internal:present(glycogen) $\longrightarrow\!\!\!\!\rightarrow_{0;0;1;200}$ output:present(glucose6P)

SD2

 input:present(ATP) $\longrightarrow\!\!\!\!\rightarrow_{0;0;200;200}$ internal:present(glycogen) & output:present(ADP) &
present(P)

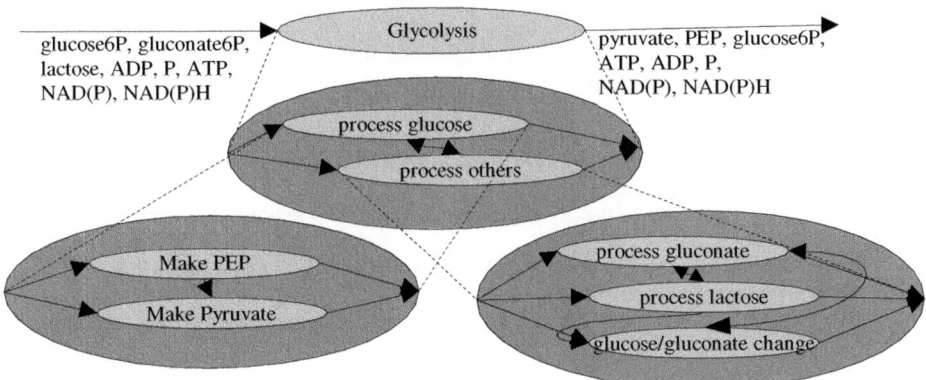

Fig. 14. Glycolysis organisation structure. For a desciption of the lower components, see
Appendix A.

Glycolysis
Input: present(glucose6P), present(gluconate6P), present(lactose), present(ADP), present(P),
present(ATP),
   present(NAD(P)), present(NAD(P)H)
Output: present(glucose6P), present(pyruvate), present(PEP), present(ATP), present(ADP),
present(P), present(NAD(P)),
   present(NAD(P)H)

GD1

(input:present(glucose6P) or present(gluconate6P) or present(lactose)) & present(ADP) & present(P) & present(NAD(P)))

$\rightarrow\!\!\!\rightarrow_{2;6;4;4}$ output:present(pyruvate) & present(glucose6P) & present(PEP) & present(ATP) & present(NAD(P)H)

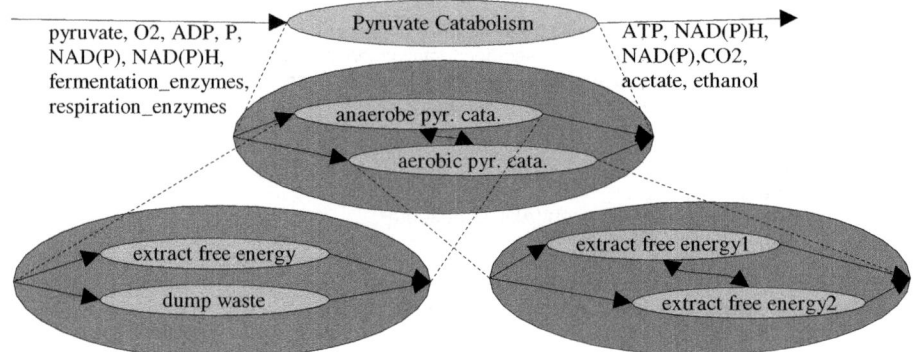

Fig. 15. Pyruvate Catabolism organisation structure. For a desciption of the lower components, see Appendix A.

Pyruvate Catabolism

Input: present(pyruvate), present(O2), present(ADP), present(P), present(NAD(P)),
present(NAD(P)H), present(fermentation_enzymes), present(respiration_enzymes)
Output: present(ATP), present(NAD(P)), present(NAD(P)H), present(CO2),
present(acetate), present(ethanol)

PD1

input:present(pyruvate) & present(ADP) & present(P) & present(NAD(P)H) & present(O2) & present(respiration_enzymes)

$\rightarrow\!\!\!\rightarrow_{0;0;4;4}$ output:present(ATP) & present(NAD(P)) & present(CO2).

PD2

input:present(pyruvate) & present(ADP) & present(P) & present(NAD(P)H) & present(fermentation_enzymes)

$\rightarrow\!\!\!\rightarrow_{0;0;4;4}$ output:present(ATP) & present(NAD(P)) & present(acetate) & present(ethanol).

Logical relationships for Catabolism

The general format provides:

DP(Glycolysis) & DP(Pyruvate-Catabolism) & DP(Glycogen-Catabolism)
& TRD(Catabolism) & IID(Catabolism)   ⇒   DP(Catabolism)

In more detail, the following relationships hold:

GD1 & PD1 & TRD(Catabolism) & IID(Catabolism) ⇒ CaD1
GD1 & PD2 & TRD(Catabolism) & IID(Catabolism) ⇒ CaD2

Appendix B *E. coli*'s Internal Dynamics: Anabolism

Within Anabolism four children roles occur: Maintenance, Intermediary Synthesis, Aminoacids Synthesis, and DNA/RNA/Protein Synthesis. The dynamics of each of these will be addressed. Lower aggregation levels can be found in the Appendix.

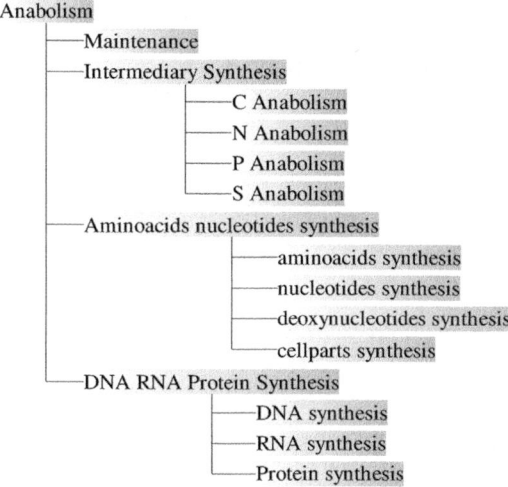

Fig. 16. Anabolism hierarchy

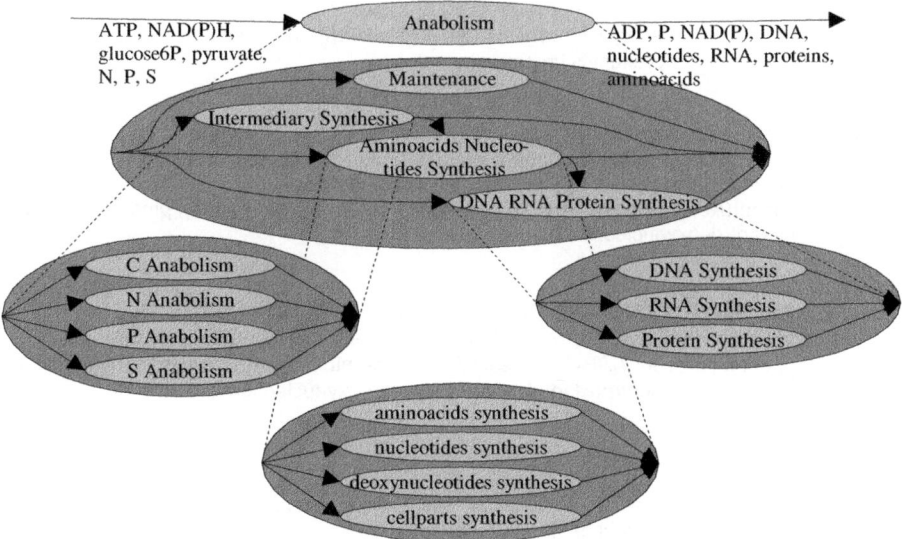

Fig. 17. Anabolism organisation structure. For a desciption of the lower components, see Appendix A.

Anabolism

Input: present(ATP), present(NAD(P)H), present(glucose6P), present(pyruvate), present(N),
            present(P), present(S)
Output: present(ADP), present(P), present(NAD(P)), present(aminoacids), present(nucleotides),
            present(DNA), present(RNA), present(proteins)

AD1
   input:present(ATP) & present(NAD(P)H) & present(glucose6P) & present(pyruvate) &
   present(N) & present(P) & present(S)
   $\twoheadrightarrow_{2;6;4;4}$ output:present(ADP) & present(P) & present(NAD(P)) &
                   present(nucleotides) & present(aminoacids)

Maintenance

Input: present(ATP).
Output: present(ADP), present(P).

MaD1
   input:present(ATP) $\twoheadrightarrow_{0;0;4;4}$ output:present(ADP) & present(P).

Intermediary Synthesis

Input: present(ATP), present(glucose6P), present(pyruvate), present(N), present(P), present(S).
Output: present(ADP), present(P), present(C_intermediaries), present(N_intermediaries),
            present(P_intermediaries), present(S_intermediaries).

ID1
   input:present(ATP) & present(glucose6P) & present(pyruvate) & present(N) & present(P)
   & present(S)
   $\twoheadrightarrow_{0;0;4;4}$ output:present(ADP) & present(P) & present(C_intermediaries) &
                   present(N_intermediaries) & present(P_intermediaries) &
                   present(S_intermediaries).

Aminoacids Nucleotides Synthesis
Input: present(ATP), present(NAD(P)H), present(C_intermediaries), present(N_intermediaries),
            present(P_intermediaries), present(S_intermediaries)
Output: present(ADP), present(P), present(NAD(P)), present(aminoacids), present(nucleotides),
            present(deoxynucleotides)

AnD1
    input:present(ATP) & present(NAD(P)H) & present(C_intermediaries) &
   present(N_intermediaries) & present(P_intermediaries) & present(S_intermediaries)
   $\twoheadrightarrow_{0;0;4;4}$ output:present(ADP) & present(P) & present(NAD(P)) & present(aminoacids) &
                   present(nucleotides) & present(deoxynucleotides)

DNA RNA Protein Synthesis

Input: present(ATP), present(NAD(P)H), present(aminoacids), present(nucleotides),
            present(deoxynucleotides)
Output: present(ADP), present(P), present(NAD(P)), present(DNA), present(RNA), present(proteins)

DD1

    input:present(ATP) & present(NAD(P)H) & present(C_aminoacids) & present(nucleotides)
    & present(deoxynucleotides)
    $\rightarrow\!\!\!\rightarrow_{0;0;4;4}$ output:present(ADP) & present(P) & present(NAD(P)) & present(DNA) &
             present(RNA) & present(proteins)

Logical relationships for Anabolism
The general pattern provides

        DP(Maintenance) & DP(Intermediary-Synthesis) &
        DP(Aminoacids-Nucleotides-Synthesis) & DP(DNA-RNA-Protein-Synthesis) &
        TRD(Anabolism) & IID(Anabolism) $\Rightarrow$ DP(Anabolism)

In more detail:

        MaD1 & ID1 & AnD1 & DD1 & TRD(Anabolism) & IID(Anabolism) $\Rightarrow$ AD1

Here, TRD(Anabolism) are the transfer dynamics within the Anabolism role, and
IID(Anabolism) are the interlevel interaction dynamics within the Anabolism role.

Appendix C *E. coli*'s Internal Dynamics: Transport

Within Transport two children roles occur: Import and Export. The dynamics of each of
these will be addressed. Furthermore, Import's children Nutrition Import and Resource
Import will be described. Lower aggregation levels can be found in the Appendix.

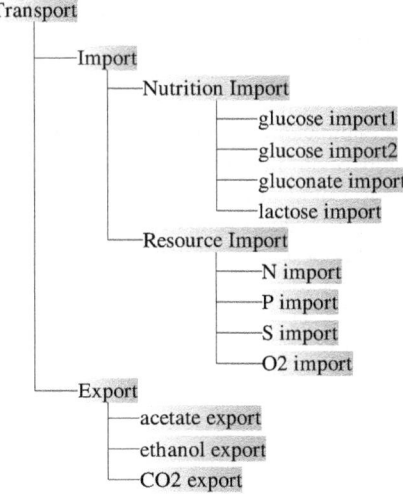

Fig. 18. Transport hierarchy

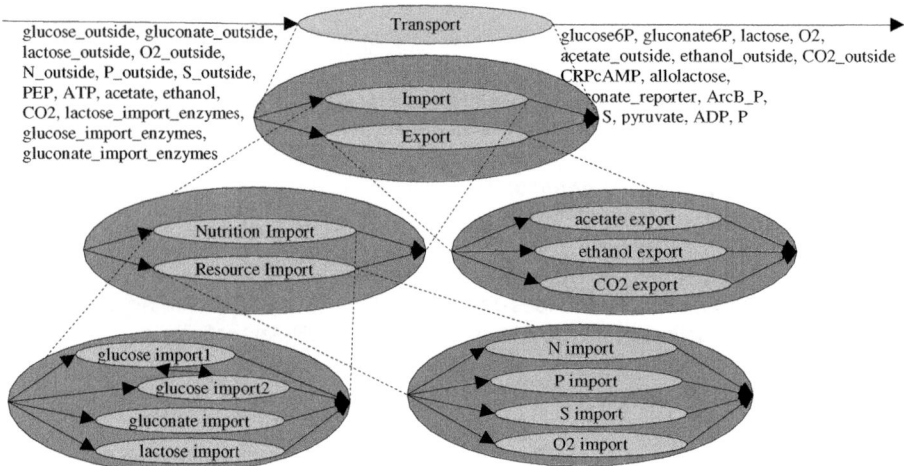

Fig. 19. Transport organisation structure. For a desciption of the lower components, see Appendix A.

Transport

Input: present(glucose_outside), present(lactose_outside), present(gluconate_outside),
present(O2_outside), present(N_outside), present(P_outside), present(S_outside),
present(PEP), present(ATP), present(acetate), present(ethanol), present(CO2),
present(lactose_import_enzymes), present(glucose_import_enzymes),
present(gluconate_import_enzymes)

Output: present(glucose6P), present(lactose), present(gluconate6P), present(O2),
present(CRPcAMP), present(allolactose), present(gluconate6P_observation_amount),
present(ArcB_P), present(N), present(P), present(S), present(pyruvate),
present(ADP), present(P), present(acetate_outside), present(ethanol_outside),
present(CO2_outside)

The timings here sometimes contain negative values. This is because the delay time only starts after the antecedent duration has passed. For example, timing –4;0;4;4 for TrD2 means that when gluconate becomes present outside at a time t0 for 4 seconds, then the delays will start to count at time t0+4. Thus the effects can happen between t0+4 + –4 seconds and t0+4 + 0 seconds, lasting at least 4 seconds. These timings thus ensure that the effects will happen at or after their causes happen.

Also note that the properties here are the combination of the properties of the Import and Export roles. For example, TrD4 is equal to ImD3. This is because the subroles Import and Export operate 'in parallel'.

TrD1
   input:present(glucose_outside) & present(PEP) & present(glucose_import_enzymes)
   $\rightarrow\!\!\rightarrow$_{-4;0;4;4} output:present(glucose6P) & present(pyruvate)

TrD2
   input:present(gluconate_outside) & present(ATP) & present(gluconate_import_enzymes)
   $\rightarrow\!\!\rightarrow$_{-4;0;4;4} output:present(gluconate6P) & present(ADP) & present(P)

TrD3
   input:present(lactose_outside) & present(ATP) & present(lactose_import_enzymes)
   $\rightarrow\!\!\rightarrow$_{-4;0;4;4} output:present(lactose) & present(ADP) & present(P)

TrD4
input:present(O2_outside) $\longrightarrow\!\!\!\!\rightarrow_{0;0;4;4}$ output:present(O2) & present(ArcB_P)
TrD5
input:present(N_outside) & present(ATP) $\longrightarrow\!\!\!\!\rightarrow_{0;0;4;4}$ output:present(N) & present(ADP) & present(P)
TrD6
input:present(P_outside) & present(ATP) $\longrightarrow\!\!\!\!\rightarrow_{0;0;4;4}$ output:present(P) & present(ADP) & present(P)
TrD7
input:present(S_outside) & present(ATP) $\longrightarrow\!\!\!\!\rightarrow_{0;0;4;4}$ output:present(S & present(ADP) & present(P)
TrD8
input:present(acetate) $\longrightarrow\!\!\!\!\rightarrow_{0;0;4;4}$ output:present(acetate_outside)
TrD9
input:present(ethanol) $\longrightarrow\!\!\!\!\rightarrow_{0;0;4;4}$ output:present(ethanol_outside)
TrD10
input:present(CO2) $\longrightarrow\!\!\!\!\rightarrow_{0;0;4;4}$ output:present(CO2_outside)
TrD11
input: not present(glucose_outside)
$\longrightarrow\!\!\!\!\rightarrow_{-4;0;4;4}$ output:present(CRPcAMP)
TrD12
input:present(lactose_outside)
$\longrightarrow\!\!\!\!\rightarrow_{0;0;0.230;0.230}$ output:present(allolactose)
TrD13
input:present(gluconate_outside)
$\longrightarrow\!\!\!\!\rightarrow_{0;0;0.230;0.230}$ output:present(gluconate6P_observation_amount)

Import

Input: present(glucose_outside), present(lactose_outside), present(gluconate_outside),
             present(O2_outside), present(N_outside), present(P_outside), present(S_outside),
             present(PEP), present(ATP), present(lactose_import_enzymes),
             present(glucose_import_enzymes), present(gluconate_import_enzymes)
Output: present(glucose6P), present(lactose), present(gluconate6P), present(O2),
             present(CRPcAMP), present(allolactose), present(gluconate6P_observation_amount),
             present(ArcB_P), present(N), present(P), present(S), present(pyruvate),
             present(ADP), present(P)

ImD1
input:present(glucose_outside) & present(PEP) & present(glucose_import_enzymes)
$\longrightarrow\!\!\!\!\rightarrow_{-4;0;4;4}$ output:present(glucose6P) &present(pyruvate)
ImD2
input:present(gluconate_outside) & present(ATP) & present(gluconate_import_enzymes)
$\longrightarrow\!\!\!\!\rightarrow_{-4;0;4;4}$ output:present(gluconate6P) & present(ADP) & present(P)
ImD3
input:present(lactose_outside) & present(ATP) & present(lactose_import_enzymes)
$\longrightarrow\!\!\!\!\rightarrow_{-4;0;4;4}$ output:present(lactose) & present(ADP) & present(P)
ImD4
input:present(O2_outside) $\longrightarrow\!\!\!\!\rightarrow_{0;0;4;4}$ output:present(O2) & present(ArcB_P)
ImD5
input:present(N_outside) & present(ATP) $\longrightarrow\!\!\!\!\rightarrow_{0;0;4;4}$ output:present(N) & present(ADP) & present(P)
ImD6
input:present(P_outside) & present(ATP) $\longrightarrow\!\!\!\!\rightarrow_{0;0;4;4}$ output:present(P) & present(ADP) & present(P)

ImD7

input:present(S_outside) & present(ATP) $\longrightarrow\!\!\!\!\rightarrow_{0;0;4;4}$ output:present(S & present(ADP) & present(P)

ImD8

input: not present(glucose_outside)

$\longrightarrow\!\!\!\!\rightarrow_{-4;0;4;4}$ output:present(CRPcAMP)

ImD9

input:present(lactose_outside)

$\longrightarrow\!\!\!\!\rightarrow_{0;0;0.230;0.230}$ output:present(allolactose)

ImD10

input:present(gluconate_outside)

$\longrightarrow\!\!\!\!\rightarrow_{0;0;0.230;0.230}$ output:present(gluconate6P_observation_amount)

Nutrition Import

Input: present(glucose_outside), present(lactose_outside), present(gluconate_outside), present(PEP), present(ATP), present(lactose_import_enzymes), present(glucose_import_enzymes), present(gluconate_import_enzymes)

Output: present(glucose6P), present(lactose), present(gluconate6P), present(CRPcAMP), present(allolactose), present(gluconate6P_observation_amount), present(pyruvate), present(ADP), present(P)

ND1

input:present(glucose_outside) & present(PEP) & present(glucose_import_enzymes)

$\longrightarrow\!\!\!\!\rightarrow_{-4;0;4;4}$ output:present(glucose6P) & present(pyruvate)

ND2

input:present(gluconate_outside) & present(ATP) & present(gluconate_import_enzymes)

$\longrightarrow\!\!\!\!\rightarrow_{-4;0;4;4}$ output:present(gluconate6P) & present(ADP) & present(P)

ND3

input:present(lactose_outside) & present(ATP) & present(lactose_import_enzymes)

$\longrightarrow\!\!\!\!\rightarrow_{-4;0;4;4}$ output:present(lactose) & present(ADP) & present(P)

ND4

input: not present(glucose_outside)

$\longrightarrow\!\!\!\!\rightarrow_{0;0;0.230;0.230}$ output:present(CRPcAMP)

ND5

input:present(lactose_outside)

$\longrightarrow\!\!\!\!\rightarrow_{0;0;0.230;0.230}$ output:present(allolactose)

ND6

input:present(gluconate_outside)

$\longrightarrow\!\!\!\!\rightarrow_{0;0;0.230;0.230}$ output:present(gluconate6P_observation_amount)

Resource Import

Input: present(O2_outside), present(N_outside), present(P_outside), present(S_outside), present(ATP)

Output: present(O2), present(ArcB_P), present(N), present(P), present(S), present(ADP), present(P)

RD1

input:present(O2_outside) $\longrightarrow\!\!\!\!\rightarrow_{0;0;4;4}$ output:present(O2) & present(ArcB_P)

RD2

input:present(N_outside) & present(ATP) $\longrightarrow\!\!\!\!\rightarrow_{0;0;4;4}$ output:present(N) & present(ADP) & present(P)

RD3

input:present(P_outside) & present(ATP) $\longrightarrow\!\!\!\!\rightarrow_{0;0;4;4}$ output:present(P) & present(ADP) & present(P)

RD4

input:present(S_outside) & present(ATP) $\longrightarrow\!\!\!\!\rightarrow_{0;0;4;4}$ output:present(S & present(ADP) & present(P)

Export
Input: present(acetate) present(ethanol) present(CO2)
Output: present(acetate_outside) present(ethanol_outside) present(CO2_outside)

ED1
   input:present(acetate) $\twoheadrightarrow_{0;0;4;4}$ output:present(acetate_outside)
ED2
   input:present(ethanol) $\twoheadrightarrow_{0;0;4;4}$ output:present(ethanol_outside)
ED3
   input:present(CO2) $\twoheadrightarrow_{0;0;4;4}$ output:present(CO2_outside)

Logical relationship for Transport

Because

$$DP(Transport) = DP(Import) \,\&\, DP(Export),$$

it trivially holds that

$$DP(Import) \,\&\, DP(Export) \,\&\, TRD(Transport) \,\&\, IID(Transport) \Rightarrow DP(Transport)$$

Logical relationship for Import

Because

$$DP(Import) = DP(Nutrition\text{-}Import) \,\&\, DP(Resource\text{-}Import),$$

it trivially holds that

$$DP(Nutrition\text{-}Import) \,\&\, DP(Resource\text{-}Import) \,\&\, TRD(Import) \,\&\, IID(Import) \Rightarrow DP(Import)$$

Appendix D More Details of Simulation Results

This example simulation follows what is described in Appendix A.

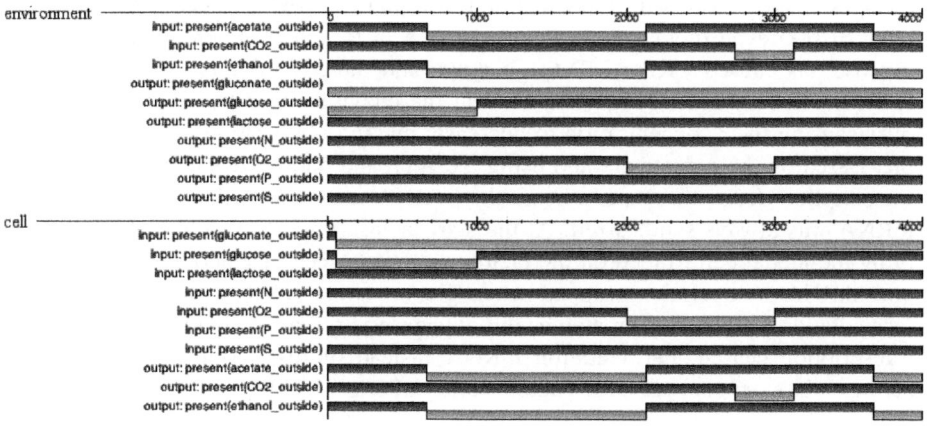

The environment was slowly changing over time. Lactose was always present, as were N, P and S. Gluconate was absent. At the start oxygen was present and glucose was absent. At time 1000 (seconds) glucose was added to the environment. At the start, all values on the inputs were set to true for 60 seconds, including for example gluconate outside. This could be specified in more detail, if another particular initialisation state were desired. At time 2000 oxygen was removed from the environment. The oxygen was added again at time 3000. The outputs of the environment are decided beforehand for the experiment, the outputs of the cell indicate the response of the bacterium. The output of the cell to the environment caused acetate, ethanol and CO_2 production at the very beginning, but as the cell adapted to the situation only CO_2 was produced. As oxygen was removed the CO_2 emissions stopped after a while, and acetate and ethanol were produced instead. After the oxygen was added again the cell adapted by stopping the acetate and ethanol emissions and returning to CO_2 production.

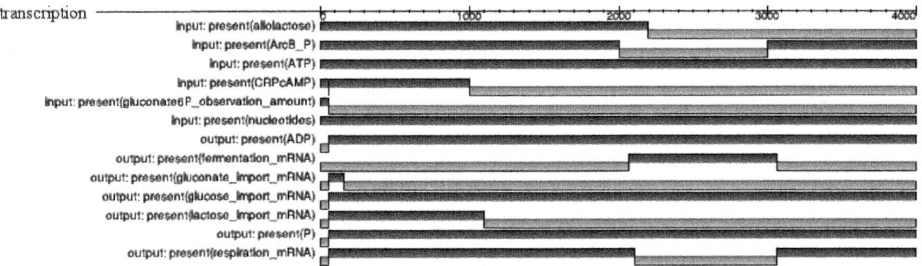

Inside the cell, the metabolism, the translation and the transcription are considered. Note that for example the ATP is not consumed, in general in this model substrates are not consumed, and products have a minimum lifetime assigned. Consumption of ATP could be added by putting the removal of ATP as the consequent of the dynamical properties. The transcription shows the detector molecules allolactose, ArcB-P and CRPcAMP doing their jobs. At first allolactose is present because lactose is present in the environment. Also ArcB-P is present, because there is oxygen. CRPcAMP is present because there is no glucose. There is no internal gluconate (a reporter of the presence of external gluconate) either. The detector molecules then change, observing the changes in the world, with the exception of allolactose, which disappears some time after t=2000 even though there is still lactose in the environment. The presence of glucose has caused CRPcAMP to go down and thereby inhibits the lactose import enzymes to be synthesized. After a while the enzymes have been diluted or turned over causing their concentration to decrease, making observation of lactose impossible. Based on these detectors and using the ATP and nucleotides that are input to the transcription from the metabolism, the mRNA was transcribed. Glucose import mRNA was always synthesized. At the start lactose-import mRNA was created enabling the model cell to feed on the lactose in the absence of glucose. The lactose import mRNA transcription stopped when glucose was added to the medium. Later, fermentation mRNA was created as the oxygen was removed, and respiration-mRNA transcription ceased. Fermentation mRNA instead of respiration mRNA was transcribed when oxygen was added again shortly after t = 3000.

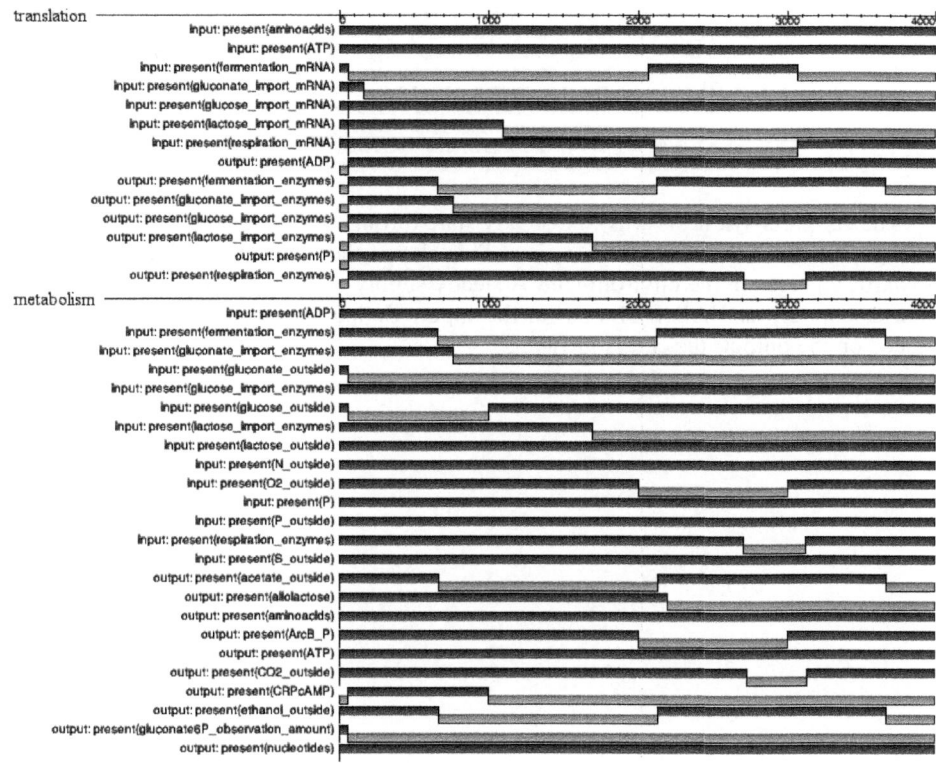

The translation takes the mRNA from the transcription and uses ATP and aminoacids from the metabolism to translate the mRNA to proteins. The enzymes among the latter catalyze the metabolism. The metabolism takes ADP and P from the translation and transcription, as well as input from the environment. It makes free energy available, detects substances in the environment and provides building blocks, such as aminoacids and nucleotides to the translation and transcription. Waste CO_2, acetate and ethanol were output to the environment. In the simulated trace, steady states established as the cell adapted to each externally defined state. When lactose was the only carbon substrate, the lactose was detected, and the the enzymes from translation regulated the metabolism to perform lactose uptake. When glucose was been added the glucose import enzymes were already there, the corresponding gene expression being constitutive. Respiration and fermentation enzyme levels adjusted to the oxygen conditions outside. CO_2 was produced when oxygen was present, but as the latter was removed, the cell quickly turned to fermentation.

More detail can be seen when inspecting components further down the hierarchy, see e.g. the cellparts synthesis:

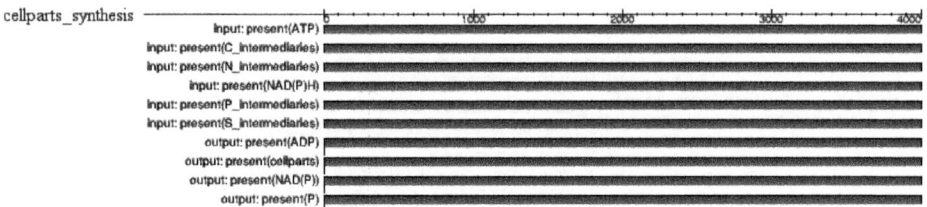

The cellparts synthesis was in a steady state throughout the entire simulation, even though the environment was changing. This shows the robustness of the model cell towards changes in the environment. A steady supply of ATP, C, N, P and S intermediaries as well as NAD(P)H was on the input. Cellparts are continually being produced on the output: the cell is growing.

Author Index

GPSR Compliance

The European Union's (EU) General Product Safety Regulation (GPSR) is a set of rules that requires consumer products to be safe and our obligations to ensure this.

If you have any concerns about our products, you can contact us on ProductSafety@springernature.com

In case Publisher is established outside the EU, the EU authorized representative is:

Springer Nature Customer Service Center GmbH
Europaplatz 3
69115 Heidelberg, Germany

Batch number: 09490872

Printed by Printforce, the Netherlands